Black Religious Landscaping in Africa and the United States

This book is part of the Peter Lang Political Science, Economics, and Law list.
Every volume is peer reviewed and meets
the highest quality standards for content and production.

PETER LANG
New York • Bern • Berlin
Brussels • Vienna • Oxford • Warsaw

Black Religious Landscaping in Africa and the United States

Edited by
Joy R. Bostic, Itumeleng D. Mothoagae,
and Tamelyn Tucker-Worgs

PETER LANG
New York • Bern • Berlin
Brussels • Vienna • Oxford • Warsaw

Library of Congress Cataloging-in-Publication Data

Names: Bostic, Joy R., editor. | Mothoagae, Itumeleng Daniel, editor. |
Tucker-Worgs, Tamelyn, editor.
Title: Black religious landscaping in Africa and the United States / Joy R. Bostic,
Itumeleng D. Mothoagae, Tamelyn N. Tucker-Worgs.
Description: New York: Peter Lang, 2021.
Includes bibliographical references and index.
Identifiers: LCCN 2020033407 (print) | LCCN 2020033408 (ebook)
ISBN 978-1-4331-7258-8 (hardback) | ISBN 978-1-4331-7255-7 (ebook pdf)
ISBN 978-1-4331-7256-4 (epub) | ISBN 978-1-4331-7257-1 (mobi)
Subjects: LCSH: African Americans—Religion. | African Americans—Social
conditions. | African Americans—Race identity. | African diaspora. |
Africans—Migrations. | Africa—Religion.
Classification: LCC BL2525 .B75 2021 (print) | LCC BL2525 (ebook) |
DDC 200.89/96073—dc23
LC record available at https://lccn.loc.gov/2020033407
LC ebook record available at https://lccn.loc.gov/2020033408
DOI 10.3726/b17884

Bibliographic information published by **Die Deutsche Nationalbibliothek**.
Die Deutsche Nationalbibliothek lists this publication in the "Deutsche
Nationalbibliografie"; detailed bibliographic data are available
on the Internet at http://dnb.d-nb.de/.

80 Broad Street, 5th floor, New York, NY 10004
www.peterlang.com

Table of Contents

Part II: Sites of Religious Landscaping: Black Churches and African Independent Churches

Acknowledgements

The production of this volume would have not happened without the support of many persons. We are deeply grateful for their contributions. We extend our heartfelt thanks to the contributors, this includes the conference participants who served as interlocutors when these chapters were presented at the 2014 Transatlantic Roundtable on Religion and Race (TRRR). This conference was held in collaboration with the Voice and Voicelessness Project 2011–2015 sponsored by the University of South Africa, Pretoria. We want to thank Dr. R. Drew Smith and all of the TRRR co-conveners without whom this book would not be possible. We also want to express our appreciation to the College of Human Sciences, University of South Africa, for the support the College provided for the conference. Special thanks also goes to Case Western Reserve University's (CWRU) Department of Religious Studies in Cleveland, Ohio (United States) and CWRU's Baker-Nord Center for the Humanities for travel grant support as well as Hood College Office of the Provost in Frederick, Maryland (United States) for an international travel grant. Finally, we want to express our thanks to the Diepsloot community leaders in South Africa as well as the broader community members for opening your space, and sharing with us the struggles and triumphs experienced by the community. We would also like to express our deep appreciation for the communities of Baltimore, Pittsburgh and other local spaces for sharing your stories of religious landscaping. We hope that this volume and these stories will inspire diverse communities to continue the ongoing work of community activism and social change.

Introduction

Over the centuries, black struggles against white supremacy and patriarchal power have occupied physical, psychological, cultural and religious space. During the twentieth century, these struggles for freedom brought about sweeping changes across the continent of Africa and the Americas. From the beginning of the twentieth century these struggles took on various forms in the pursuit of resisting colonization and struggling for political rights. For example, black people in the United States struggled for an expansion of political rights, against lynching, and against an array of discriminatory practices and policies. In the Caribbean and Latin America, black people were also making demands for greater political and economic rights. At the same time, Africans on the Continent were struggling against European imperialism and colonization in a variety of ways. By mid-century these persistent struggles yielded extraordinary achievements as black people on the Continent and throughout the diaspora began to win greater civil and political rights. Beginning in the 1950s many predominately black nations achieved political independence. For example, Ghana became independent in 1957 and in 1960—what many refer to as the year of Africa—nations like Cameroon, Senegal and Nigeria and over a dozen other African nations achieved their independence. Throughout the 1960s and 1970s dozens more countries in the Caribbean and on the African continent gained their independence including Trinidad and Tobago, Jamaica, and Uganda in 1962; Barbados and Botswana in 1966; Mozambique and Angola in 1975; and culminating with Zimbabwe in 1980. These movements for independence transformed the cartographical space of black freedom on the Continent of Africa and in the Americas.

While South Africa gained independence from Britain in 1910, the black majority nation remained under a white minority rule for most of the twentieth century. It was not until 1994 that the nation's first black president, Nelson Mandela, took office along with a multi-racial coalition led by the African National Congress (ANC). Therefore, it wasn't until the end of the twentieth century that South Africa became the last nation on the African continent to elect a black president.

Meanwhile the geographical mappings of black empowerment continued to shift during the twentieth century as black people in the United States, fought for and gained important civil rights. In the 1950s and 1960s, mass protests by black Americans resulted in the passing of voting rights legislation and the legal desegregation of public and private institutions. The attainment of civil rights or the dismantling of apartheid did not, however, put an end to white supremacy or lead to full equality among blacks and whites in the United States or South Africa. In both countries, discrimination in housing policy, wealth disparity, job discrimination, land ownership, educational inequities and racial violence and intimidation prevailed. Despite the election of Nelson Mandela as South Africa's first black president in 1994 and the unforeseen election of Barack Hussein Obama as the first black president of the United States in 2008, these times of apparent black empowerment do not offer simple solutions to the problem of black oppression. Moreover, these spaces of post-independence for African and Caribbean nations, Post-Mandela times for South Africa and a Post-Obama era in United States have given rise to paradoxes of empowerment that continue to impact black people around the world.

The political independence of predominantly black nation-states during the twentieth century and the election of a black president of a majority white nation at the beginning of the twenty-first provide historical markers for signs of black empowerment that have led to the establishment of classes of black elites who have attained positions of power at local or national levels. The African and Caribbean—countries that gained independence during the twentieth century established and reestablished geo-political, governmental, and social structures, boundaries, and balances of power. Even though positions of power within these nations have been occupied by black (although predominantly male) bodies, political and geographical changes within these nation-states have not necessarily translated into systemic changes that provide economic, political and social empowerment for most black people within their respective borders. The paradox of empowerment means that despite legal, political and economic changes, black people on the African continent and in its diaspora, continue to face various forms of injustice and deprivation on multiple levels across the globe. This injustice and deprivation takes not only racial, political and economic forms but also gendered, environmental, sexual, psychic, cultural, spiritual and religious forms as well.

This ongoing state of geo-political injustice with respect to black and African people, is due in part to, as Edward Soja suggests, the fact that historical "[(in)justice] has a *consequential geography*."[1] As Soja goes on to explain, the consequences of geographical injustice involve not only geographies of physical and political boundaries but also involves the geographical mappings of ideas, images, and normative structures. Therefore, mere changes in the phenotypes of those who occupy political positions of power within the physical boundaries of a nation state cannot, in one stroke, eradicate the history of injustices done to the bodies, lands and cultures of those who live there. Black lives in independent nation-states on the African continent and in its diaspora have been complicated by histories of colonialism, ongoing forms of neocolonialism, segregation, gendered and sexual oppression, and economic exploitation and violence. These nations continue to bear the marks of the "dominant geographies"[2] of Western, white, colonial narratives and histories that have resulted in a legacy of violence, marginalization and attempts at erasure of black political, cultural, religious and intellectual practices and ideas. The legacy of this violence (both physical and symbolic) and its consequential effects are indelibly etched into the landscapes of black communities and homelands. Colonial, neocolonial and white supremacist religious practices and theologies have played a central role in the mystification of imperial tactics and have served to justify forms of physical, economic and social violence against black people. In some cases, black leadership has taken on authoritarian dimensions and one-state parties that betray the original hopes and goals of struggles for independence. Thus, despite the advances made during times of apparent black empowerment, the colonial legacies of white supremacy, black disenfranchisement and poverty, and the marginalization of and violence against black women and men persist and continue to manifest in the geographical, political and cultural landscapes of spaces occupied by black people.

Notwithstanding, however, the ongoing violence of geographical oppression and injustice, black people have engaged in what Katherine McKittrick describes as "cartographies of struggle" in which they continue to claim and reclaim black homelands, black religion and black ideas from the grip of historical colonial and white supremacist power. Black bodies through means of protest, action and agency continue to rail against racial, economic and political injustice wherever they stand. In order to be effective, these cartographic struggles against the legacies of dominant geographies are often organized against geographic injustices that are, as described by Edward Soja, "situated and contextualized in three overlapping and interactive levels of geographical resolution" that include (1) the "external creation of unjust geographies through boundary making and the political organization of space"; (2) the local (including interpersonal) "distribution of inequalities" and "discriminatory decision making by individuals, firms, and institutions"; and (3) middle scale forms of regional or meso-geographical exploitation associated with "uneven development" and " the globalization of injustice."[3]

Black cartographies of struggle result in the exercise of geographical agency in ways that counter the dominate geographies of the colonial past on all three of these interactive levels. This agency involves the physical mapping of black ancestral homelands and sacred spaces. It involves political power in relationship to these physical geographies as well as methods of black social control and bodily freedom. It also involves struggles over ownership, control and distribution of profits regarding the mining of African resources and financial capital. Finally, black cartographies of struggle not only involve geographical locations and physical territories but also involves reclaiming black social, political and imaginative spaces and the integrity and validation of black bodies, black languages and religious and cultural practices within those spaces. These cartographies of struggle have profound implications for broader notions of black empowerment, identity and community.

Toward this end, black people across the globe have engaged in cultural and religious practices and constructed theological sites that enable them to construct and embody identities and notions of community that serve to counter geographical injustice. Rachel Harding suggests that within the context of the diaspora, people of African descent use "physical, cultural, psychic, and ritual-religious locations"[4] as a way of creating and recreating "relationships and countercultural identities" that contest white supremacist ideas about Africa and blackness.—This creation and re-creation of physical, religious and cultural space is critical to the widespread empowerment of black people affected by oppressive historical legacies. Black religious spaces, which are the focus of this volume, serve as sites of creation and re-creation of black identity, community and the imaginative spaces of "an-other world."[5] In the creation of "an-other" world, black people create emancipatory spaces that work to undermine dominant geographies. In creating other worlds through religious practice and theological construction, black people, as Jualynne Dodson argues, "[construct] assemblages of shared awareness that articulate a three-dimensional symbolic expression of the body of knowledge that undergirds [Black peoples'] comprehensions about life and being in the world"[6] within specific locales and, comparatively, across geographical and cultural borders. In other words, black people embody different forms of knowledge and enflesh[7] theological ideas within these physical and imaginative spaces. Thus, black geographies and environmental landscapes express, establish, and reestablish bases for knowledge, expression and meaning in the lives of black people and the communities in which they live. Below, we provide two examples of what black people face—one in South Africa and the other the United States—as they engage in cartographic struggles against the dominant geographies they have inherited even as they attempt to employ and "construct assemblages of shared awareness" that provide remedies to the destructive effects of racial oppression.

Diepsloot, South Africa

In South Africa under the system of Apartheid, the white-controlled government created black townships that were separate from so-called white neighborhoods. These townships were created to prohibit black people from living in proximity to whites. Limiting black bodies to living in townships was a reminder to black people that they were not citizens of South Africa, and that they cannot occupy the same spaces as white people. In addition, the spaces black people occupied in the black township were temporary. Under apartheid, black townships were leased for 100 years. This meant that even with the segregated townships, blacks could not maintain total ownership. Failure to pay rent in these townships meant that the family could be evicted from their home or if the head of the family died, the family would be expected to vacate the house. The townships also served as reservoirs for cheap labor. Black South Africans were then relegated to live in permanent areas of what was referred to as Bantustans. In the 1970s, the South African government declared four of the Bantustans "independent." These were the Transkei in 1976, Bophuthatswana in 1977, Venda in 1979, and Ciskei in 1981. The remaining Bantustans remained self-governing, but had no independent rights. Eventually, Bantustans were to become independent from South Africa.[8]

These were the geographical complexities of black people living within the then white-controlled, South African borders. It is within this context that we need to understand the formation of informal settlements. The Native Resettlement Act of 1954 gave the state the power to override local municipalities and to forcibly remove Africans and relocate them into spaces that were separate from that of white people. These spaces would later come to be known as townships. Scott reminds us that,

> In the "struggle for the city", which began in earnest in the early twentieth century in South African towns, the mutually exclusive, and implicitly racial categories, of "formal" and "informal" formed a broad implicit framework within which municipal authorities devised policies and legislation for replacing informal settlements with formal planned developments which were appropriate to the emerging industrial order.[9]

At the same time, it can be argued that the informal settlements were not only formed by those that were living in the white Republic of South Africa as a space of displacement and dislocation, but informal settlement also became a space of fortitude and a labor reservoir for the white minority. Butler et al argue that "the homelands served as labour reservoirs, housing the unemployed and releasing them when their labour was needed in white South Africa."[10]

One of the first victims was the African freehold areas of western Johannesburg in Sophiatown, whose residents were relocated to the new township at Soweto in 1955. Most of Soweto was built within a short space of time in the 1950s and early 1960s. Although the area was only given its present name in 1963, the first African township in modern Soweto was established in 1905. Initially called Klipspruit it subsequently changed to Pimville, the name that the original township of Soweto is known by today.[11] South African geo-political, socioeconomic and geo-religious locations emerge from these spaces occupied by both white colonial masters entitled to the privileges that comes with being white, and the cartographic struggles of the black people who reconstruct these spaces and map out responses to the "absurd" reality of what it means to be a "citizen" but not have access to the actual privileges that should come with citizenship.[12]

It is within this context that the economic, political and social landscape of Diepsloot and other shantytowns such as Khayalitsha, Nyanga in Cape Town as well as South Western Townships (affectionately known as SOWETO) around Johannesburg arise. It is remarkable that it has been one hundred and eight years since the land act of 1913; and it has been twenty-seven years since the 1994 negotiated settlement that took place at the Convention for a Democratic South Africa II (CODESA) between the African National Congress and the National Party (NP). The National Party government was resistant in concluding the "package deal" that linked agreement on phase one of the transition (an interim government) to phase two (a constituent assembly). What this meant was that the National Party government wanted an open ended agreement on power sharing before they would commit to the uncertainty of an elected constituent assembly. It is crucial to point out that this led partly to the failure of CODESA II. It was at this point that the ANC led alliance produced a document entitled *Negotiation: A Strategic Perspective* by Joe Slovo, a member of the South African Communist Party. Amongst the things that formed part of the negotiated settlement was a five year "sunset clause." It is within this context that the so-called dawn of democracy arose. Twenty-one years after the signing of the South African constitution into law black people remain marginalized within their own country. Despite the achievements of the last one hundred years, black bodies continue to be relegated to the periphery of the white-privileged space in South Africa.

Although the liberation struggle was successful in achieving the legal eradication of racism and the dismantling of the apparatus of apartheid, the achievements of 1994 did not necessarily bring with it all the rights and privileges that should be afforded to everyday citizens. These are some of the issues with which black people in South Africa in an era of "Black Empowerment Times" still must contend. In addition, the practices of segregation, torture, "othering" have not ended with gains in political freedom (the right to vote). Although we are no longer experiencing the violence of a formal apartheid system, there is still state violence and police violence. Apartheid as a system and the geographical injustice it has engendered, therefore, still exists. Black people who have attained full legal citizenship within a post-apartheid South Africa continue to be treated as the "other." The student protest under the banner #feesmustfall, #decolonization of curriculum, and #Rhodesmustfall, have reawakened what the negotiated settlement attempted to bury in the subconscious of the black populace. These student protests are a part of the cartographies of struggle that remind black bodies of the unfinished business of "liberation."

Diepsloot is located in a northern section of Johannesburg. It is a sprawling, densely populated settlement made up of formal and informal settlements. It was established in 1995-a year after the first black president of a new South African democratic government was elected. It was intended to be a temporary (informal) settlement, or a "squatters' camp" for people who were evicted from the white suburbs of Honeydew and Sevenfontein and the densely populated black township of Alexandra. It is in these squatter camps that the social struggle of the dislocated and alienated black bodies is experienced. For example, suburbs such as Sandton City, which is opposite Alexandra, is one of the richest cities on the African continent. While other townships including Diepsloot and Alexandra to name but a few do not have access to sanitation, electricity and clean water and experience high levels of unemployment. The South African statistics on poverty and inequality depict very bleak conditions for black people living below the poverty line.[13] The majority of the households in Diepsloot shared water and sewage and had no electricity; the unemployment rate was 54%; and HIV prevalence was over 50%.[14]

Shortfall in Services

While the landscape of the Diepsloot has had many changes in terms of the expansion of the settlement like many other informal settlements, it can be said that in terms of the economic landscape there has been minimal economic growth. As mentioned previously, the slowness of the economic growth in many informal settlements like Diepsloot is the gross reality of abject poverty, inadequate housing; high levels of unemployment, crime and diseases. Much of the economic activity in the area is what can be branded survivalist strategy. This mode of survival consists of low profit commerce, insufficient to get people out of the abject poverty in which they find themselves. While the government has attempted to improve the lives of the people of Diepsloot, it is undeniable that the economic landscape of the community is dire. Yet, a shopping mall was opened in Diepsloot just outside extension 9 in 2007 and some major South African brands (e.g., Absa, Nedbank, Standard Bank, FNB bank, and Pep among others) moved in. More mid-level businesses also moved into the mall. It is commendable what the investors have done by bringing some of the big brands to the community. This meant that they would not use their hard earned money to travel long distances to access these services. However, it must be pointed out that, this move also had serious consequences for local businesses; they would in the process lose their customers rather than incorporating them into the business sector. It can therefore be argued that the harshness of poverty in the community is not necessarily addressed. Yet at the same time this could be an indicator of the potential the population in Diepsloot offers for big businesses. Recently the national government erected a police station in Diepsloot with the hope of providing the much needed police services in the community to curb the levels of crime, rape, and murder cases.

These shortfalls point to the value of black lives in "Black Empowerment" times. Despite these circumstances there are numerous stories of resilience, entrepreneurship, courage and hope through faith-based activism. It is through decolonization that the dismantling of relations of power and conceptions of knowledge that generate the reproduction of racial, gender, and geo-political hierarchies that came into being or found new and more powerful forms of expression in the modern-colonial world.[3]

Baltimore, United States of America

In April 2015, Freddie Gray, a young African American male was taken into custody by Baltimore City Police in the Baltimore neighborhood, Sandtown-Winchester, where Gray lived in the Gilmor housing complex. Police assert that Gray first made eye contact and then ran from them. They chased and arrested him and put him into a police transport on the floor of the van shackled by both hands and feet. When police arrived at the booking station with Gray, he was not responsive and they refused to book him. He was then transported to the hospital, where he died 7 days later, apparently from a spinal injury. The medical examiner said that the cause of death was homicide. All of this happened in the context of heightened awareness of police brutality and the poor relationship between police and black communities across the country. Freddie Gray's death in police custody incensed members of the black community who already had been protesting over police brutality incidents in Baltimore and those across the United States.

After Gray's funeral, people (mostly school children) got into altercations with the police at a local shopping center—Modowmin Mall, which also serves as a transportation hub for school children. This led to unrest across much of West Baltimore. More than 500 were arrested. Fifteen buildings and 144 cars were set on fire. The U.S. National Guard was called in to patrol the city of Baltimore and there was a curfew for the week. Six Baltimore police officers were charged with Gray's death but they were eventually all released and the charges dropped. The death of Freddie Gray and the unrest that followed continued the national conversation on race and policing. Baltimore joined Ferguson, New York, Baton Rouge, and localities which in recent years have all erupted in civil unrest over the killing of unarmed black people by police officers.

The arrest of Freddie Gray, a young black man in the Baltimore City neighborhood of Sandtown-Winchester was not an anomaly or unusual occurrence. Black communities in the United States many assert are "over policed." The neighborhood where Freddie Gray lived, and was arrested, has among the highest number of juvenile arrests in the city. It also has among the highest proportions of its residents on parole or probation in the city (10.4%) of the residents, which is double the rate in the city of Baltimore (5.3%).[15]

The events of April 27th, sparked a U.S. Justice Department investigation of the Baltimore Police Department and their policing practices. The Justice Department's report found that the Baltimore Police Department was in serious need of reform and must enter into a consent decree with the federal government to make these reforms. The U.S. Justice Department found that the Baltimore Police Department regularly violated residents' 1st, 4th and 14th amendment constitutional rights by doing the following: "(1) making unconstitutional stops, searches, and arrests; (2) using enforcement strategies that produce severe and unjustified disparities in the rates of stops, searches and arrests of African Americans; (3) using excessive force; and (4) retaliating against people engaging in constitutionally-protected expression." They also regularly failed to investigate sex crimes against women and failed to investigate citizens' allegations against Baltimore City police officers. While the Justice Department investigation covered the entire city, the bulk of the violations occurred in one particular police precinct—the Western District. Freddie Gray's Sandtown-Winchester neighborhood is in the Western District. There is clearly a spatial element to the condition of black poor/working class people in Baltimore. In certain neighborhoods like Sandtown-Winchester, police/community relationships were found to be particularly egregious.[16]

Arguably, there has been black political incorporation (meaning black people have had political power) in Baltimore for over 30 years. The first black elected mayor of Baltimore, Kirk Schmoke, was elected in 1983. The majority of city council members are black as are most other city officials. At the time of Gray's arrest and death, the mayor was black, as were the city state's attorney, the city council president, the city's Maryland state delegates and senators, the US Congressional representative, and the police chief. Despite this, the condition of Freddie Gray's neighborhood, Sandtown-Winchester, is but one symbol of the persistent spatial, economic and racial oppression that still occurs in the era of so-called black empowerment. The killing of Gray was a spark that lit an already rife situation in Baltimore city. It can be argued that the more root cause was disinvestment in the black neighborhoods in Baltimore City which has led to deep and persistent disparities among neighborhoods.[17]

Sandtown-Winchester is one of the most economically depressed neighborhoods in the city. The median household income in Sandtown-Winchester was $24,374 in 2014 compared to $41,819 in the City of Baltimore. The percent of children living below the poverty line in Sandtown-Winchester was 52% compared to 34.6% in Baltimore City. The unemployment rate was 22.2% compared to 14.2% city wide. Sandtown-Winchester has among the highest percentage of families receiving Temporary Assistance for Needy Families (TANF) benefits in the city and is one of the neighborhoods with the lowest percent of births where the mother received early prenatal care. The neighborhood also has disproportionate percentage of abandoned and unsafe housing. In 2014 it had the highest number of residential properties that were vacant or abandoned in the city—35%. Over one third of the neighborhood housing was abandoned. This is compared to 8.1% citywide.[18] This quick look at some of the Sandtown-Winchester neighborhood statistics makes Soja's concept of geo-spatial disparities and injustice painfully clear.

In the immediate aftermath of the Freddie Gray uprisings, there were attempts by individuals and community organizations to transform these communities through "landscaping." For example, local artists and activists painted several murals at key locations in the neighborhood (e.g., the exact place where Gray was arrested, across the street from the Gilmor Homes) and in the larger West Baltimore area. These murals commemorate Gray's life and also commemorate and celebrate black protest. They are clear examples of "landscaping" in that they alter the physical space. These artworks stand in contrast to the visibly decayed physical structures that surround them. Moreover, they stand as symbols commemorating black resistance in spaces that are often defined by the oppressive forces of disinvestment, exploitation, economic marginalization and racist policies.

There are also examples landscaping led by religious activists in the wake of the Freddie Gray uprisings. For example, Empowerment Temple African Methodist Episcopal Church (a black church in Baltimore) partnered with a local Boys and Girls Club to create the Freddie Gray Youth Empowerment Center which housed a summer camp, served meals and sponsored local activities for children. In another example, Rev. Heber Brown, a local Baltimore minister and activist organized the Black Church Food Security Network to address issues of food security and food justice in local communities. The Network encourages churches to serve as points of distribution for food produced by black farmers outside the city and also encourages and provides support for black churches to develop community gardens on church land.

Perhaps the best example of religious landscaping in the aftermath of the Freddie Gray uprisings was the development of the Tubman House (named for Harriet Tubman), a community center in Sandtown-Winchester, organized by a coalition of local activists and led by Dominque Stevenson. Stevenson was working with the American Friends Service Committee, doing community programs at the Gilmor Homes. Stevenson was looking for a place to house community programs when the uprisings occurred. She and others decided to seize a condemned house directly across the street from the Gilmor Homes, rather than let it be torn down and become another vacant lot. When seized, the house did not have electricity or plumbing, however they used it as a community resource as they ran youth programs, sponsored community celebrations and built thriving community gardens that provided fresh fruit and vegetables for the Sandtown-Winchester Community. Tubman House sees its work as "reclaiming local land and resources so as to secure and improve community life." In Sandtown-Winchester the Tubman House serves as both a practical transformation of the physical space and a symbol of resistance and empowerment in the face of oppressive forces and spatial injustice. The impact of dominant geographies and the black demand for geographical justice in Diepsloot and Baltimore are but two examples of the cartographies of struggles black people are engaged in around the world.

Volume Overview

This volume uses the prism of spatial theory to explore the analyses of various aspects of black landscapes on the African continent and black Atlantic diasporic locations to "disclose the underside, unapparent histories and stories that name the world and black personhood"[19] and amplify the forms of empowerment and liberation black people have constructed as counter actions and narratives to dominant geographies. We endeavor to present diverse representations of the black creative impulse to form religious landscapes and construct social, economic and political spaces that are habitable for black people and black bodies. These landscapes and spaces are physical, psychological and conceptual. They are gendered and racialized in ways that are shaped by their specific religious, geographic and sociohistorical contexts. These contexts are influenced by colonial systems and institutions of modern slavery. The landscapes that people of African descent struggle to construct, reshape and inhabit are intended to counter the effects of these oppressive systems and institutions and often include attempts to reclaim and adapt sources, concepts, tools and techniques that are indigenous to specific geographical contexts or ethno-racial groups. We hope in this volume to offer a look at how the cartographic struggles and constructive engagements within these black-inhabited spaces are rooted in black movements that support the emancipation of black lives and black bodies from the oppressive forces of dominant geographies. At the same time, we are also aware that some practices and constructs that arise out of exercises in black agency can serve as obstacles to black freedom and liberation.

Most of the essays in this volume have evolved from papers delivered at the Transatlantic Roundtable on Religion and Race Conference in Pretoria, South Africa. The theme for the conference was "Social Struggle and Faith-Based Activism in 'Black Empowerment' Times." These essays explore examples of black people struggling to shape and reshape the geographical landscapes in which they live to make life better and increase life chances for themselves and their communities as they exist within the paradox of "black empowerment times." The chapters are divided into two parts. The chapters in "Part I: Aesthetical, Psychological, and Religio-Cultural Landscaping," examine the ways in which religious counter narratives attempt to address psychological, aesthetical, theological and religio-cultural landscaping. These chapters examine the ways in which symbols, language and ritual have been used in attempts to colonize the minds of black people as well as the ways in which black people have reclaimed and reconfigured symbols and language in ways that counter coloniality. In Chapter 1, Tracey E. Hucks explores the religious significance of the ways in which black people establish and reimagine physical space in "In Search of a 'Land Language': Explorations of Race and Land in the African Diaspora." In the opening chapter, Hucks argues that black people in North America have been alienated from land and have struggled to connect with historical and geographical spaces to call "home." She goes on to describe how, despite this alienation, black North Americans claim physical spaces to construct identities and exercise the power to name themselves. In Chapter 2 "The Struggle for the African Soul in the Interface between *Koma* (Christian Missions) and *Thuto* (Basotho Traditions)", Maarman S. Tshehla explores the ways in which modern Christian missions have shaped African landscapes in the form of literacy. Christian missionaries assumed that the local Basotho traditions were hindrances to the propagation of the Christian faith. Tshehla, uncovers the ways in which Basotho disciples of these Christian missionaries used avenues of literacy to construct a Christian faith that could coexist with Basotho institutions and worldview. In Chapter 3 "The Role of Religion in the Formation of White Nationalism: Exclusion, Race, and Ethnicity in Shaping Democratic South Africa's Identity," Itumeleng Daniel Mothoagae reflects on the persistent ideology of white supremacist nationalism in South Africa. He argues that the foundation of white supremacy and nationalism in South Africa is fundamentally linked to the pseudo-understanding of Calvinist Theology from the beginning of white settler arrival. He maintains that though South Africa has a liberal constitution, there are sections in the Constitution that are aimed at maintaining and sustaining the 1994 accord signed between the African National Congress, National Party and Freedom Front on the self-determination of the Afrikaners. The Constitution, according to Mothoagae does not redress the ideology of white supremacy and nationalism expressed in settlements such as Orania. According to Mothoagae, religion has contributed to such ideologies and has shaped the identity of the democratic South Africa post-1994. Boitumelo Senokoane and Mofenyi L. Mataboge discuss the crisis of developing young Africans in Chapter 4 "Back to Africa: Towards a Re-imagination of "Youth" in Africa." In this chapter, they maintain that youth are caught up in a transported hegemonic as opposed to the African worldview. Thus, constructions of colonial knowledge are imposed on the consciousness of young Africans and has led to the dislocation and alienation of young Africans. In Chapter 5, Melinda Contreras-Byrd's "A Psychologist's Perspective on Becoming Agents of an Unruly Transformation" discusses the ways in which religious and healthcare professionals have not thoroughly understood and, thus, have not been able to affectively address the toll that oppression has taken on black bodies and black minds. In response,

Contreras-Byrd begins to map the methods used within these professional landscapes and outlines their limitations in dealing with the emotional and psychological ills of a people who have been affected by racism, sexism and violence. She calls upon these professionals to construct spaces that can effectively support and empower black people. Karen Crozier, in "Affirmative Action and the New Jim Crow: Listening for and Living from the Sound of the Genuine," focuses upon her local community's (Fresno California) use of Peace Light Circles. This community transformed the urban landscape by engaging in a community dialogue centered on Michelle Alexander's book *The New Jim Crow: Mass Incarceration in the Age of Colorblindness.* The community dialogue, which was attended by a range of members from the area, is included in this volume as a model for how groups can transform religious, social and political landscapes and create opportunities for collective exchange and empowerment.

The chapters in "Part II: Sites of Religious Landscaping: Black Churches and African Independent Churches," explore black religious institutions: black churches and African Independent Churches (AICs) in the United States, Cameroon and Zimbabwe. The authors explore examples of religious institutions facilitating collective action in local communities to make the lives and conditions of black people more habitable and address disparities and deprivation such as educational crises, mass incarceration, economic development and government corruption in the age of so-called black empowerment times. They also examine how some of the traditions, practices and theological orientations that black religious institutions have embraced can serve as obstacles to liberation. Several important themes carry through the chapters in this volume: land and spatial injustice; religious landscaping; legacies of colonialism, slavery, apartheid and segregation; and the role of black churches and AICs in countering or cooperating with oppression. In Chapter 7, Donn Worgs focuses on the ways in which black people engage in a kind of geographical "landscaping" through faith-based organizations. In his chapter, " 'To Be Relevant': Black Churches, Education and Productive Engagement," Worgs puts forward the idea of "productive democracy" and argues that black communities through their churches and religious organizations try to improve the life chances of black people through the development of schools and other education programs-- sometimes collaborating with government or minding the gap for government when it was either "absent or hostile" to black community needs. But they do it to remain "relevant" and see their work as a theological obligation. In Chapter 8, "The Reconnectional Hope: Interfaith Transformation of Recidivism to Regeneration of Community," Ronald Peters demonstrates that disproportionately black people in Pittsburgh, PA are caught up in the criminal justice system. Peters addresses the many factors that contribute to this problem. He also shows how local faith-based organizations through Project Hope tries to prevent recidivism and transform community spaces so that the formerly incarcerated can be successfully integrated back into their communities. In Chapter 9 "Leadership Succession Practices in African Independent Churches in Zimbabwe," Clemence Makamure and Vengesai Chimininge address the question of leadership succession within the African Independent Churches in Zimbabwe. They maintain that succession planning is necessary for the stability and progression of these churches, failure to focus on leadership succession is detrimental to African Independent Churches. Vengesai Chimininge and Clemence Makamure in Chapter 10 "The Place of Women in African-Initiated Churches in Zimbabwe," chart the gendered religious landscape of Zimbabwean African Initiated Churches with a focus on Zionist and Apostolic churches. While this chapter gives attention to the gendered and racialized terrains of colonial imposed systems of oppression, it also problematizes current and traditional ethnic practices that may provide sources for increased gender empowerment but also may carry with them gendered practices that maintain women's exclusion from leadership roles. Daniel Pratt Morris-Chapman in "Pick Up Your Cash and Follow Me: Pentecostalism, Prosperity and Socioeconomic Empowerment in Southwest Cameroon," examines whether the prosperity gospel has served as a source for empowerment in Cameroon. He concludes that in the Cameroonian context the prosperity gospel in some ways is empowering. It encourages thrift and hard work and economically productive activity. It also promotes some level of equality for women. However, neo-Pentecostal churches do not address government corruption, which is the main challenge for economic growth and prosperity in Cameroon.

Notes

1 Edward W. Soja, *Seeking Spatial Justice*, Globalization and Community Series (Minneapolis: University of Minnesota Press, 2010), 1.
2 See Katherine McKittrick, *Demonic Grounds: Black Women and the Cartographies of Struggle* (Minneapolis: University of Minnesota Press, 2006), xxii–xxi.
3 Soja, *Seeking Spatial Justice*, 8-9.
4 Rachel E. Harding, *A Refuge in Thunder: Candomblé and Alternative Spaces Blackness* (Bloomington: Indiana University Press, 2003).
5 Charles H. Long. "Perspectives for a Study of Afro-American Religion in America" in *Significations* (Minneapolis: Fortress Press, 1995), 191.

6 Jualynne E. Dodson and José Millet Batista, *Sacred Spaces and Religious Traditions in Oriente Cuba* (Albuquerque: University of New Mexico Press, 2008), 62.
7 See M. Shawn Copeland, *Enfleshing Freedom: Body, Race and Being* (Minneapolis: Fortress Press, 2009).
8 Terreblanche Sampie, *A History of Inequality in South Africa, 1652–2002* (Natal: University of KwaZulu Natal Press, 2002).
9 Dianne Scott, "The Destruction of Clairwood: A Case Study on the Transformation of Communal Living Space," in *The Apartheid City and Beyond Urbanization and Social Change in South Africa*, ed. David M. Smith (London: Routledge, 1992), 89–100.
10 Jeffrey Butler, Robert I. Rotberg, and John Adams, *The Blacks Homelands of South Africa: The Political and Economic Development of Bophuthatswana and Kwa-Zulu* (Berkeley: University of California Press, 1978).
11 P. Bonner and L. Segal, *Soweto: A History* (Cape Town: Maskew Longman, 1998), 10.
12 Terreblanche Sampie, *A History of Inequality in South Africa 1652–2002* (Pietermaritzburg: University of Natal Press, 2002).
13 Maluleke Risenga, Inequality Trends in South Africa: A Multidimensional Diagnostic of Inequality (Pretoria: Statistics South Africa, 2019).
14 SACN, *State of South African Cities Report 2016* (Johannesburg: SACN, 2016), 50.
15 Baltimore Neighborhood Indicators Alliance. 2016. *Vital Signs 14 Spring 2016.* Neighborhood Statistical Report (Baltimore: Jacob Francis Institute University of Baltimore).
16 U.S. Department of Justice Civil Rights Division (2016). *Investigation of the Baltimore City Police Department* (Washington, DC: U.S. Department of Justice).
17 Baltimore Neighborhood Indicators Alliance. 2016. *Vital Signs 14 Spring 2016.* Neighborhood Statistical Report (Baltimore: Jacob Francis Institute University of Baltimore).
18 Baltimore Neighborhood Indicators Alliance. 2016. *Vital Signs 14 Spring 2016.* Neighborhood Statistical Report (Baltimore: Jacob Francis Institute University of Baltimore).
19 Katherine McKittrick, *Demonic Grounds: Black Women and the Cartographies of Struggle* (Minneapolis: University of Minnesota Press, 2006), xxii.

Part I: Psychological, Aesthetical, and Religio-Cultural Landscaping

1. *In Search of a "Land Language": Explorations of Race and Land in the African Diaspora*

TRACEY E. HUCKS

Introduction

Africana Religious Studies—an emerging subfield of inquiry within the discipline of religion—concentrates on African diasporic traditions in North America, South America, Central America, and the Caribbean. Situated at a disciplinary nexus between the social sciences and the humanities, the study of African diasporic religious cultures focuses closely on the ways that "Africa," as a contested category and cultural resource, has been at the center of Atlantic cross-fertilizations, the basis of innovative processes and practices, as well as a symbol and strategy for religious recovery, re-humanization, and self-authentication in the African diaspora. Within inhospitable Atlantic environments, African Americans navigate the social and political challenges of diasporan existence and create systems and modes of re-humanization through the material and discursive meanings of religion. In this quest for a renewed humanity and revalued materiality in the Atlantic world, the physicality of land has been an important spatial and spiritual symbol for diasporan re-rootedness.

Africa: A Theory of Land

Charles H. Long, author of *Significations: Signs, Symbols and Images in the Interpretation of Religion*, has been hugely impactful in theorizing Africa as a symbol for religious nationalism and social activism. For Africans in the Diaspora, Long takes the exilic historical moment of the transatlantic slave trade as his point of departure in reflecting on the meaning of Africa, land, and religion. "By being slaves," Long writes, "black persons were isolated from any self-determined legitimacy in the society of which they were a part and were recognized by their physiological characteristics. This constituted a complexity of experience revolving around the relationship between their physical being and their origins. So even if they had no conscious memory of Africa," Long continues, "the image of Africa played an enormous part in the religion of the blacks. The image of Africa, an image related to historical beginnings, has been one of the primordial religious images of greater significance. It constitutes the religious revalorization of the land, a place where the natural and ordinary gestures of the blacks were and could be authenticated. In this connection," Long writes further, "one can trace almost every nationalistic movement among the blacks and find Africa to be the dominating and guiding image. . . . The image of Africa as it appears in black religion is unique, for the black community in America is a landless people. . . . Their image of the land points to the religious meaning of land even in the absence of these forms of authentication. It thus emerges as an image that is always invested with historical and religious possibilities."[1]

In response to their identity as a displaced population grappling with ambiguous questions of origin, nationhood, and identity, African people in the Diaspora have engaged consistently in finding a new "land language" through which to politically, culturally, economically, and religiously encode a meaningful existence. Physical geographies of "land language" ultimately symbolize the distinct need for security, self-governance, and free citizenry.[2] Whether nineteenth-century black townships and settlements in the United States and Canada or twentieth century reclamation movements such as the African Hebrew Israelites of Jerusalem or Oyotunji African Village in South Carolina, negotiating a new land language for black diasporic communities has meant occupying new physical landscapes that combat exile, displacement, and alienation. In these re-inhabited territories, African-descended populations have sought to reconnect to primordial roots and utilize religion, culture, or ethno-nationalisms in order to imbue land and space with meaning and authentication.

Since slavery, the African continent has been a formative physical and symbolic land language for Africans in the Atlantic world. Africa within a diasporan context had to be re-landed. Thus, Charles Long explains, "the significance, power, and necessity of a 'place to be called home' for millions of persons of African descent who were separated from their original homeland and denied authenticity as human beings in North America" became an essential aim. The African continent, "their place of origin," Long explains further, "was remembered, invented, symbolized, and remade within the new spaces and times of North America as a foundation for their humanness as well as a vision for a viable human future."[3]

Black Land Language in Nineteenth-Century North America

Fugitive slaves and freed blacks in the United States and Canada attempted several physical land languages prior to ratification of the Thirteenth Amendment, ending American racial slavery, in 1865. These collective North American black communities offered protection and independence amidst alien geographies of insecurity and bondage. In 1828, for example, a group of black Canadians drafted a petition to the royal monarchy of Britain. The group requested a land grant in order to create an all-black community to thwart "the system of kidnapping which is now carried on through his Majesty's provinces by the Georgia and Virginia kidnappers from the Southern states of America." By uniting "themselves together" and establishing this alternative community, or "township," the petitioners believed they "could become useful to [their present] king and country." However, the community they envisioned had a broader importance. As indicated in the petition, land-language metaphors such as township, village, and kingdom were important nineteenth-century designators of territorial organization and cohesion.[4]

Conceptions such as freedom, welfare, autonomy, and safety permeated black thought in relation to land that could be owned and territory that could be governed. Aby Jones, formerly enslaved in Kentucky, whose brother purchased his freedom, desired to "migrate to some place where I could be really a FREE MAN."[5] Not unlike numerous others, Canada was the *place* that Jones selected. His and related acts of self-emancipation constellated in the establishment of black settlements such as Africville. Formed as recompense for blacks who had sided with Britain during the War of 1812, Africville was a township, or community, whose residents desired to "live in privacy, relatively free from the racist attitudes of the predominately white population."[6] Their desire proved that, whether voluntary or through intentional escape, migration and movement were central to black pursuits for landed autonomy and collective independence. As scholars William and Jane Pease once noted, autonomous "Negro communities [such as Africville] were dedicated to training their inhabitants in the virtues of self-reliance, individualism, and independence."[7]

Of course, the majority of black people who endured slavery in the United States never made it to Canada or to any other so-called promised land before ratification of the Thirteenth Amendment in 1865. After ratification, countless newly minted African Americans began to index the complex meanings of citizenship, safety, and home through the acquisition of land. This process continued throughout the remainder of the nineteenth century. In 1889, for example, black attorney, land developer, and Republican politician Edwin McCabe ventured from Kansas to Oklahoma in search of a suitable site for an all-black township similar to Nicodemus and others established by the Exodusters of Kansas (McCabe, an influential Exoduster, had served as a public official in Nicodemus before relocating to Oklahoma). While surveying the terrain of Oklahoma, he declared fervently: "I mean to make a *home* for my people."[8]

McCabe's declaration reflected the evolution in his thought process about black autonomy. No longer was he desirous of an all-black township; he desired an all-black state. In 1890, he journeyed to Washington, DC, to pitch his idea of black independent statehood to federal officials. To amass support for this venture, McCabe passionately argued: "Why not a Negro State? We desire to remove from the surroundings that so disgrace my people. We are not only loyal citizens but capable of advancement. In a new country [meaning a black independent state within the United States], new lands, a climate suited to our race, we desire to show that we are men and women capable of self-government."[9]

The prospect of significant land acquisition and self-government in the American West seemed feasible to many blacks during the early 1890s. Elsewhere, and particularly in the former slaveholding South, these blacks noted, conservative whites were trying hard to negate the gains that African Americans had made since emancipation. Political disenfranchisement, social ostracism, and physical violence were three common means to achieve this vile aim. The West, then, might provide an effect counterbalance to Jim Crow. In fact, there were some African Americans who viewed the development of black settlements on the Southwestern and Midwestern frontiers as intermediary stops before their final migration to Africa. In 1891, A.G. Belton expressed this sentiment when he wrote, "We as a people are oppressed and disfranchised. We are still working hard and our rights are taken from us. Times are hard and getting harder every year. We as a people believe that Africa is the place but to get from under bondage we are thinking of Oklahoma as this is our nearest place of safety."[10]

By the 1890s, the formation of black towns in the West and repatriation to Africa had become two important ways African Americans responded to Jim Crow. Black leaders such as Henry McNeal Turner of Georgia—a bishop in the African Methodist Episcopal Church, Union war veteran, and onetime politician—believed strongly that true freedom and independence for African Americans could only be found on the continent of Africa. In 1895, Turner told black Oklahomans that there was "no manhood future in the United States for the Negro. He may eke out an existence for generations to come, but he can never be a man—full, symmetrical and undwarfed."[11] Whereas Turner and other emigration advocates suggested that Liberia and Sierra Leone were fine places to resettle and enjoy full humanity, historian Carl Hunt recalls that large numbers of black Americans "never looked to Africa as the place where they could control their own cultural destiny [or] be able to wield political power and influence"; the formation of all-black townships *within* the United States predominated their thinking about free territorial configurations.[12] The names of the following towns encapsulated these black Americans' persistent desire to exercise autonomy in the land of their birth: Independence Heights, Texas; Arkansas Colored, Oklahoma; New Zion, Kentucky; North Folk Colored, Oklahoma; Bookertee, Oklahoma; Blackdom, New Mexico; and Africa Town, Alabama.[13]

"Oyo Rises Again": The Contemporary Land Language of Oyotunji African Village

African Americans continued to conjoin both language and meaning of race and land well into the twentieth century. Oyotunji African Village founded at Sheldon (Beaufort County), South Carolina, in 1970 offers a prime example of this continuum. The Yoruba and Dahomey ethnicities of West Africa inspired the village's founder, an *oba*(king) named Efuntola Oseijeman Adelabu Adefunmi, to seek a "purposeful reconceptualization" of African American agency. In particular, Adefunmi re-envisioned the landscape of the American South by re-territorializing it as an expression of religious-based activism. In so doing, Adefunmi expanded a Yoruba-based cultural movement that African Americans, Cubans, Nigerians, and other diasporan populations in the United States had begun in the 1950s. Because this movement was foundational to the 1970s work of Adefunmi generally and Oyotunji African Village specifically, the movement deserves extended notice.[14]

Leaders of the Yoruba-based movement of the 1950s strove to de-center the black Christian church and cultivate African traditions as alternative sources of religious meaning. Whereas the Christian faith-based activism of the civil rights movement emphasized social integration, Christian universality, and inclusive American citizenry within the existing contours of the United States, Yoruba religious cultures supplied African-descended communities in the United States with a distinct paradigm for territorial nationalism and social activism based on global Pan-African perspectives of nationhood and sovereignty, decolonized approaches to Anglo-cultural dominance, and broader Atlantic renaissances of the indigenous religions of Africa. Yoruba religion and its diasporan configurations in the United States introduced a new religiosity that included African deity, ancestral veneration, new modes of divination and herbal healing, animal sacrifice, the ritualizing of deities through drum and dance, and union with spirits through trance possession.

During the 1950s, African Americans engaged Yoruba religion as a threshold to a pre-Atlantic past as well as a resource for Africanizing diasporan terrains. Even though Africa was their original homeland, they strove to create an ultimate homeland—a "New Africa"—in the United States. This movement gained momentum during the 1960s into the 1970s. Black territorial nationalists and organizations such as the Republic of New Africa (who often shared overlapping memberships with practicing Yorubas) sought to chart a new geographical cartography in the United States, thereby making space for the demarcation of New Africa. Oba Efuntola Oseijeman Adelabu Adefunmi was one of these nationalists. In 1970, he founded Oyotunji African Village to introduce Yoruba culture to the black American South. He expressly wanted to model a residential community that would be self-governing on its own land; provide alternative African models of polity, society, and national belonging; and foster religious and cultural transformations from American Christianity to African-based practices. A sign at the entrance of the village makes clear these distinguishing factors and Adefunmi's religio-cultural and nationalist goals: "You are leaving the U.S. You are entering the Yoruba Kingdom. In the name of His Highness Efuntola, peace. Welcome to the sacred Yoruba Village of Oyotunji. The only village in North America built by priests of the Vodun cults as a tribute to our ancestors. These priests preserve the customs, laws, and religion of the African race[.] Welcome to our Land!"[15]

Representing a geographical inscription of Africa American religious nationalism, Oyotunji African Village affixes an entire ancestral framework to a diasporan landscape. According to the village's present leadership, a crucial difference between Oyotunji and the rest of North America is not just geographical, cultural, and political; Oyotunji African Village also is different psychologically and spiritually. Oba Adejuyigbe Adefunmi II explains, "The psychology, above all, is what is different. You're leaving the United States" when you enter the village. In Oyotunji, citizens revere and enshrine African gods. They also fashion novel forms of government, honor priestly lineages, and establish new African monarchies. Villagers likewise ritualize the ancestors of Africa as well as those of the Diaspora.[16]

Of equal significance, Oyotunji African Village makes linkages between the materiality of land and the materiality of the black body. Within its physical contours, the black body is transformed from a historically objectified American commodity as slave chattel (a thing) to a historically superlative African cultural and artistic tapestry (a human). By offering African Americans a humanizing materiality and a revalued ontology, the Yoruba religion practiced in Oyotunji African Village serves to rescue blackness from a maligned American history of devaluation, perverse physicality, and defiled phenotype. Similar to the belief of art historian Babatunde Lawal, who insists the human body can become a canvas on which religion, politics, and culture can be mapped and emblematized, the citizens of Oyotunji African Village believe the black body can become a lived site of aesthetic culture. The villagers' natural hairstyles; traditional African garb, head, and body adornments; and beaded *eleke* necklaces collectively formed pictograms, or image texts, of readable code that reclaim vital meanings of Africa historically withheld from them in North America.[17] Thus, languages of land, religion, and black materiality converge within the physical boundaries of Oyotunji in transformative and enduring ways.

Conclusion

The creation of diasporan land languages in the Atlantic world were first and foremost about inscribing new interpretations and formulations of home and home*land* in the Atlantic. From nineteenth-century black townships to contemporary restorations of African village life, African Americans in North America have symbolized a relational approach to land as a way of assuaging historical diasporicity and social discontent. These diverse land languages of the Diaspora continue to demand new interpretations of humanity and freedom now more than two decades into the twenty-first century.

Notes

1 Charles H. Long, *Significations: Signs, Symbols, and Images in the Interpretation of Religion* (Philadelphia, PA: Fortress Press, 1986), 176.
2 African American members of the African Hebrew Israelites of Jerusalem used the term *land language* to define their quest for a holy land. See, for example, *The Village of Peace*, dir. Ben Schuder and Niko Philipides, 68 mins., Infinity Vision, 2014, DVD.
3 Charles H. Long, quoted in Tracey E. Hucks, *Yoruba Traditions and African American Religious Nationalism* (Albuquerque: University of New Mexico Press, 2012), xiii–xiv.
4 William H. Pease and Jane H. Pease, *Black Utopia: Negro Communal Experiments in America* (Madison: State Historical Society of Wisconsin, 1963), 6.

5 Ibid.
6 Angel David Nieves, "Memories of Africville: Urban Renewal, Reparations, and the Africadian Diaspora," in *Black Geographies and the Politics of Place*, ed. Katherine McKittrick and Clyde Woods (Cambridge, MA: South End Press, 2007), 88.
7 Pease and Pease, *Black Utopia*, 6.
8 Faye Mathews, "Dream of a Black State," *Sepia* 21 (March 1972): 69.
9 Ibid.
10 William Loren Katz, *The Black West: A Documentary and Pictorial History of the African American Role in the Westward Expansion of the United States* (New York: Simon and Schuster, 1987), 250.
11 Ibid., 254.
12 Carl M. Hunt, *Oyotunji Village: The Yoruba Movement in America* (Washington, DC: University Press of America, 1979), 2.
13 See Kenneth Marvin Hamilton, *Black Towns and Profit: Promotion and Development in the Trans-Appalachian West, 1877–1915* (Urbana: University of Illinois Press, 1991), 153; and Currie Ballard, "The Camera Speaks for Them," *American Legacy* 2 (summer 1996): 42–47 (offering a pictorial account of Black townships in Oklahoma).
14 John L. Jackson Jr., *Thin Description: Ethnography and the African Hebrew Israelites of Jerusalem* (Cambridge, MA: Harvard University Press, 2013), 6.
15 Michelle M. Commander, *Afro-Atlantic Flight: Speculative Returns and the Black Fantastic* (Durham, NC: Duke University Press, 2017). Other sources offer slightly variations of the sign at the entrance of Oyotunji African Village. One version reads: "NOTICE. YOU ARE LEAVING THE U.S. YOU ARE ENTERING YORUBA KINGDOM. Welcome to the Sacred Yoruba Village of Oyo-Tunji. The only village in N. Amerika built by Priests of the Orisha-Voodoo Cults. As a tribute to our Ancestors the Priests preserve the customs, laws and religion of the Afrikan Race. WELCOME TO OUR LAND!" Harry G. Lefever, "Leaving the United States: The Black Nationalist Themes of OrishaVodu," *Journal of Black Studies* 31 (November 2000): 174. See also Hucks, *Yoruba Traditions and African American Religious Nationalism*, 168.
16 Oba Adejuyigbe Adefunmi II, personal interview with the author, September 19, 2008.
17 Babatunde Lawal, "Art and Architecture, History of African," in *Encyclopedia of African History*, Vol. 1: A–G, ed. Kevin Shillington (New York: Fitzboy Dearborn, 2005), 103–108.

2. *The Struggle for the African Soul in the Interface between* Koma *(Christian Missions) and* Thuto *(Basotho Traditions)*

Maarman S. Tshehla

A little over a decade ago, Tinyiko Maluleke argued that Africanization was "more complex than sheer translation or indigenization"; instead, he urged, it involved "a combination of combat and construction."[1] Are not Africans' efforts to demonstrate compatibility or continuity between Africa's religious past and her Christian present, after all, a response to particular brands of hostile and domineering Christian expression?[2] In other words, anyone seeking "to appreciate the emergence of African theologies" must also "understand the negative impact of the colonial system in Africa" because, by and large, African theological maneuvers amount to "a creative response that seeks to authenticate the essence and relevance of the Christian gospel" to Africa's realities.[3] Even as Africans enthusiastically take up Christian faith despite the circumstances surrounding its modern propagation, they also engage in contemplation of that espousal's implications on their individual and communal identities.

Africa's embrace of Christianity is thoroughgoing. Instead of a simple "the more religious options the better for us" attitude, Africans appear to have always sought a genuine meaningful integration between Christian faith and African realities. So, Kwame Bediako can confidently point out the "Christianization of the African past" phase.[4] Put differently, Africans are able to look past nineteenth century missions' shortcomings because their Christian roots go far deeper than those of the West. In a nutshell then, and without discounting other pertinent factors, the struggle over Africa's soul is essentially "the problem of Christian identity in the African context."[5] Precise jargon is secondary here; moreover, "the two processes – Christianisation and Africanisation – have not and cannot be artificially separated."[6] To speak of "a combination of combat and construction," therefore, is to concede that the waters have been troubled and concordant action is all that is called for.

An admirable attempt to marry combat and construction is here gleaned from a seminal article penned in Sesotho by a Mosotho writer belonging to the first generation of literate Basotho.[7] This chapter contends that the author Filemon Rapetloane's work illustrates a manner of going about the task of engendering a cohesive African Christian identity that is fairly typical of the African response. While skillfully holding both contenders in critical balance, Rapetloane demonstrates a perspective that enriches through challenge and admiration both the traditional African and the Christian missionary. A pithy summary of the very limited extant detail about this remarkable writer precedes our interested reading of the article he penned way back in 1863. The reading itself is informed by Sesotho nuance, which is sometimes awkward for non-Sesotho readers, as much as it is further limited by my own blind spots and partialities.

In a word, this chapter asserts that African engagements with Christian faith have from the earliest days always been creative. More especially when drawing from African mother tongues as was the case across most of the Continent, there was in practice scarcely any discord between the emerging Christian self-understanding on the one hand and African consciousness on the other. An expatriate Christian missionary reading Rapetloane's piece will applaud the extent to which this disciple both commends the gospel and is critically aware of world events. An African auditing Rapetloane will be moved by the beauty of his Sesotho oratorical skill as well as by his intrepid affirmation of traditional cultural institutions. Christianity finds accommodation within the African world while the African acquires a language and competencies that can be used to uphold the beauty of her soul. The landscape Rapetloane paints is African and complex; African responses to modern Christian missions involved way more than European missionaries envisaged even while African converts employed mission tools.

Ntate Rapetloane

A feature that records from nineteenth century South Africa often share with postcolonial critiques of such archives is the privileging of individual European actors accentuated by the facelessness of so-called native agents. Accordingly, the mission newspaper wherein Rapetloane's piece appears does not indicate his authorship. In fact, since this was the lead article of *Leselinyana la*

Lesotho's launch issue, the impression arises fairly naturally that the piece is an Editorial instead of the Op-Ed that it in fact was. Thankfully, however, such an illusion dissipates fairly quickly once one starts reading the piece itself. The oral tones and aural beauty, the loaded vocabulary that presumes so much cultural awareness, the beaming confidence in things Sesotho, the overall style of the article has an air about it which would be rare among recent adult students of the language; an air by which *Leselinyana's* founding editor, Adolphe Mabille, was scarcely buoyed.[8]

Whether or not expatriate missionaries did it deliberately, the eclipsing of native intellectuals was exacerbated by the reality "that social action amongst the Basotho was communal and the traditional institutions, religious and otherwise, promoted this communality."[9] In other words, the Basotho cared only that their voices had been heard, and not necessarily whether each individual speaker was acknowledged by name. Self-effacing though the Basotho may be, knowing something about Rapetloane surely enhances appreciation of the depth of his argument. For this feat a debt is owed to the expatriate missionary editor's biographer:

> The first number of *Leselinyana* ... appeared in September, 1863. With some interruption it has gone on appearing all though the years—it has the distinction of being the oldest Native newspaper in South Africa. Filemone Rapetloane wrote the introduction to the first number but all the rest of it was, it seems, written by Mabille and he set up the type and printed it with his own hands.[10]

Rapetloane dared not eclipse Adolphe Mabille! After all, at the time of writing his erudite piece, he worked as Mabille's right hand man at Morija. In this capacity, he more than helped out with the translation into Sesotho of both the Old Testament and *The Pilgrim's Progress* among others.[11] Here was a man fully formed in literary work, actively involved in the arduous work of translating the Bible across languages and cultures, an indubitable Mosotho who acceded to Christian faith as an adult. Rapetloane is certainly part of the reason it is now widely accepted that, "as a rule, the most striking achievement of nineteenth-century missionaries was not the conversion of individual Africans .... The most successful evangelists were African Christians themselves."[12]

My Fellow Basotho

> True and dependable Basotho! Long, long ago, this place where we now reside, used to be called "Far, far away, over at Quthing". It was such a marvel when Mohlomi travelled this far. Shaka's land, Bopedi, Mabutswanyaneng, Botlokwa, Kgolokwe, Basieng, Kalahari—all those places seemed like the

> ends of the earth. Whoever came from those regions was a spectacle, admiringly referred to as "One from over yonder".

Nineteenth-century Basotho at the interface found their identity challenged on two fronts. In Molema's parlance, on the one hand, "Communality was the basis of social organization in Lesotho and Ancestor-veneration was its ideological justification."[13] Cultural self-understanding revolved around community; thought, speech, or any other activity proceeded with the community in mind and for the sake of community. Owing to aggressive and tactless presentation strategies, Christian missions "threatened customs that were religiously observed to placate the Ancestors and to ensure harmony within the society," and they "also challenged constituted authority which derived its justification from these same Ancestors."[14] For Rapetloane to address the piece to genuine Basotho then was to acknowledge issues surrounding the state of their identity politics. To affirm their genuineness in relation to *koma* ("mountain school") was to side with them against the missionary assault on Basotho institutions.[15]

To identify with the Basotho, for one who belonged for all intents and purposes with the aggressive mission enterprise, was a self-conscious statement regarding the compatibility of Christianity with Sesotho. Those who were literate among the Basotho would have attended mission schools and been taught by persons such as Emile Rolland (see note 15); "the schools were missionary controlled and the condition for attending them was acceptance of Christianity."[16] The degree to which school attendance transformed such a student would be a matter of interest to both traditional Basotho and missionary teachers. This tension informs Rapetloane's piece, and to ignore it is to miss the nuance with which he maneuvers between the supposedly conflicting worlds that he inhabits.

Rapetloane's poetic license is best appreciated in his Sesotho parlance; we can nevertheless here only deal with my English approximation thereof. His goal is to commend *Leselinyana* to Basotho ears—"Sesotho prose has an air of being listened to and not of being read."[17] Addressing them as *Basotho ba mannete a koma* (here rendered *true and dependable Basotho*), Rapetloane is consciously reaching well beyond the small fraction of Basotho who can read and write; he has in mind the entire nation. In other words, he takes it for granted that those Basotho who are armed with literacy do indeed take pride in mediating written messages to their unlettered relatives and fellow citizens. Basotho's *Pitso*[18] culture had ensured that no Mosotho could be unconcerned about the goings on of his or her day. Accordingly, he addresses the hearers of *Leselinyana* contents just as a Mosotho man would address any august *pitso*, which was itself Basotho men's oratorical school and rhetorical performance platform.

Having identified his audience as well as having identified with his audience by paying homage to ***koma***, one of the institutions that occupy the heart of Sesotho identity and thus was expatriate missionaries' enemy number one, Rapetloane then goes on to engage in some overt landscaping. Quthing, which the French missionaries had renamed Morija, though only some 40km away from Thaba Bosiu, where King Moshoeshoe resided, used to appear to be worlds away. Thanks to the exploits first of Morena Mohlomi—who was mentor of the eventual King Moshoeshoe—and, subsequently, of the Paris Evangelical Missionaries, Quthing has now drawn closer to Thaba Bosiu, closer to the hearts of the Basotho.

This careful maneuvering by Rapetloane is as significant as it is deliberate. Chief Mohlomi represents several associations to every Mosotho's mind, just as does Quthing now baptized Morija. The mention of Mohlomi's name amounts to saluting the Basotho paramountcy. Not only was Mohlomi of royal lineage, he had tutored the greatest Mosotho yet—Morena Moshoeshoe himself. Mohlomi was also a renowned diviner, a traveler-explorer, and an enthusiastic collector of wisdoms from near and far; in the eyes of some students of history, these traits earned him the title of "religious and political reformer."[19]

Through molding the young Moshoeshoe, Mohlomi's influence on the evolution of Sesotho had been cemented. For instance, Basotho practiced cousin marriage, a way of ensuring that family wealth circulated within the extended family. Mohlomi is credited with making a systematic case for the practice of marrying outside one's immediate clan.[20] When one throws polygyny into the mix, as Rapetloane does anon, then emerges a model which the Basotho applied even to spiritual matters: your homestead is strengthened by taking one from closer home, another from over there, a couple more from further still. How frustrating this approach to life proved to be for the *baruti* who needed their converts to choose one way or the other! To this very day Moshoeshoe's refusal to convert on missionary terms remains the bane of both Protestant and Catholic missionary legacy in Lesotho.[21]

Quthing, and indeed any other place on earth, has been brought closer to the purview of the Basotho. It is now possible to know what is going on anywhere on earth thanks to the work of men and women whose command center is Morija. It is significant that Quthing has been renamed, and the new name signifies the positive effects coming out of Protestant missing headquarters. But to the Basotho it remains Quthing; it continues to bear both its pre-missions history and its Sesotho history alongside Christian missions. Rapetloane could have easily found a way to use the new name, *Morija*, but it was important to him that his Basotho audience appreciated that the renaming was cosmetic rather than obliterative.

Christian mission projects have produced a cohort of Basotho who can read for, as well as teach, their fellow Basotho knowledges of various kinds. Whereas persons coming from physically far-off places used to be a spectacle on account of Basotho's ignorance of what went on whence they came, those who now opt out of engagement with the changes that are taking place among the Basotho will be the ones about whose ignorance people will be taken aback. *Leselinyana* is here to ensure that the Basotho are not left behind from history's forward march.

In essence, the defining qualities of "true and dependable Basotho" are transforming. Being a genuine Mosotho used to revolve around knowledge of Sesotho values, history and customs transmitted across generations via *koma* and related edifices.[22] Now, while valuing from where one has come still remains critical,[23] authentic Sesotho identity has grown to include knowledge about, and interaction with, peoples and places that were once considered alien and beyond human reach. To be sure, both inimical and amiable forces are behind these changes to people's worlds and worldviews, but the question is whether one is acclimatizing.

Change Is Inevitable

> Then calamity arose. It scattered people. Nations intermingled. Lesotho's rulership got consolidated. Then the gun appeared, that is to say, the Koranna. They took people down as though they were shooting animals. Next came baruti, bringing thuto, coming as though they were a medicine. And yes it is so; the medicine is God's word. Then wars ceased. Basotho even returned from Makgoweng as well as from Bokone. From Makgoweng they brought with them cattle, goats, sheep, horses and guns. Some even had wives and children. We said, "Wow, on what manner of sojourn have you been, returning now as you do driving flocks?" They replied, "Well, that's the kind of peace which exists over there; where people are remunerated in cattle. We even bought horses and guns and all manner of cloth."
>
> What more should I recount? Dear Basotho, let us gladly receive Leselinyana la Lesotho.
>
> Ignoramus: What does it help?
> Wisdom: Pshaw, you love wheat, and wheat-chaff, but you refuse news!
> Ignoramus: News about pass documents?
> Wisdom: Folly sure is death.
>
> Then Leselinyana la Lesotho answered them and said: "What are you two quarrelling about? I shall be welcomed at the palace, at Ramohato's place, the very one who communicates through letters. He enjoys the protection of the Queen of the whites, with whom he converses through letters. I shall be to Letsie like his sephatho, to Molapo a serethe as well; just as to Masopha

> too I shall be a tlhakwana. Mopeli will skip like a horse when he sees me. Sekgonyana in turn will say, 'That's what I'm talking about.' To Qadi's Mabeoana, Tsholo, I will say, 'How can people who now grind gunpowder lack a newspaper?' All the headmen and elders will welcome me; I will enlighten Mokoteli's domain with my little light. Great joy will come to believers. You ask what I come bearing. Well, I have news pertaining to various nations. I have come to remind you about your Creator, who is also the Creator of the whites, and of all other nations. Greetings, I am Leselinyana la Lesotho. This is what I am about."

Leselinyana will disseminate information among the Basotho, but it will not shy away from the tougher issues of life. The manner of Basotho it envisages have as much to give as they have to receive; they have a promising future as much as a proud past. Presuming whatever editorial touch-ups were enacted, Rapetloane's piece cannot be accused of either shirking controversial questions or capitulating to expatriate missionaries' demands and standards. So much more than a mere bricoleur, here is a genuine creator and pioneer within Sesotho literature. The article's peerless quality is accentuated by the fact that it had no Sesotho precedent after which to be modeled.

Rapetloane's second paragraph deals with a number of recent historical developments about which history books of subsequent generations are replete. These include the *Lifacane* (or *Difaqane*) that mottled Southern African tribes, the gun that proved so much more effective than the spear, along with Moshoeshoe's consolidating several petty chiefdoms around the navel of South Africa into a formidable force known as the Basotho. In a move that is by no means "loud flattery," Rapetloane grants the arrival of the Gospel as the pinnacle development of those days. He recognizes *baruti's* role as its agents. But by calling the Gospel *God's word*, and so distinguishing it from *thuto* (literate evangelical Christianity), Rapetloane intimates that the medicine the Basotho needed was necessarily the former. There should be no confusion. *Thuto* represents the Gospel as interpreted and propagated by the *baruti*. But *God's word* is the ultimate medicine to which the Basotho enjoy independent access, for which access they have *thuto* to thank. In such a scenario, what is to stop God's word engaging *koma* after the same manner that the Gospel's engagement with European edifices resulted in *thuto*? This erudite reasoning has not always been matched within subsequent African theological endeavors. That has been in part because colonization has succeeded in duping Africans into believing that they can dispense with reflecting in their own mother tongues.

Rapetloane insists that credit for the cessation of wars and the welcome return of migrant laborers should go to the effectiveness of the Gospel. This distinction between the Gospel and its time- and culture-bound carriers obviously applies to all missionaries, both black and white. But in Rapetloane's day it cut more deeply into the white missionary's ego, for the latter was persuaded that "Christian civilization" as "he" understood it was normative for all peoples. From *thuto*, argues Rapetloane, true and dependable Basotho are free to assimilate what they find desirable, thereby Christianizing their worlds. In the final analysis however, not *thuto* but *God's word* is the definitive remedy and a formidable partner in their efforts to engender an authentic African Christianity!

Migrants are able to return home because peace now prevails in Lesotho. But not even King Moshoeshoe, who is famed for considering peace to be his sister,[24] can claim sole agency for the prevailing stability. Peace, it must be emphasized, prevails ultimately because of the agency of *God's word*. Thanks to this peace, Lesotho will benefit from the worldly goods and skills and implements which the returnees come bearing. One of the things these migrant laborers picked up in *Makgoweng* (industrialized towns characterized by white settlements) is the reality of newspapers; they have come to appreciate the value of being kept abreast on a regular basis about developments both near and far. For that reason these erstwhile migrants should be among the first people to welcome *Leselinyana la Lesotho*. Not only will Leselinyana help keep them in touch with the distant worlds they have known, the newspaper will also enrich their participation at the nation's *pitso's*.

Leselinyana has come about in order to make it unnecessary for people to travel far in order to learn news of happenings all around the world. The respect which was accorded persons such as Chief Mohlomi before *Leselinyana's* advent can now belong to all Basotho provided they let *Leselinyana* transport them near and far without the treacherous drain of physical travel. For this reason, *Leselinyana* is confident that it will be as welcome in the King's courts as in the junior chiefs' homes. After all, King Moshoeshoe already enjoys the symbolic honor of being the first Mosotho author[25] and a regular writer of letters to the British queen. Indeed, even beyond the royal households, *Leselinyana* will be welcomed among the various decision-makers and opinion-shapers of the day, not least among whom are the believers themselves. For this reason, *Leselinyana* will not apologize for its religious content; after all there is only one Creator who is interested in the welfare of all.

Several words with which Rapetloane's piece concludes defy translation. *Leselinyana* presents itself to the heir-apparent, Prince Letsie, as a *sephatho*. Moshoeshoe was 79 years old when *Leselinyana* launched, and therefore Letsie was increasingly the person through whom to influence the nations' direction. A *sephatho* is the chief's favorite person; the one to whom the prince is always likely to give an ear; a chief advisor if you will. Such a person is clearly very influential and is often used by others to either soften or harden the leader's heart regarding particular issues. *Leselinyana* sees itself from the onset as created to play this enviable role in the life of the king-in-waiting. That is Rapetloane's bold challenge to the Basotho royalty, if they will take it up. As for *Leselinyana*, she is competent and eager to play that role.

The younger princes Molapo and Masopha also should gladly receive *Leselinyana* as their *serethe* and *tlhakwana* respectively. Having affirmed *koma* at the beginning of his piece, Rapetloane now concludes through approving references to polygyny. *Serethe* and *tlhakwana* are tags used for junior wives within polygamous Basotho families. In true *dikoma* style, *serethe* (a heel) and *tlhakwana* (a small hoof) are simultaneously both doting and euphemistic expressions. You can tell by the anatomical position of the parts alluded to that the female referents and their offspring enjoy a lower status in regard to the running of the family or, in the case of these two princes, the running of the kingdom. But their value in propping up the family is undeniable. It seemed better for Basotho that consorts be known and formalized than that they be entertained in secret.[26] Rapetloane unapologetically offers *Leselinyana*—a Christian missionary newspaper—in this capacity of a junior wife.

In this charged mission context, *sethepu* (polygyny), like *koma*, was so frowned upon that even Morena Moshoeshoe himself had had to succumb to some of his believing junior wives' demands for divorce. As against *koma*, Mabille was equally vociferous against *sethepu* (polygyny). So passionate was he that the entire May 1872 number of the *Little Light* was made up of his one article entitled "Cattle Marriage, I"; the treatise was continued in the subsequent two numbers. The series systematically expounds six points in all, but the crux of his argument was that *lobola* ("bride-price") encourages polygamy: "A polygamist who has sold a daughter to advantage" he concludes, "will always be able to purchase an additional wife with the proceeds, and parents attracted by the price offered, will always find ways and means of coercing the will of their daughters if necessary."

It was in the face of constant and consistent expatriate missionaries' submissions against *dikoma* and *sethepu* that Rapetloane penned the telling piece we have just glanced. What a confident assertion of independent thought subtended by honesty to self! What an example for posterity! The confidence he exhibits permeates even the last lines. "Mopeli will skip like a horse when he sees me. Sekgonyana in turn will say, 'That's what I'm talking about!'. . ." And on he goes about the various prominent Basotho households and what they stand to gain from associating with *Leselinyana*; all this being regardless of whether *baruti* approve of the types of associations involved. Rapetloane's rhetoric is practically always representational; reading, or rather hearing it in its original tones, transports one to the courts of the palace where a feast is afoot and the crème de la crème of Basotho speakers are on stage.

Cracks Are Inevitable

The above reading of Rapetloane's outstanding article has been too admiring. Two reasons are responsible for this. First, in negative terms, native sources tend to be treated as anecdotal evidence of something other than what they were meant to be by those who produced them. So, for instance, it is easier to treat Rapetloane's article as instance of nascent literary production. This author is persuaded that much gets missed when these sources are not accorded the respect they asserted themselves to be deserving. Secondly, in positive terms, it is vital that African students who continue to this day to grapple with the question of their African Christian identity are both made aware of the existence of predecessors such as Rapetloane and indeed get introduced to those predecessors' thoughtful reflections.

In other words, the criticality displayed in the foregoing reading of Rapetloane's article is directed at the academy and its assumptions. The challenge of combining combat and construction demands more than a comfortable armchair criticality. It calls for involvement, for the creative embrace of those who constructively and dynamically welcomed Christian faith despite whatever else attended it. It presupposes the privileging of voices hitherto relegated to the margins by the boisterous self-proclaimed authoritative voices of history.[27] The slow unexciting process of listening to the otherwise marginalized needs to be done properly before the rush to demolish or build theories can occur. In a word, it is as futile to hear the marginalized through the agency of the privileged (rather than via their own authentic voices) as it is to hurriedly subject them to schemas developed elsewhere without due appreciation of the insights they made.

Gaps will certainly be encountered in their argumentations and presentations. But their approaches for tackling the identity question at the interface are matchless reward. It may just turn out that some of the hang-ups we have today are based on misunderstandings that occurred as concepts were communicated across cultures. So, for instance, while I admire the extent to which *koma*, *sethepu* and *thuto* are at home in Rapetloane's self-understanding, I struggle to visualize how in practice he actually managed to genuinely be all things to all people. More digging awaits.

Concluding Thought

Nineteenth century Christian missions have shaped modern Africa's landscape in lasting ways. One of their key contributions was the introduction and propagation of literacy. It was a form of literacy so closely tied to Christian faith that the Sesotho word for "learning," *thuto*, cannot shed its Christian undertones; to this day the noun for "teachers," *baruti*, is reserved for clergy. Missionaries working among the Basotho perceived several traditional institutions to be standing in the way of Christian missions' success, and they regularly isolated those structures for special attack. But because traditional institutions fed off one another, their supposedly straightforward argumentations failed to dissuade their Basotho disciples. Instead, the Basotho sought to create room for Christian belief within and alongside established Basotho institutions. Such coexistence of apparently incompatible worldviews persists to date, and it will do African Theology a lot of good to go back to sources such as Filemone Rapetloane to glean mindsets and attitudes whereby to process such conundrums.

Among various lessons, nineteenth century Basotho sources illustrate what it means to retain a communal sense of self in all of one's toils. It is because modern African societies have been bewitched by sorceries such as capitalist consumerism that especially Christians are the least exemplary when it comes to exploiting *thuto* for the benefit of their very own communities. *Thuto*, if it is to have lasting local meaning, needs authentic Sesotho self-expression as much as it incorporates international customs. And the risk involved in bringing Sesotho on board has just been boldly illustrated in *Leselinyana's* leading article. He made *Leselinyana* speak on behalf of the Basotho as much as it spoke to their hearts. Such feats are near impossible to attain if the premises from which we launch are foreign. We are able to engage honestly because as one seasoned missionary put it: "we cannot do anything against the truth, but only for the truth."[28]

Notes

1 T.S. Maluleke, "The Africanization of Theological Education: Does Theological Education Equip You to Help Your Sister?" in *Inculturation and Postcolonial Discourse in African Theology*, ed. E.P. Antonio (Peter Lang, 2006), 70.

2 "Within our context Christianity was the religion of European colonization, and the nineteenth century missionary movement benefited greatly from the colonial subjugation of the region." (J. de Gruchy, "From Cairo to the Cape: The Significance of Coptic Christianity for African Christianity," *JTSA* 99 (1997): 36).

3 B. Goba, "The Hermeneutics of African Theologies," *Journal of Black Theology in South Africa* 12, no. 2 (1998): 19.

4 Bediako submits, for instance, that "So far as Mbiti is concerned, Christianity's deep roots 'in the history of our continent'... is a fact of great significance .... For it means that there is a sense in which the success of the modern missionary enterprise of the nineteenth and twentieth centuries may be seen as the fuller establishing of what, after all, 'can rightly be described as an indigenous, traditional and African religion'." (K. Bediako, *Theology and Identity: The Impact of Culture upon Christian Thought in the Second Century and in Modern Africa* (Regnum, 1992), 304).

5 K. Bediako, *Theology and Identity*, 10.

6 T.S. Maluleke, "Half a Century of African Christian Theologies: Elements of an Emerging Agenda for the Twenty-First Century," *JTSA* 99 (1997): 13.

7 An individual member of this amalgamation of southern African ethnicities is a *Mosotho*; their tongue and culture are known as *Sesotho*. While *Lesotho* is their symbolic home, southern Africa is the *Basotho's* actual home. (Unless otherwise stated, all translations from Sesotho sources are mine.)

8 His biographer reveals how Mabille was "a man of action ... impatient .... No one would rank him as a thinker, a theologian. He did not philosophise." (E.W. Smith, *Mabilles of Basutoland* (Morija, 1939), 235).

9 L.S. Molema, *The Image of Christianity in Sesotho Literature: Thomas Mofolo and his Contemporaries* (Hamburg: Buske, 1989), 130.

10 The point is clearer if the passage is quoted *fullishly*: "Soon after Mabille arrived at Morija, a gentleman in England named Brown ... sent him out a small press .... He knew nothing about printing; but Mr. Ellenberger gave him some lessons and he soon mastered the art .... The first number of *Leselinyana* ... appeared in September, 1863. With some interruption it has gone on appearing all though the years – it has the distinction of being the oldest Native newspaper in South Africa. Filemone Rapetloane wrote the introduction to the first number but all the rest of it was, *it seems*, written by Mabille and he set up the type and printed it with his own hands. By June, 1864, his apprentice, David, had made such good progress that all the printing could be entrusted to him, and Mabille had only the 'copy' to furnish and read the proofs. In his writings, as in his oral teaching, Mabille was confronted by difficulties inherent in the use of a language which as yet was insufficiently developed to express all the ideas which he wished to convey." (Smith, *Mabilles*, 127–128).

11 He had earlier been more hands-on with various mission activities, but "While helping to place the new roof on the church he had fallen and been hurt rather seriously. Since he was incapacitated for other work, Mabille took him into the school. So infirm that sometimes he had to lie upon his back while teaching, and quite untrained though he was, Filemone was zealous and faithful and for many years rendered good service. Mr. and Mrs. Mabille gave him lessons out of school hours and in return he helped Mr. Mabille in his literary work." (Smith, *Mabilles*, 125).

12 H. Giliomee, "A Proper British Colony," in *New History of South Africa*, ed. H. Giliomee and B. Mbenga (Cape Town: Tafelberg, 2007), 100.

13 L.S. Molema, *Image of Christianity*, 131.

14 Ibid., 132.

15 Though born and raised in Lesotho, Emile Rolland was vehement that *koma* was "the starting point of heathenism," nothing less than "the school of Satan" where "the grand corrupting and seductive influence in the country" was propagated. (quoted in Machobane, "Basotho Religious Beliefs and Western Thought," in *Essays on Religion and Culture among Basotho (1800–1900)*, ed. L.B.B.J. Machobane and T.L. Manyeli (Lesotho: Mazenod, 2001), 44–50).

16 L.S. Molema, *Image of Christianity*, 136.

17 L.S. Molema, *Image of Christianity*, 115.

18 *Pitso* is a meeting called by the chief or king in order to discuss developments of public interest. Even Nelson Mandela could not pass the opportunity to address the *Pitso* in Maseru on 13 July 1995.

19 A.F. Walls, "Moshoeshoe (also Moshesh, and Various Other Spellings)," in *Biographical Dictionary of Christian Missions* (BDCM), ed. G.H. Anderson (Grand Rapids, MI: Eerdmans, 1998), 475.

20 S.J. Gill, *A Short History of Lesotho* (Morija Museum & Archives, 1993), 59–61. The practice of marrying beyond one's immediate relatives is as old among the Basotho as their memory according to Thoahlane, in relation to Morena Mokgeseng, also known as Ratladi. But it was Chief Mohlomi who weaved much more systematic reasoning into its benefits (A.B. Thoahlane, *Makumane a Histori ea Lesotho* (Morija Sesuto Book Depot, 1978), 5).

21 See, e.g., S.J. Gill, *Short History*, 93; V. Ellenberger, *Landmarks in the Story of the French Protestant Church in Basutoland during the First Hundred Years of Its Existence, 1833–1933* (Morija Sesuto Book Depot, 1933), 21; A.F. Walls, "Moshoeshoe," 475.

22 *Koma* entails the language of the initiated and, thus, the rhetoric of mature and dependable Basotho. Its intricacy is stupendous, as one Mosotho researcher celebrated the preservation while also lamenting the impenetrability of *dikoma* (*likoma* in Lesotho orthography): "Basotho sacred songs known as *likoma* or *lifela* (hymns) are a good example of African cultural elements which have managed to retain their purity amidst many missionaries' attempts to either trivialize or mock them. Although these are, as we have said, the best sources in as far as tracing genuine African religious thought is concerned, a serious problem is encountered when one has to find and analyze those which are shrouded in secrecy such as those associated with initiation in the case of Basotho." (F. Rakotsoane, *The Southern Sotho's Ultimate Object of Worship: Sky-Divinity or Water-Divinity?* (University of Cape Town, Doctoral Thesis), 2001).

23 At the traditional initiation school (*lebollo*) Basotho youth are taught *dikoma* (sacred lyrics) whose function is to preserve and communicate age-old truths reserved only for the initiated. Before the advent of the Christian missionaries, *koma* functioned as the most critical qualification of a true and dependable Mosotho. Familiarity with *koma* separated men from boys, women from girls. Furthermore, as a cultural institution, *koma* bound generations of Basotho to both their rulers (as loyal regiments) and their ancestors (as grateful heirs and custodians of tradition and custom). Armed with *dikoma*, initiates could be presumed schooled in the best of Basotho folklore/history, customs/ways and values/ethics. Among such "circumcision songs," argues Mabafokeng Makara, we find for instance "those that narrate the origins of the Basotho." (M. Makara, *Management of Indigenous Knowledge in Lesotho: Prospects and Challenges for Information Professionals* (Pretoria: SCECSAL Conference Proceedings, 2002), 38).

24 Thoahlane, *Makumane*, 33; Gill, *Short History*, 82–84; Ellenberger, *Landmarks*, 5–8; M.B. Khaketla, *Moshoeshoe le Baruti* (Morija, 1954); T. Couzens, *Murder at Morija* (Johannesburg: Random House, 2003), 89; D. Ambrose and A. Brutsch, "Introduction" to T Arbousset, *Missionary Excursion into the Blue Mountains: Being an Account of King Moshoeshoe's Expedition from Thaba-Bosiu to the Sources of Malibamatšo River in the Year 1840* (Lesotho: Morija Archives, 1991), 9.

25 S. Willet and D. Ambrose, *Lesotho: A Comprehensive Bibliography* (Oxford: Clio Press, 1980), xxiii.

26 Once cattle have been exchanged, there can be no such thing as even a paternity dispute: "once a woman has been legally married it is impossible to speak of her children

as illegitimate even where it is clear that they were not fathered by her legal husband." (P.M. Bereng, *I Am a Mosotho* (Morija Printing Works, 1987), 66; cf. M. Epprecht, *This Matter of Women Is Getting Very Serious: Gender, Development and Politics in Colonial Lesotho* (Pietermaritzburg: University of Natal Press, 2000), 16–26).

27 "The validity of an interpretation does not depend on positing an alternative reading or supporting it with new data. Simply replacing a metropolitan reading with a subaltern one does not make the latter more legitimate than the one it tries to dislodge. Combating one set of data with a counter set is not enough to unsettle hegemonic readings. Instead, the discursive modes through which narratives and facts are produced must *also* be called into question. The crucial question is not to do with one set of data replacing the other, but with which text, theory or author is relevant and meaningful to the context in which they are appropriated." (R.S. Sugirtharajah, *The Bible and the Third World: Precolonial, Colonial and Postcolonial Encounters* (Cambridge University Press, 2001), 280).

28 2 Corinthians 13:8, RSV. The immediate literary context is one colored by phrases like: "examine yourselves, to see whether you are holding on to your faith," "beware the test," "examine our work and find out whether or not we have failed in our endeavors among you." The overall quest is for righteousness and not whether 'we' or 'you' come out justified; my God-given authority as missionary is for building up and not for tearing down, and so forth.

3. *The Role of Religion in the Formation of White Nationalism: Exclusion, Race, Ethnicity and Identity in Shaping Democratic South Africa's Identity*

ITUMELENG D. MOTHOAGAE

Introduction

The construction of white supremacy and the intention of exterminating people of color could be traced to modernity and philosophical rationalization of white supremacy and inferiority of anyone who does not originate from Europe. It is for this reason that Hegel maintains the following regarding African people:

> Africa is in general a closed land, and it maintains this fundamental character. It is characteristic of the blacks that their consciousness has not yet even arrived at the intuition of any objectivity, as for example, of God or the law, in which humanity relates to the world and intuits its essence. He [the black person] is a human being in the rough.[1] (Hegel 1830, 1975: 176–177)

Notions of white nationalism and white supremacy in the context of South Africa continues to haunt the country. Religion as a vehicle to sustain these discursive practices has not been critically engaged. While scholars such as Boesak have argued that Apartheid was a heresy, the theological foundations of white nationalism embedded within the policy of apartheid are still to be critically engaged. Since 1994, South Africa as a country has still not critically engaged with the race issue head on. The lack of critical engagement has paralyzed the debate. The recent racial attacks on black people indicate the deeper problem of white supremacy in the country. For example, an estate agent by the name of Vicky Momberg was caught on camera hurling the k-word at black police officers and 10111[2] operators after she was the victim of a smash-and-grab robbery. She used the k-word more than 48 times. The clip went viral and Momberg was arrested.

These incidents have further prompted the Department of Justice and Constitutional Development to draft a bill that criminalizes racism.[3] The move to criminalize racism does not address the problem of white supremacy, instead it places the victim and the perpetrator on the same level. Furthermore, such a move fails to recognize the various racial markers that have formed part of the foundation of white nationalism.

Blackness continues to be interrogated; on the other hand, whiteness and its privileges are still perceived as a norm. As a young black man, I have to work twice as hard as a white compatriot does as a white man. Thus, blackness and whiteness are still the determining factors regarding who is interrogated. Grosfoguel defines racism in the following manner:

> Depending on the different colonial histories in diverse regions of the world, the hierarchy of superiority/inferiority along the line of the human can be constructed through various racial markers. Racism can be marked by color, ethnicity, language, culture and/or religion.[4]

The above citation points to the construction of identities and ethnicities. It also points to the subversion of African spirituality. When looking at the definition of race, according to Grosfoguel, African spirituality is viewed as inferior and categorized as such. One can draw on an example from one of the missionaries, Robert Moffat, who said the following regarding the religion of Batswana:

> Satan is obviously the author of polytheism of other nations, he has employed his agency with fatal success in erasing every vestige of religious impression from the mind of Bechuan, Hottentots and Bushmen, leaving them without a single link to unite them to the skies. Thus the missionary could not make appeal to legends, or altars, or to an unknown God or to ideas kindred, to those he wished to import ...). Their religious system like those streams in the wilderness, which lose themselves in the sand had entirely disappeared, and devolved on the missionary to prepare for the gracious distribution of the waters of salvation in that desert soil, sowing the seed of the word, breathing many prayers, and shedding many a tear, till the Spirit of God should cause it to vegetate, and yield fruits of righteousness.[5]

The above statement by Moffat, without any doubt, points out how African religion[6] was perceived. Above all, it indicates how African spirituality, as a form of religious expression, is categorized and marked by what Grosfoguel refers to as,

> The hierarchy of superiority and inferiority along the line of the human politically, culturally and economically produced and reproduced for centuries by the institutions of the "capitalist/patriarchal westerncentric, / Christian-centric modern/colonial world-system".[7]

It is for this reason that in this chapter I will use Black Liberation Theology and the Intersectionality theory to argue that racism, ethnicity, gender and spirituality center on the person of color. In other words, the system is made in such a way that it continues to locate people of color within the "zone of no-being"; thus, subjecting them to perpetual scrutiny. It is within this context that I follow Tshaka's definition of Black Liberation Theology as cited by Mothoagae:

> First and foremost, it must continue to assert its guerrilla nature. This is to say it must never lose sight of structural racism which in essence justified its existence as a means towards understanding why God created differences. Secondly, a Black Liberation Theology that is not inward looking is one that is able to make the needed assessments in present day South Africa.[8]

The first-century Christian writers, Mark and Matthew, use ethnic formation in their gospel to separate the Christians from Jews, Gentiles and the Roman. Riches makes the following assertion regarding the role of identity in Mark's Gospel:

> Many of the central images and motifs in Matthew and Mark suggest that our text comes from a group with a strong sense of identity as a distinctive from all other groups in the world. It is a community of the sighted, by contrast with the rest of the world which is blind; it is the family of God, by contrast with all others who do not do his will. It enjoys knowledge of the Mystery of God's purposes for the world.[9]

Riches argues that, Matthew, on the one hand, seems to be sensitive to Mark's concerns of developing a community with a strong sense of its own identity against broader society; on the other hand, Matthew makes a shift from ethnic groups definitions with their invocations of (real/ or supposed) physical descent from common ancestors (sons of Abraham). To achieve this, Riches argues that Matthew uses allegorical kinship in the following manner:

> To allegorical kinship definitions (brothers and sisters of Jesus) tends to a more radical division of the world into two. The Great Church, by contrast, takes up the allegorizing strain in Matthew's Gospel, seeing itself as the family of God, which is grounded in its call and instruction by Jesus. Jesus' genealogy and the witness of the Old Testament ensure their place in scared history … the kingdom is been given away from the people of Israel and given to a new nation, whose task is to make disciples of all nations, Jews and Gentiles alike.[10]

In her book *Bodies and Souls*, Jennifer Glancy, argues that, *Sōma*, the Greek word for body, is a synonym for slave. According to her, slaves were considered to be without honor and were the sexual property of their owners.[11] In the Roman Empire slaves were vulnerable to physical control, coercion and abuse in settings, such as a public space, at the auction block and even at a private place such as the bedroom. They were owned, they had no right to their own life. This form of power according to Foucault is sovereign power.[12] The right to take life and to punish. They resembled docile bodies. Peter Garnsey cited by Glancy argues that:

> Paul seems to have Roman law on slaves, sons, and inheritance in mind in the third and fourth chapters of Galatians. Indeed, apparent erasure of division between slave and free that Paul proclaims in 3:28 is only a cover-up, as Paul goes on to reinscribe customary and legal distinctions between slave and free.[13]

Snyman points to what could be identified as the two theological implications of religion as a construction of race. Firstly, Calvinism stressed that all authority came from God. Thus, in matters of state, God's ruling had to be followed. It is for this reason that if one had to find out what God wants, one would have to go to the Bible. The Bible became central in the construction of the "Afrikaner" identity and the subsequent racial divide of the nation.[14] It is evident from the above citation that religion played a role in identity-making and construction of race particularly the making of white nationalism and supremacy. Such an ideology that has been centered on the biblical texts also functioned as modes of disciplinary power and surveillance of society. Secondly, Kuyper's interpretation of God's creation as a creation of diversity of races, colors and cultures formed the basis for a Christian Nationalist white supremacy based on a hierarchy of races. It is for this reason that the biblical paradigm was employed extensively to the benefit of a white nationalist identity referred to as the "Afrikaner" people.[15]

This formed a religious framework that contributed to the discourse of race, identity and ethnicity in South Africa. The determination to have an exclusive white space, regulated and guided by the religious belief of self-determination to sustain their nationalistic view of exclusion and resistance to integration is expressed in the idea of a white exclusive space referred to as Orania. Furthermore, the religious pilgrimage to the Voortrekker Monument that takes place yearly on December 16th to mark the day, according to white nationalistic view, as the day of the covenant between the "Afrikaner" and God, is still held by those communities such as those like Orania and Afri-Forum. This is done on the same day of the year as the country's celebration of the Day of Reconciliation, South Africa's public holiday marking the end of Apartheid and calling for national unity. It is these events that raise questions about the notion of a "rainbow nation" and the national Constitution. These events further point to the paralysis that characterizes the country as a result of the issues of racism and the role of religion in legitimizing racism. In the next section I will discuss the making of racial hierarchy in the context of South Africa.

Situating Religion, Race and Ethnicity in the Context of South Africa

When situating the role of religion and its effects on race and ethnicity in the context of South Africa, it is imperative to consider how the pseudo-interpretation of Calvinist theology formed the consciousness of the Dutch settlers. This includes the importance of religious belief in shaping Afrikaner ethical convictions. By contextualizing the above, one comes to appreciate the complexity of Afrikaner history and race relations in South Africa. The arrival of the Dutch settlers in the Cape resulted in the history of South Africa to be seen through the eyes of a pseudo-interpretation of Calvinism theology. This is pseudo-interpretation finds its genesis on the symbolism of concepts such as "the people of God," "Exodus," the "Covenant," and the "sovereignty of God" as it is characterized through language, symbols and theological outlook that asserted the privileged status of the Afrikaner race within the Dutch Reformed Church.[16]

In his article "From Apartheid to Liberation," Timothy Renick begins with the following assertion by situating the apartheid regime ideology with Dutch Calvinism theology by arguing that:

> Despite the fact that over eighty percent of the south African population is self-avowedly Christian, despite the fact that South Africa is a nation whose very constitution defers to "the Sovereignty and Providence of [the Christian] God in guiding the affairs of the nations, social-scientific analyses of the origins and nature of apartheid have tended to ignore or minimize the role played by Christian theology.[17]

One cannot ignore the role and impact of religion, specifically in South Africa, on the ideologies of nationalisms of exclusion and that of resistance. When one refers to the role of Christian theology what comes to mind is the Dutch Calvinist theology. It is because Dutch Calvinism and the Reformed theology espoused the development of South African ethics, including its racial attitudes. This advocacy is seen in the various theological interpretations of their historical events, such as, the belief of the 1700s that the Dutch settlers, later called the Afrikaners, were literally following the footsteps of the ancient Israelites: The naming of the hill; the Tower of Babel; and their discovery of some stone cairns along the Fish River that they believed were monuments left behind by the ancient Israelites. Later on, the Afrikaners depicted the British restrictions as an "oppression led by Pharaoh."[18] Kruger in his speech links the Hebrew Scriptures with the Afrikaner people in the following manner:

> Unbelievers say God does not do signs and winders as in the days of the old Covenant, but I can show you from our own history that the dear Lord does everything to give a good time to those that are people of the Lord. Kruger went on to cite God's words to Abraham in Genesis (17:7): "the Covenant which I made with you and your descendants, excluding none, shall remain before you and your seed from now until eternity.[19]

The language and symbols used by Paul Kruger in his speech cemented, to a large extent, the notion of nationalism of exclusion founded on being the "people of God" and a covenant with God that shall never end. Such a theology continues to play this specific role although it is subtle. This is evident because there are those Afrikaners who still ascribe to this type of theology, like those who started their own town called Orania[20] situated in the Northern Cape. Here they still have the colors of the old national flag and live on their own. They cite Chapter 14 section 235 that reads as follows:

> The right of the South African people as a whole to self-determination, as manifested in this Constitution, does not preclude, within the framework of this right, recognition of the notion of the right to self-determination of any community sharing a common cultural and language heritage, within a territorial entity in the Republic or in any other way, determined by national legislation.[21]

The above citation reflects the compromises that the ANC acceded to. Furthermore, this has got to be understood within the context of a prior settlement that the ANC, National Party and the Freedom Front signed on April 23, 1994, prior to the elections. The 1994 accord deals with the self-determination of the Afrikaners. It recognizes the right of the Afrikaner people on self-determination. This was to be later put into law, in the constitution of the Republic.[22] The agreement I would argue, sustains the ideological agenda of nationalism and white supremacy. It also illustrates the weakness of the Constitution as it did not challenge such notions of "the chosen race"—"us" vs "them." Such a concept is observed by Fatton according to Renick, who argues as follows, "the Afrikaner program of apartheid is an oppressive system of labor exploitation determined by a particular pattern of class domination."[23]

Renick further maintains that race, class and the capitalist economy contingently combine to create and uphold the system of white domination in South Africa. Twenty-five years into democracy the majority of people who occupy senior managerial positions are white and earn the highest family income according to the South African statistics. Yet the country claims to be liberated and proclaims equality while the remnants of race, class and identity are as vivid as 300 years ago. Renick states that it is imperative to link the South African work ethic to Dutch Calvinist theology. Renick cites Enquist who makes the following remark regarding the "secular bias":

> Of much Western scholarship, perhaps one should not be surprised to find economic, political and racial factors cited in lieu of theological beliefs as crucial ingredients in the development of South African ethical attitudes.[24]

It is evident from the above discussion that religion, as a social construct, has to a large extent affected how race was rationalized in the context of South Africa. Such a belief formed and sustained the assumption that, as human beings, we are made to be separate and that there are those who are destined to be superior and that they should rule and be served thus, crafting a supremacist mentality based on the ideological notion of a nationalism of exclusion. Such a notion was a conscious and unconscious reality. This is precisely because there was an element of ethnic mobilization.[25] Through rational choice ethnicity can be seen instrumentally. Rational choice focuses primarily on how leaders strategically manipulate ethnicity for the sake of power, as I have previously argued.

This includes the mobilization of ethnic identity; and in this way ethnicity becomes the focal point that facilitates convergence of individual expectations; and can be useful as a mobilization strategy.[26] This is illustrated by Kritzinger's assertion that it was in the church that he first became aware of racism. This is because the church opened his eyes to the existence and the wrongness of racism, that is based on white nationalism and supremacy.[27] I will now turn to the issue of the nationalism of exclusion and resistance. These two ideologies form an integral part of understanding the effects of religion on race, ethnicity and identity in South Africa. They further point to how the Dutch Reformed Church, as an institution, promoted racism and found it theologically sound to do so. It is without a doubt that one has to consider the effects of religion in the construction of race and ethnicity when dealing with the issue of racism in the context of South Africa.

It is for this reason that de Gruchy asserts that the missionaries also provided the settler community with familiar symbols, rituals and values. One can say that the church, as de Gruchy rightly points out, "became a cultural link with the 'old country'."[28] Yet, at the same time the missionaries also saw themselves as agents of change by evangelizing the "heathens" and in the process constructing a different identity contrary to what they have, turning them into "civilized persons," "spiritual," "purified" beings.[29] I would like to argue that the missionary activity accelerated colonialism and the subversion of the Tswana traditions and spirituality. It is for this reason that de Gruchy makes the following assertion regarding Christianity in South Africa:

> If the missionaries always found themselves as the servants of the colonialism, the settlers were colonists, the "settler churches" a significant element within the process of colonization.[30]

It is within this context that one can speak of racialism. The notion of racialism, as I have shown in the discussion above, emanates from the prejudice that one's culture, knowledge, spirituality or religion is superior to that of the "Other."[31] Snyder defines racialism in the following manner:

> Racialism, a relatively recent phenomenon, is historically a concomitant movement with modern nationalism and imperialism. There was little consciousness of race before the sixteenth century. The ancient world was a small world in which physical differences of peoples were not noticeable. Germanic barbarians were not very different in physical character. Until the rise of national states in the late medieval and early modern eras, antagonisms between peoples were motivated chiefly by cultural, religious, and linguistic differences. Little was understood about intermarriage and racial intermixture.[32]

The above citation sums up the attitude of the western world towards those who are nonwhite by categorizing them, using the following markers: cultural, religious and linguistically different. It is worthwhile at this point to link the above discussion with the lived experience of Fanon. In his book (1952) Fanon makes the following assertion:

> But I too am guilty, here I am talking of Apollo! There is no help for it: I am a white man. For unconsciously I distrust what is black in me, that is, the whole of my being. I am a Negro—but of course I do not know it, simply because I am one. When I am at home my mother sings me French love songs in which there is never a word about Negroes. When I disobey, when I make too much noise, I am told to "stop acting like a nigger."[33]

The above citation points to the creation of myth about what makes a non-European and a European different. Foucault, cited by Carter argues as follows; "In *History of Sexuality* he observes that what came to mediate the shift from the administration of power through 'a symbolics of blood' to its administration through 'an analystics of sexuality' was race."[34]

It therefore follows how in the case of South Africa blood forms part of the myth in the discourse of racism, because the wars were created in such a way that they suggested that Africans were the cause of these wars. The wars were orchestrated in such a way that they dislocate African people from their identity and their land; and turned them into objects of exploitation and cheap labor.[35]

Nationalism of Exclusion and of Resistance

The notion of the nationalism of exclusion in the context of South Africa emerged from the premise that the white settlers were biologically different from the indigenous people; and that they were "chosen people of God," "a nation set aside." Such an ideological premise foregrounded white nationalism and supremacist mentality. Notice that I use biblical connotations to illustrate the "otherness" of the indigenous people. It was "us" and "them." The mobilization of the rest of the community on the basis that they were ethnically different from the "Others" led to the nationalism of exclusion and resistance. South Africa may claim to be nonracial, but racism is still an integral part of the country's fiber. An organization such as Afri-forum and communities such as Orania apply Article 235 of the South African Constitution to maintain white nationalist and supremacist agenda. It can be argued that nationalism of exclusion based on ethnicity and identity can be an equivalent to Balkan "ethnic cleansing."

The personification of biblical characters played a fundamental role in the construction of racial differences and the subjugation of the natives and the slaves in South Africa.[36] This is expressed in the writings of Totius, as cited in Snyman, in which the creation and maintenance of an "Afrikaner" identity can evidently be seen in his paper at the People's Congress on race policies in 1944. The use of Colossians 3:11 by Totius serves as an example of how religion is an identity-maker and a constructor of race. Renick makes the following observation regarding the role of religion:

> If the Afrikaner people exist, they exist by God's will. If the Afrikaner people exist despite great historical odds, their preservation must be an indication of their privileged status in God's eyes.[37]

The above citation points to how race is constructed based on the theological premise that some people are created to be superior and others are created to be inferior. Grosfoguel maintains that such a premise finds its point of departure in 1492 when several centuries of Occidentalism in the world created the epistemic privilege and hegemonic "identity politics" of the West over the rest to judge and produce knowledge about the "others" in the zone of nonbeing. The ego-politics of knowledge of Rene Descartes in the seventeenth century where the "God-eye view" of Western men replaced God as the foundation of knowledge is the foundational basis of modern Western philosophy argues Grosfoguel.[38] This view is maintained by Volf in which he argues as follows:

> Segregation, holocaust and apartheid are Western equivalents of Balkan "ethnic cleansing" from more recent past that match in inhumanity anything we encounter outside the boundaries of the West. The exclusion signified in "ethnic cleansing" as a metaphor, is not about barbarity "then" as opposed to civilization "now" and not about evil "out there" as opposed to goodness "here". Exclusion is barbarity within civilization, evil among the good, crime against the other right within the walls of the self.[39]

It is without doubt that there are certain steps that one would have to follow to achieve, what Volf states in the above citation: ethnic mobilization, cultural identity and ethnic behavior. According to Varshney, the nationalism of exclusion thrives when there is ethnic mobilization, cultural identity and ethnic behavior. He further argues the following:

> Ethnic mobilization cannot proceed on value-rational grounds alone. Strategies are necessary; coalitions must be formed; the response of the adversary—the state, the opposed ethnic group, the in-group dissenters—must be anticipated.[40]

It is evident that in the context of South Africa post-1994, a similar pattern can be observed with the formation of these minority groups claiming autonomy and hegemony for themselves to the extent of not using the national flag but creating their own. This flag is said to be designed by the whole country and it should be a symbol of where the country comes from and where it is heading. In other words, its main purpose is to unify the country. On the contrary, a nationalism of exclusion in South Africa for the past 360 years has been about the dominant group within society that seeks to impose its own values on the various groups and to exclude, sometimes violently, other ethnic groups from the portals of power. Such an expression of dominance is illustrated by enforcing language, religion, or culture via control of the state or excluding groups from power on the basis of their ethnic characteristics only.

I submit that one cannot speak of nationalism of exclusion without nationalism of resistance. In the case of South Africa prior to 1994, the liberation movements represented this kind of resistance that stands against discrimination and exploitation. While we see a different type of resistance post-1994; the white minority community, such as the Oranian community, that resists inclusive and non-racialism by utilizing the very Constitution to advocate for their resistance. The notion of being the "elect," "people of God" based on the mythological interpretation of the Bible and their identity formation form the basis of their nationalism of resistance. This is evident in their flag, the link between the past, present and the future. Varshney makes the following observation regarding nationalism of exclusion:

> It is reasonable to suppose that the nationalism of exclusion is driven substantially by hatred and/or deep-rooted condescension: Afrikaner nationalism in South Africa, the anti-Semitism of Hitler, and Hindu nationalism in India would be some examples.[41]

It is evident that for one to tackle the issue of nationalism of exclusion and resistance it is imperative that symbolic exclusion is dealt with. This is precisely because symbolic exclusion is often a distortion of the other, according to Volf. Furthermore, it is not simply ignorance about the other; rather it is a willful misconstruction and failure of knowledge. Volf further asserts that:

> We demonize and bestialize not because we do not know better, but because we refuse to know what is manifest and choose to know what serves our interests. The practice of exclusion and the language of exclusion go hand in hand with a whole array of emotional responses to the other, ranging from hatred to indifference; these exclusions both call forth emotional responses and are sustained by them.[42]

It can be argued that, although religion has contributed to nationalism of exclusion, race, ethnicity and identity formation prior to 1994 and post-apartheid, one thing that cannot be overlooked is that the long history of segregation was seen as necessary for a dynamic identity of the self in relation to the other. The flip side of it is that the one segregating slides into exclusion that seeks to affirm identity at the expense of the other. By using the Constitution to resist and exclude the rest of the country, communities, such as Orania, by their own act of exclusion, have excluded themselves from all relationships from the land below, from God above, from the people around. Volf argues that such exclusion does not belong because, according to him, one cannot speak of exclusion and belonging in the same breath. This is precisely what these movements have become. Such a condition could be summarized in Pearce's words regarding Philo in Egypt in the following manner "Belonging and not belonging."[43]

Non-racialism: A Dream or Reality Post-1994

Bonilla-Silva problematizes the notion of non-racialism or what in the United States is referred to as color-blind racism. He contends that such a notion is another form of racism, and those categories that were used to "other" black people as mentally, morally and intellectually inferior have morphed into what can be referred to today as color-blind racism. He remarks:

> However, this does not mean the "end of racism," as a few conservative commentators have suggested. Instead, a new powerful ideology has emerged to defend the contemporary racial order: the ideology of color-blind racism. Yet, color-blind racism is a curious racial ideology. Although it engages, as all ideologies do, in "blaming the victim," it does so in a very indirect, "now you see it, now you don't" style that matches the character of the new racism.[44]

Although Bonilla-Silva's analysis is made in the context of the United States of America, it can also be applied to the South African context. The idea of non-racialism is a form of idealism. The problem with such an approach is that it assumes that the past should remain in the past as if the present is not the product of the past. How can one speak of non-racism as if racism is a thing of the past and does not constitute continual white privilege? It is for this reason that Snyman in his article (2005) points out that the issues of racism continue to dominate public discourse like 25 years ago. As a result, he argues that it affects how people relate to one another as persons, this also includes how they relate with God in terms of their spirituality. Furthermore, he raises the question regarding the possibility of transcending racialized discourse:

> If the African body remains a black body out there and the white body always already infused with racist ideology? Has this perception something to do with the way we see our identities, fixed and immutable?[45]

Perhaps this is why myths about their inferior moral, intellectual, behavior and features developed and facilitated exclusion and any competition with the children of a "higher God." It can be argued that race is made equivalent to and the dominant source of human identity superseding all other aspects of identity. The national identity of South Africa as a rainbow nation remains an ideal, a dream to be dreamt at night for as long as the Constitution, religion and ethnicity dominate the race discourse in South Africa. Vice reflects on how whites in the country have not accounted for the atrocities that brought into play white privilege founded on the ideologies of white nationalism and supremacy. She states:

> The Truth and Reconciliation Commission (TRC) raised the question of white South Africans' mundane complicity in the Apartheid regime, even though it did not adequately explore it (and probably could not, given its remit). The focus on certain key figures in Apartheid atrocities allowed some whites to escape feelings of guilt—the crimes of Apartheid were performed not by them, but by

> certain figures of apparently inhuman evil (perhaps the most infamous example is Eugene de Kock, commander of the government's death squad, "Vlakplaas" 20). Whites could insist with some degree of sincerity however naïve that they knew nothing of the violence taking place daily and routinely at the hands of the security police.[46]

Following the argument by Vice, it can be argued that the ideal expressed in the Constitution remains an ideal, as the key issues that have determined the kind of narrative in the construction of a nationalistic view, have not only racialized the country, but also have created a sense of privilege to the extent that, the Truth and Reconciliation Commission did not necessitate this type of restoration. Instead, white privilege provides for the perpetrator a space to claim ignorance and shift of responsibility. Resulting in the victim becoming the perpetrator and the victim at the same time. McKaiser argues that white South Africans need to do the following:

> [B]e mindful of how your whiteness still benefits you and gives you unearned privileges. Engage black South Africans with humility, and be mindful of not reinforcing whiteness as normative [. . .].[47]

The above citation further points to the problems of the Constitution and the denial that whiteness is still associated with power, economy and the spirituality of superiority conscious or unconsciously so. Snyman argues that reading The Africana Bible reminded him of James Perkinson's book *White Theology Outing Supremacy in Modernity.* In that he argues that:

> Part of coming to consciousness of oneself as white, [. . .], involves daring to look into black eyes and not deny the reflection. The first moment in elaborating a white theology is one of hearing and internalizing black critiques that are both overt and oblique. It entails confrontation with the embarrassment of having already been "found out" by one's (in this case) most frightening other.[48]

It is for this reason that it is imperative for white people to look into black eyes and see the embarrassment, so that: "The expression of the vulnerability within a coloniality of being ethically compels a coloniality of power, whiteness, to become accountable, that is, 'responsible not only for the choice of theoretical interpretive models but also for the ethical consequences of the biblical text and its meanings.' "[49]

The issues of whiteness, spirituality, race, exclusion and resistance continue to characterize the South African discourse. It is without doubt that, without addressing these issues and engaging with them publicly, we will not be able to challenge the continual coloniality that is found in the system and the structures of society and government. This view by Snyman is also held by Vice. She labels it as guilt as according to her guilt cuts to the bone. She states:

> Despite this focus on serious individual wrongdoing in the TRC, issues of collective guilt certainly arose, and there is in South Africa much talk, usually dismissive, of "white guilt." These issues are complex, but there is always the risk of disingenuously absolving oneself from blame, and so guilt, by ignoring the other ways in which one, as a white person, participated in and upheld violent and demeaning structures. There are many ways of being unjust, and it is too easy to jump off the moral hook by focusing on the obvious crimes of the apartheid death squads. I am not denying that whites here acted reprehensibly, and that some still do, but I am more interested in ways of being and acting that at least do not look obviously unjust and are not intended to be discriminatory and harmful.[50]

In other words, public engagement of these issues will deconstruct and reconstruct the paralysis found in society and theological concepts such as reconciliation, human dignity, spirituality, elect, chosen people, theoretical interpretative models and ethical consequences of the biblical text and its meanings. I maintain that, without grappling with these issues as a country, the Constitution will remain a document that does not facilitate the kind of human dignity that is envisioned. Rather, it will continue to serve the minority and maintain white privilege. Thus, sustain whiteness as a norm, authority and an authentic race over and above other races.

Conclusion

In his article "Social Construction," Magubane argues that the politics and economics of empire cannot be separated. Thus, to understand the notion of white supremacy in South Africa, it is imperative for one to locate within the racist doctrine of Kaffir-work, the land monopoly by whites and the mines super-incumbent was theorized in this classic formulation by Lord Milner.[51] According to Magubane, Milner sees racial divide as so essential to sustaining the notions of white supremacy that whites had to be, by a process of social engineering, constituted as racial aristocracy:

> Our welfare depends upon increasing the quantity of our white population, but not at the expense of its quality. We do not want a white proletariat in this country. The position of the whites among the vastly more numerous black population requires that even the lowest ranks should be able to maintain a standard of living far above that of the poorest section of the population of a purely white country. However you look at the matter, you always come back to the root principle *the urgency of that development which alone can make this a white man's country in the only sense in which South Africa can become one, and that is, not a country of poor white, but one in which a largely increased white population can live in decency and comfort.* That development requires capital, but it also requires a large amount of rough labuor. And that labour can not to any extent

> be white, if only because, pending development and subsequent reduction in the cost of living, white labour is much to dear. (*My Italics*)

In this chapter, I sought to deliberate on the role of religion and its effects on nationalism of exclusion, race, ethnicity and identity in shaping democratic South Africa's identity. I argued that since the dawn of democracy the country has not started to engage critically on matters of race, religion, ethnicity and identity. As a result, the Constitution, as a document that is supposed to facilitate things has not done so. Instead, it is the very Constitution that sustains those who have exercised exclusion, exploitation and white privilege to continue to do so. While at the same time there continues to be ethnic mobilization in resisting the protection of white privilege by the Constitution. Such spiritual mobilization is seen in various church organizations, civil movements and labor movements.

I have further argued that for the Constitution to be meaningful and to serve those who were previously and continue to be underprivileged,there is a clear need of revisiting certain aspects of the Constitution. In other words, South Africa, despite the legal end of white rule, racial oppression and class inequalities remain deeply rooted. Color-blindness criticizes government-sponsored programs to alleviate structural injustices of capitalism and ignores 350 years of white domination and dispossession. This, in itself, is not surprising, what is shocking is that those who benefited from the injustices of white supremacy and colonial dispossession remain inured to their own privileges. They are unable to and are unwilling to recognize the realities and the fundamental historical injustices of the society that gave them all the benefits they now take for granted. It is for this reason that according to Magubane:

> Indeed, after a transition to democracy characterized by breathtaking magnanimity on the part of the black majority, after more than three years of devastating Truth and Reconciliation Commission testimonies documenting the appalling parameters of apartheid inhumanity, white society seems resolutely unwilling to acknowledge those truths or to respond with caring and generosity. Better to forget the past, deny the present, and to use a favorite phrase, get on with our lives.[52]

The metaphor of the Two Nations cannot be understood without understanding the class divisions inherent in the capitalist mode of production. The democratic breakthrough of 1994 makes this very clear. I argued that democracy without liberation is futile. This is because in the case of South Africa, the country attained democracy not liberation. Racist practices such as the denial of the vote, intensified the degree of powerless among blacks. It is not the only reason the black South Africans fought for. It is through democracy and liberation that South Africa as a country can create a society and/ or nation based on genuine equality of opportunity for all persons. Consequently, this requires examining the connections between racism and capitalist production and accumulation. Power derives from control over the means of production. Magubane cites West who argues the following:

> Class position contributes more than racial status to the basic form of powerlessness .... Only class divisions can explain the gross disparity between rich and power, the immense benefits accruing to the [white] and the depravity of the [black].[53]

Thus, the role of religion in facilitating such a transaction is fundamental. I will therefore submit that all the above issues that I outlined in this article intersect with the black person and as a result produce a different type of spirituality. This spirituality brings a different dimension of God as someone who is intrinsically active in the lives of those who experience hardship and exploitation. It is therefore then the task of Black Liberation Theology to rescue theological concepts that were used to categorize black people as inferior and white people as superior. Furthermore, as Tshaka maintains in his definition of Black Liberation Theology, unless black theology remains outside of the structured systems and becomes the property of the people and reflect on the black experiences, and emerging spiritualties. It is through such reflections that religious consciousness will begin. Black Liberation Theology will not be able to make meaning for the marginalizedand raise religious awareness if it fails to identify its interlocutors and only redefines paralyzed theological concepts that have been hijacked by the colonialism and continued with coloniality. As a result, it will be a hand maid of the systems that continues to exploit, exclude and categorize people as master and servant.

Notes

1 See Ben Magubane, "Social Construction of Race and Citizenship in South Africa," in *Conference Paper* (Durban, South Africa: United Nations Research Institute for Social Development, September 3–5, 2001), 23.

2 This is an emergency number used to contact the police.

3 Department of Justice and Constitutional Development, Revised Draft National Action Plan-Draft 12, 2013 *National Action Plan to Combat Racism, Racial Discrimination, Xenophobia and Related Intolerance Revised Draft 12 Version*, 2013, South Africa.

4 Ramon Grosfoguel, " 'Racism,' Intersectionality and Migration Studies," Summer School Lecture, College of Human Sciences University of South Africa, January 7, 2014.

5 Robert Moffat, *Missionary Labours and Scenes in Southern Africa* (London: J Snow, 1842), 294.

6 In defining religion, I follow Coleman's definition of religion as: a set of symbolic forms and acts which relate man to the ultimate conditions of his existence. Religion provides a general identity to individuals by helping them to cope with questions of ultimate meaning or frustrations of death and suffering. Religion reinforces personal identity by suggesting "limit images" of conduct, self-conception and role (John A. Coleman, "Civil Religion," *Sociological Analysis* 31, no. 2 1970).
7 Grosfoguel, " 'Racism', Intersectionality," 2014.
8 Itumeleng D. Mothoagae, "Expelled and Peripheral: The Resistance of the Black Marginalised Majority and the Call for New Liberation in Post-Apartheid South Africa." *Scriptura Journal* 112, no. 1 (2013): 2.
9 John K. Riches, *Conflicting Mythologies: Identity Formation in the Gospels of Mark and Matthew* (Edinburgh: T & T Clark, 2000), 111.
10 Riches, *Conflicting Mythologies*, 228.
11 Jennifer Glancy, *Bodies and Souls: Slavery in Early Christianity* (Oxford: Oxford Publishers, 2002), 10.
12 Michel Foucault *The History of Sexuality*. New York: Pantheon Books, 1980.
13 Glancy, *Bodies and Souls*, 35.
14 Gerrie Snyman, "Constructing and Deconstructing Identities in Post-apartheid South Africa: A Case for Hybridity Versus Untained Afrinicity?" *OTE* 18, no. 2 (2005): 326.
15 Snyman, "Constructing and Deconstructing," 327.
16 Timothy. M Renick, "From Apartheid to Liberation: Calvinism and the shaping of Ethical Belief in South Africa," *Sociological Focus* 24, no. 2 (1991): 129–143.
17 Renick, "From Apartheid to Liberation," 129.
18 Ibid., 133.
19 Ibid., 134.
20 Bruce Berry, "Orania Flag" December 08, 2006, http://flagspot.net/flags/za%7Dorani.html (accessed June 28, 2013).
The homeland they plan for the Afrikaners is between the river Orange River and the Atlantic Ocean, so part of the Cape, not the Free State or Transvaal. Their flag is not totally based on that of the old Transvaal as the red is changed to orange for the Orange Free State. According to Boere Data the *Vryheidsvlag* or new *Vierkleur* was first hoisted in the night of April 26/27, 1994 (when the apartheid was officially abolished!). It's not only a combination of the design of the flag of the South African Republic (Transvaal) with the orange from the flag of Orange Free State but also incorporates the orange-white-blue of the *Prinzenvlag* of the *Dietse* ancestors of the Boers and the former flag of South Africa, but with a green stripe at the hoist. See Appendix 1.
21 Constitution of the Republic of South Africa 1996.
22 Article 235 of the South African Constitution recognizes a community's self-determination within the framework of the Constitution and the law.
23 Renick, "From Apartheid to Liberation," 130.
24 Ibid.
25 By ethnic I follow Varshney's definition of ethnicity as meaning the following both from the narrower and from the broader perspective "Ethnicity is used in two different ways. In the narrower, popularly understood sense, ethnic, groups are racial or linguistic groups. There is however, a broader meaning as well. As Donald Horowitz

suggest all conflicts based on ascriptive (birth-based) group identities, real or imagined-race, language, religion, tribe, or caste—can be called ethnic.

26 Vashney Ashutosh, "Nationalism, Ethnic conflict, and Rationality," *The American Political Science Association* 1, no. 1 (2003): 88.

27 Johannes Kritzinger, Becoming aware of Racism in the Church: The story of a personal journey (unpublished paper 1999).

28 John W. De Gruchy, "Settler Christianity," in *Living Faiths in South Africa*, ed. Martin Prozesky and John de Gruchy (Cape Town: Clyson Printers, 1995), 29.

29 De Gruchy, "Settler Christianity," 29.

30 Ibid.

31 The term 'Other' is applied to people of African descent.

32 Louis L. Snyder, "The Idea of Racialism: Its Meaning and History," in *Racism: Essential Readings*, ed. Ellis Cashmore and James Jennings (London: SAGE Publications, 2001), 91.

33 Frantz Fanon, *Black Skin White Mask* (France: Editions de Seuil, 1952), 148.

34 J. Kameron Carter, *Race: A Theological Account* (Oxford: University Press, 2008), 68.

35 Here one can point to the *Bambatha* rebellion. In 1887 Zululand was annexed by the colony of Natal and the Zulu were gradually stripped of most of their arable land. There was widespread poverty, made worse by a series of natural disasters. In 1903 an epidemic of East Coast fever decimated the cattle, there were swarms of locusts and enormous damage was caused by a severe hailstorm in 1905. All these factors led it a serious economic depression. Africans had to pay a Hut Tax and a Dog Tax, and were subjected to a system of forced labor called *isibalo*, which caused widespread hardship and resentment. White farmers occupied more and more land, establishing farms and sugar plantations. After the South African War there was a shortage of agricultural labor. Rather than work for the white farmers, the black workforce was increasingly attracted to the gold mines of the Witwatersrand, where they could earn better wages. In 1905, in an attempt to increase the supply of labor and force more black men into becoming agricultural laborers, the Natal government under Charles Smythe, imposed a Poll Tax of £1 on all men over the age of 18. To pay the tax, African men would have to work for cash. Gandhi captured the proletraisation process in his book, Satyagraha in South Africa. In order to increase the Negro's wants or to teach him the value of labor a hut tax has been imposed on him. If these imposts were not levied, this race of agriculturists living on their farms would not enter mines hundreds of feet deep in order to extract gold or diamonds, and if their labor were not available for the mines, gold as well as diamonds would remain in the bowels of the earth. Like, the Europeans would find it difficult to get any servants, if no such tax was imposed (http://www.sahistory.org.za/events-leading-bambatha-rebellion).

36 Glancy, *Bodies and Souls*, 327.

37 Ibid., 136.

38 Ramon Grosfoguel, "The Epistemic Decolonial Turn," 27–28.

39 Volf Miroslav, *Exclusion & Embrace: A Theological Exploration of Identity, otherness, and Reconciliation* (Nashville: Abingdon Press, 1996), 39.

40 Varshney, Nationalism, Ethnic Conflict," 88.

41 Ibid., 86.

42 Volf, *Exclusion & Embrace*, 53.

43 Sarah Jones Pearce, "Belonging and Not Belonging: Local Perspectives in Philo of Alexandria," in *Jewish local Patriotism and Self-Identification in the Graeco-Roman Period*, ed. Sian Jones and Sarah Pearce (London: Sheffield Academic Press, 1998), 79–105.
44 Bonilla-Silva Eduardo, *Racism without Racists: Color-blind Racism and the Persistence of Racial Inequality in America* (Maryland: Rowman & Littlefield, 2018), 53.
45 Snyman, "Constructing and Deconstructing," 340.
46 Samantha Vice, "How Do I Live in This Strange Place?" *Journal of Social Philosophy*, 41, no. 3 (2010): 327.
47 Eusebius McKaiser, "Confronting Whiteness," n.p. [cited July 2, 2011.] Mail & Guardian online, July 1, 2011. Online: http://mg.co.za/article/2011-07-01-confronting-whiteness. Samantha Vice, "How Do I Live in This Strange Place?" *Journal of Social Philosophy* 41, no. 3 (2010): 323–342.
48 James Perkinson, *White Theology Outing Supremacy in Modernity* (New York: Palgrave, 2004), 3–4. The book challenges white theologians to learn how to confess and redress white power in their intellectual work. It is a continuous confrontation with white privilege in terms of socioeconomic frameworks, personal power, cultural habit and erotic embodiment. Perkinson argues that whiteness functions as a "surrogate form of 'salvation,' a mythic presumption of wholeness."
49 Snyman Gerrie, "Looking into Black Eyes and Feel the Embarrassment. A Selected and Selective Reading of the Africana Bible." *Old Testament Essays* 24, no. 2 (2011): 488.
50 Vice, "How Do I Live," 327.
51 Magubane, "Social Construction of Race," 23.
52 Ibid., 32.
53 Ibid., 33.

4. *Back to Africa: Towards a Re-imagination of "Youth" in Africa*

Boitumelo Senokoane and Mofenyi L. Mataboge

Introduction

Since the colonial expansion project began in Africa, African societies have been forced to accept knowledge about themselves that is foreign. The imposition of Western knowledge on African people and societies emanates from what Nkrumah notes as subtle methods of coercion.[1] According to Nkrumah, subtle methods of coercion can be found in the historical accounts of European scholars on Africa.[2] The European's historical accounts maliciously mischaracterize African people and their identity, to such an extent that they deny them their history.[3] Without a history, the landscape is set where Africans only exist through the knowledge and pen of the European scholars. In the context of this chapter, the European narrative on the identity of African people is considered with respect to African youth, and how this narrative landscape alienates them from their authentic self.

Now, African society as Keita observes is not only characterized by European colonization but also by African indigenous tradition, and Islamic religious cultural inputs.[4] This is known as Africa's triple heritage. The third segment, already mentioned in part, of Africa's triple heritage is rooted in Western culture and the traditions of Christianity.[5] For According to Nkrumah, this third segment was primarily brought in through colonialism.[6] For Nkrumah, each of the segments of Africa's triple heritage is animated by competing ideologies.[7] However, given the dynamic nature of society only one of the competing ideologies can be acceptable as a reflection of society's dynamism.[8] In some instances, the dominant ideology may insist on its axiomatic status through violence. In most colonized societies, Western culture, through Christianity, represents the mores of the day. Thus, this chapter argues that the conceptual position of the term "youth" in relation to Africa indicates this precise epistemic dominance of Western forms of knowledge in Africa. This chapter aims to show that a true meaningful reflection and understanding of African youth should find its departure in the African context. We posit that starting with Africa as the fundamental departure point may assist us in reaching a true understanding of African youth identity.

The primary methodological process adopted in this chapter was Serequeberhan's philosophical hermeneutics. The authors relied on deconstruction to meander through the history and meaning of colonization, colonialism, and youth identity. The next aim was reconstruction premised on African philosophy. The chapter gives a brief historical overview of colonization, colonialism, and epistemic violence in relation to African youth identity in scholarship. We aim to show how Western knowledge (especially pertaining to identity and identification) was imposed on Africa youth. The following section aims to locate the emergence and meaning of the concept "youth" in a particular geographical, philosophical and political context. This section follows logically from the brief historical overview mentioned above. The last aim of this chapter is reconstruction; it proposes a re-imaging of African youth from an Africanist perspective.

A Brief Contextual View Leading to the Misunderstanding of the Young Africans

This chapter's point of departure is a much-discussed area in African intellectual discourse and historiography, namely the introduction of European colonization in Africa, and the subsequent effects. These effects have been observed and documented in literature by authors such as Mudimbe, Smith and Quijano.[9] Literature shows how European colonization transformed, distorted, developed and advanced various socio-religious, cultural, political and economic systems of African native societies. Mudimbe notes that although the colonial experience represents but a brief moment in the history of Africa, this moment is still charged and controversial. Largely the imperial colonial experience still represents and explains Africa's modern societies.[10]

Literature on the subject of colonization and colonialism is vast and varying, and definitions of these concepts vary from author to author. In this chapter, we use Smith's perspective on colonialism. Smith argues that although imperialism and colonialism are interconnected concepts, it is generally agreed that colonialism is but one expression of imperialism.[11] For a narrower understanding of colonialism, and for the purposes of this chapter, we opt to work with Mudimbe's conceptualization of colonialism and colonization: Mudimbe notes that colonialism and colonization mean organization and arrangement.[12] In addition, he states that the two words are derived from the Latin word *colere*, meaning to cultivate or to design. Understood as such, we posit that it was the precise intention of colonists to organize and transform non-European areas into fundamentally European constructions.[13] They wanted to produce after their own kind. To be able to effectively organize and design their newfound territories, the colonists needed to have an organizing principle to arrange their newfound territory. This principle would drive and inspire the colonists to settle and prosper in their newly formed territories. It would also underpin colonialist procedures to acquire, distribute and exploit lands in the colonies; inspire the policies of domesticating natives; and determine how ancient organizations would be managed and new modes of production implemented.[14] The intended consequence of colonization as Quijano observes is to create specific power structures of dominance.[15] Quijano argues that colonial power structures produce specific social discriminations that codify themselves as racial, ethnic and anthropological systems, and that differ according to times, agents and populations.[16]

According to Wallerstein, these (social) discriminations foster zonal distinctions that create core and peripheral production processes within economies.[17] For one to understand how the colonial power structure operates and succeeds in creating social and economic discriminations, one should critically look at "whiteness" and its position in the colonial power structure.[18] Kincheloe and Steinberg inform us that whiteness hides and re-inscribes itself in differing contexts of times, social agents, and populations,[19] the covert ability of whiteness allows to engineer and dictate power realities in differing social horizons. In our particular thesis, it is how whiteness secretly signifies and determines African youth in the contested space of identity politics.

It is now common knowledge in critical whiteness studies, that through colonial expansion, whiteness was able to extend itself as a naturalized universal axiom. According to authors such as Kincheloe and Steinberg, whiteness has been able to achieve this through the insistence of its long Western philosophical tradition of reason and rationality.[20] Nkrumah notes that the origin of this insistence rises during the European Renaissance where man became the center of the universe, the human mind and the ways it might fix the limits of what is real became the primary concerns of philosophy.[21] According to Nkrumah, the rise of rationalism was one stream of thought, and perhaps belief, which kept reality firmly in the light of reason.[22] In addition, Nkrumah submits that the origin of the cut of the individual can be traced to the Protagoras dictum, "man is the measure of all things."[23]

However, Nkrumah contends that Protagoras' view was perverted by lesser minds into a grasping idealistic subjectivism.[24] In the era of rationalism, reason is *whitened* and human nature itself is grounded upon this reasoning capacity.[25] According to, Kincheloe and Steinberg whiteness began to establish itself in its rationalistic womb as a norm that represents authoritative, delimited and hierarchical modes of thought.[26] Similarly, Ramose notes how (European) self-consciousness is articulated and epitomized in Aristotle's writing that "man is a rational animal."[27] The Aristotelian position becomes the metaphysical idea of European existence as qualitatively superior human to others.[28]

Whiteness is thus able to create contexts that accommodate and promote its being-and-knowing-in-the-world. Whiteness becomes culture and culture is whiteness. Ani, correctly notes that Europeans discovered the secret that culture carries rules for thinking, and if you could impose your culture on your victims, you could limit the creativity of their vision and destroy their ability to act in their own interest with will and intent. Cultural imposition must be understood as the tendency by another group to impose its values and patterns of behavior on others.[29] This view of culture becomes important for colonists and colonialists aiming to redesign colonial territories. In order to design and extend its cultural logic, whiteness engaged in brutal violence to establish itself. For Ani, this cultural logic functions in four ways: Firstly, it teaches its logic and worldview to the ordinary participants, who then assimilate it, assume it and push it beneath the surface, from where it influences their collective behavior and responses.[30] Secondly, the special members of the culture—those regarded as intellectuals, scholars, theorists—retrieve the assumptions of this worldview and represent them as the tenets of a universal system of thought, one that presents standards of logic, rationality and truth to the world.[31] Thirdly, the European worldview takes on ideological force within and outside the culture, since it can be imposed as universal, speculative and self-conscious.[32] Fourthly, this culture and its parochial and axiological character remain well hidden and camouflaged beneath pseudo-universalism.[33]

To Ani's second point, we add Kincheloe and Steinberg's observation that whiteness is shaped and confirmed by its close association and belief in science.[34] As the result of this close association, whiteness favors mind over body; intellectual ways of knowing over experiential ways of knowing; and mental abstractions over passion, bodily sensations and tactile understanding.[35] The impact of this view on knowledge means that indigenous knowledge is subordinated to the colonial world system of knowledge.[36] Subsequently, Europeans become the source of knowledge and Europeans the only knowers.[37] However, to subdue and discard indigenous knowledge successfully, whiteness has to classify the natives or indigenous people as the Other. The intention of Othering is to culturally traumatize indigenous people permanently. Smelser explains cultural trauma as follows:

> A cultural trauma refers to an invasive and overwhelming event that is believed to undermine or overwhelm one or several essential ingredients of a culture or the culture as a whole. The Protestant Reformation qualifies as a cultural trauma because of the fundamental threat it posed to the integrity and dominance of the Catholic cultural worldview. The imposition of Western values on colonial societies in the nineteenth and twentieth centuries provides additional examples. The exposure of migrating groups to the cultures of the host societies into which they migrate provides still more. Several other points about the concept of cultural trauma can be advanced. National cultures in complex societies are typically problematic with respect to unity and loose with respect to coherence. It follows that a claim of traumatic damage (i.e., destruction of or threat to cultural values, outlooks, norms, or, for that matter, the culture as a whole), must be established by deliberate efforts on the part of cultural carriers-cultural specialists such as a priests, politicians, intellectuals, journalists, moral entrepreneurs, and leaders of social movements. Furthermore, once a historical memory is established as a national trauma for which the society has to be held in some way responsible, its status as trauma has to be continuously and actively sustained and reproduced in order to continue in that status.[38]

Moreover, cultural trauma might also imply the feeling of shame when you are not living up to set cultural norms and expectations. It occurs when you believe that you are unworthy of love and belonging because you do not fit in. So, cultural trauma is the result of cultural messages suggesting that there is something wrong with you or that you are not good enough because you fail to live up to a cultural norm and blame yourself for that failure. Cultural trauma is essentially a painful manifestation of the myth that there is only one right way, that is the way of the imposer, and the other "other" must comply.

Said notes that the classification process of the "other" is a cultural and ideological mode of discourse supported by institutions, vocabulary, scholarship, imagery, doctrines, colonial bureaucracies and styles.[39] These discourses were particularly informed by the imaginative tales and constructions of the Rest or the Other.[40] In as much as these homilies copied a certain rationale in the West about the Rest or the Other, they also molded the self-consciousness and duplicated the West. In this case, the West would not be if it were not for the encounters it had with the Rest. However unpresumptuous the encounter, Hall reminds us that these encounters were not innocent because they were encounters between equals.[41] Based on this condition of inequality, Fanon proposes his thesis on the existential zonal categories of being and nonbeing.[42] These existential zonal categories conditioned a reality that gave the West an ontological status of being and the Rest an ontological status of nonbeing.

It is in these zonal categories that we find clear representations of the West–Whiteness–Europe and the Rest–Nonwhite–African. The West–Whiteness–Europe would exist in the zone of being characteristically signified by rationality, scientific knowledge and philosophies of mind. In the zone of nonbeing, we find the Rest–Nonwhite–Africans characterized by irrationality, indigenous knowledge and folk psychologies. We could argue that it is within the logic of zonal distinction and classifications that epistemic racism finds its grounds. Based on the same distinctions and classifications, African knowledge has been discarded as a significant contributor to academic discourses. Further, it is the contention of this chapter that the subordinated knowledge should play a central role in the construction, production and dissemination of knowledge in Africa. Another contention of this chapter is that only African knowledge can emancipate Africans from Western universal ways of knowing. In addition to emancipation from racialized epistemic forms of knowing, economic emancipation may also be realized. We postulate that if Africa can reclaim the space of knowledge production, then Africa may minimize or eradicate some of its economic maladies.

Historic Location of the Concept and Idea of "Youth"

It is considering the above brief historic overview that the concept "youth" finds its universality. According to Nsamenang, psychologists know about human development, more specifically youth development, from one cultural point of view, which give us individualistic and child-centered categories of youth development.[43] These categories predominantly emanate from Western discourse and influence. In our African context, researchers easily rely, adopt and adapt these categories to give meaning to the concept "young African." More often than not, they do so uncritically. Pence and Marfo warn us about the danger of this type of uncritical cultural juxtaposition.[44]

In order to locate its epistemological and conceptual location, we begin with the etymology of the concept "youth." Soares observes, "Youth is both a social concept created to define the particular way that human beings see themselves and others at a particular point in their lives, and a useful sociological concept."[45] We start our discussion with the etymology of the concept "youth" according to the *Oxford English Dictionary*. The word originates from the Old English word *geogup*, the Old Saxon word *jugud*, the Middle Low German and Middle Dutch word *joghet*, the Old High German word *jugund* and the German word *jugend*. It is defined as "[t]he state of being young; youngness."[46] Additionally, the concept refers to "[t]he time when one is young; the early part or period of life; more specifically, the period from puberty till the attainment of full growth, between childhood and adult" and the "[e]arly stage or period of existence."[47] According to Jones, youth is also the product of social and educational reforms that are mainly the result of the development of welfare capitalism. Based on the above, we put forward that the idea, meaning and understanding of youth are geographically and contextually out of place in Africa.[48] Researchers such as Durham note that a primary definition of youth often refers to age as the main idea-signifier of youth.[49] Additionally, Durham (citing Meyer Fortes) notes that definitional categories remain problematic for defining children and youth in this way.[50] King writes that "studies of the young [using the problematic definitions critiqued by Durham] must address the question: Do age groups have histories?"[51] Following King's argument, we note that, in other cultural contexts, "social customs rather than chronological age determined if one is called a bondservant 'boy' or 'girl'."[52]

Durham states that this view of youth is extremely problematic in Africa.[53] In the African context, the constructs and meanings of "youth" are not the equivalent to the constructs and meanings of "youth" according to Western paradigms. Translating and interpreting them to have the same, meaning is to bastardize African languages and their meaning. Insistence on speaking of "Young Africans" or "youth in Africa" legitimizes the dominance of western knowledge. The difficulty lies in trying to have meaningful discussions about the African youth without succumbing to a Western perspective. This difficulty is caused by the view that research concepts and research language used to identify African youth remain Western orientated.[54]

A Re-imagining of Youth in an African Context

In this section, we attempt to develop an identity for African youth while discarding the Western perspective. Ntarangwi argues that research in Africa should be based on Afrocentric research questions and practices.[55] Furthermore, Ntarangwi states that the social realities and environments of youth in Africa have to be considered in such research endeavors.[56] Upon hearing Ntarangwi' s suggestions, African researchers are inclined to ask how such research potentialities can be achieved. In an attempt to conceive of such an Afrocentric research paradigm, Marfo suggests the following:

> [T]he research paradigm should not be conceived as a culturally insulated enterprise cocooned in its own traditions and designed exclusively to address

> questions of local relevance but as a field that is mindful enough of the interconnectedness of the human condition across cultures to be able to benefit from and contribute to other understandings.[57]

Marfo also notes that the research paradigm "should be informed by an orientation that accentuates local relevance [that] pays priority attention to mechanisms for building a knowledge base on indigenous conceptions of childhood."[58]

That is why consensus among African scholars such as Jegede, Okebukola, Nsamenang and Ramose is that one such paradigm can be found from the perspective of an African worldview. According to Jegede and Okebukola, it is important to consider the worldview when determining the theoretical positions of an observer.[59] Furthermore, they note that the African worldview functions as a paradigm for the observer in an African context.[60] The African worldview, according to Jegede and Okebukola, is a "system of religious and philosophical beliefs that exits in traditional African societies."[61] According to Nsamenang, such a system conceives individuality as one that is relational and interdependent rather than narcissistic.[62] Additionally, Nsamenang posits that the African worldview plays a significant role at various ontogenetic points.[63] The African worldview equips the observer to understand youth and personhood in an African context. This worldview captures both ontology and epistemology in one reality.[64] When we consider the philosophical concept of Ubuntu, we see such an encapsulation of ontology and epistemology.[65] According to Ramose, the Bantu philosophy of Ubuntu sees Ubuntu as "being becoming."[66] For African developmental psychologists such an understanding of being is critical to understanding youth development and personhood.[67] This understanding of youth in Africa provides categories that are contextual and situational.[68] According to Frederiksen and Munive, the being of African youth is one that is a socially constructed,[69] and this social ontogeny draws from African life journeys.[70] For Nsamenang these life journeys are the spiritual selfhood, social selfhood and ancestral selfhood.[71]

An African worldview would be able to treat an African youth as a social shifter. This chapter concurs with Durham's assertions that African youth as social shifters would mean that "to call someone a youth is to position him or her in terms of a variety of social attributes, including not only age but also independence-dependence, authority, rights, abilities, knowledge, responsibilities, and so on."[72] When considering the Young African as social shifter, the possibility arises of seeing the youth as proactive agents of change in society.[73] However, this is not always the case, as dominant perceptions of the youth are that they are passive agents in need of adult supervision.[74] Diouf states that this perception and intervention has had disastrous consequences for some African youths. Some of these consequences have been huge numbers of unemployed youths in Africa, youths living in poverty, youths involved in gangsterism, poor levels of literacy and so on.[75] This gives us a context of the living environment of the African youth.

That is why the formulation and implementation of effective youth capacity-building plans are imperative. For us to have an effective youth capacity then it will require a new approach and to create new leadership with a different active rather than passive role. Igue's description is helpful and in order as he argues that: The new African leaders will play an essential role in these different aspects of social capital. This is the reason why they must meet several requirements in terms of training and ability, such as: boldness and the ability to anticipate through management and control of change; loyalty to themselves and the people; respect for leadership principles like duty, honor, national commitment, insight and so on; and establishment of a more equitable system of partnership with the rest of the world.[76]

We agree with Campinha-Bacote that in the process of providing service delivery to a particular social group such as children or youth, the service provider(s) ought to be culturally competent.[77] Extending her thesis, Campinha-Bacote argued that cultural competency was equally important to diverse racial groups found in societies, in her paper it was the necessity of cultural competence in providing care to African American people.[78] In her thesis, Campinha-Bacote cultural competence is "an ongoing process, not an event, in which [the service provider] continuously strives to achieve the ability to effectively work within the cultural context of the community."[79] According to, Campinha-Bacote, this ongoing process involves the integration of cultural awareness, cultural knowledge, cultural skill, cultural encounters, and cultural desire.[80] Adapting some of her work, we postulate that an endeavor to re-identify and provide quality service to African youth the following basic ideas ought to be considered: cultural consciousness and cultural knowledge.

Cultural Hunger

Cultural hunger is defined as positions itself opposite the sensation of "having to" participate in this process. Cultural hunger is the critical key paradigm of cultural competence, for it is the Young African hunger that arouses the entire development of cultural competence. This hunger must come from Young African ambition and not from anxiety.

Cultural hunger encompasses the notion of consciousness, as it comprises an unpretentious appetite to be exposed and flexible to the teachings of an African worldview, and a willingness to learn from African elders as cultural informants. This category of erudition is a life-long progression that is referred to as cultural modesty.

Cultural hunger also encompasses the obligation of the Young African to care for all Africans, regardless of their cultural values, beliefs, customs or practices. Of course, because culture evolves, sometimes there might be difficulties when caring for challenging elders whose behaviors (e.g., child abuse, substance abuse and sexual addiction) may be in direct political and moral conflict with the Young African ideal.

Cultural Consciousness

Cultural consciousness involves the self-examination and in-depth exploration of your own cultural background.[81] It involves the appreciation of one's biases, prejudices and assumptions about your own culture. Without being aware of the influence of his or her own cultural values, there is risk that the Young African becomes absorbed in cultural assimilation and hate. Cultural assimilation and hate are the tendencies to hate your own beliefs, values and patterns of behavior, and to exchange them for the beliefs, values and behaviors of another culture that is regarded as superior.

We must state that there are those Young Africans who are consciously disabled or unconscious of their own being as Africans. We deliberately use the term "consciously disabled" to capture a contemporary shift and modern-day self-hate. The Young African must be forced to ask continuously, "Do my views and behaviour as an African support the stigma, isolation and devaluation of Africa? Am I sensitive to the cultural uniqueness and beauty of an African worldview in response to Africanization and in support of the African agenda?" Young Africans must know that effective interactions with their African ancestors, elders and the communities will give them access to personal consciousness of their own thoughts and feelings.

Cultural Acquaintance

Cultural acquaintance is the quest for, and location of, sound knowledge of African culture and one's own ethnic group. African traditions explain how Young Africans should interpret their worldview and how it determines their thinking, doing and being. They believe that the most important quality of consciousness disability is not the lack or nonexistence of tradition, but rather hunger for and participation in the ancestral culture that is based on African traditions; this is where African values and pride reside. Acquaintance with the cultural values of the African worldview can help Young Africans to use their usual inferiority accusations and responses during identity questions and concerns.

In seeking knowledge about African culture, it has to be clear that African Youths have to go through four stages: unconscious stupidity, conscious stupidity, conscious aptitude and unconscious aptitude. Unconscious stupidity is being unaware that you lack cultural acquaintance. These Young Africans have no awareness of cultural differences between themselves and European descendants. Conscious stupidity is the awareness that you are lacking knowledge about African culture. Young Africans may recognize this stupidity when they attend cultural ceremonies (e.g., funerals, marriages and initiations) or have direct cross-cultural experiences with fellow Africans. They possess the "know that" of knowledge, but not the "know how" of knowledge. They discern that culture plays an important role in Africa, but do not know how to use this understanding. Conscious aptitude is the African act of studying the Young African culture, corroborating over-generalization and providing culturally reactive, relevant mediations. Unconscious aptitude is the aptitude of the Young African to offer culturally appropriate solutions to the problems facing Africa and Africans. An unconsciously competent Young African appears to be "a natural" when their interaction with youths from alien cultures is observed.

Conclusion

In closing, we must say to Young Africans that in obtaining cultural acquaintance, it is critical to remember the concept of intracultural disparity–there are more dissimilarities within cultural groups than across cultural groups. To ease the crisis of meaning and misunderstanding of Young Africans and scholarship, Young Africans need to reconcile themselves to the African tradition, reality and worldview. The marginalization of the African worldview is the reason why most Young Africans adhere simultaneously to both African or Western definitions and practices when they have to contend with cultural challenges. The task involves that the Young African should engage and invest heavily in hermeneutics.

Notes

1 Kwame Nkrumah, *Consciencism: Philosophy and Ideology for De-colonization* (New York: Monthly Review Press, 1970), 62.
2 Ibid.
3 Ibid.

4 Lasana Keita, "Africa's Triple Heritage: Unique or Universal?," *Présence Africaine Nouvelle série* 3, no. 143 (1987): 2.
5 Nkrumah, *Consciencism*, 68.
6 Ibid.
7 Ibid.
8 Ibid.
9 Valentin-Yves Mudimbe, *The Invention of Africa: Gnosis, Philosophy, and the Order of Knowledge* (Indianapolis: Indiana University Press, 1988); Linda Tuhiwai Smith, *Decolonizing Methodologies: Research and Indigenous Peoples* (London and New York: Zed Books, 1999); Annibal Quijano, "Coloniality and Modernity/Rationality," *Cultural Studies, Special Issue: Globalization and the De-Colonial Option* 21, no. 2–3 (2007): 168–179. Accessed July 9, 2014, https://www.tandfonline.com/doi/full/10.1080/09502380601164353.
10 Mudimbe, *The Invention of Africa*, 14.
11 Smith, *Decolonizing Methodologies*, 21. See also, "Quijano, Coloniality and Modernity/Rationality," 168.
12 Mudimbe, *The Invention of Africa*, 14.
13 Ibid.
14 Ibid., 15.
15 Quijano, "Coloniality and Modernity/Rationality," 168.
16 Ibid.
17 Immanuel Wallerstein, *World-Systems Analysis: An Introduction* (Durham, NC and London: Duke University Press, 2004).
18 Joe Kincheloe and Shirley Steinberg, "Addressing the Crisis of Whiteness: Reconfiguring White Identity in a Pedagogy of Whites," in *White Reign: Deploying Whiteness in America*, ed. Kincheloe, Joe, Shirley Steinberg, Nelson Rodriguez, and Ronald Chennault (New York: St. Martin's Griffin, 1998), 4.
According to Kincheloe and Steinberg, no one really knows what whiteness is, but most would agree that it is intimately involved with issues of power and power differences between white and nonwhite people. Thus whiteness cannot be separated from hegemony; it is profoundly influenced by demographic changes, political realignments and economic cycles.
19 Kincheloe and Steinberg, "Addressing the Crisis of Whiteness," 4.
20 Ibid., 5.
21 Nkrumah, *Consciencism*, 30.
22 Ibid.
23 Ibid., 39.
24 Ibid.
25 Kincheloe and Steinberg, *Addressing the Crisis of Whiteness*, 5.
26 Ibid.
27 Mogobe Ramose, *African Philosophy through Ubuntu* (Indiana: Mond Books, 1999), 5.
28 Tsenay Serequeberhan, "The Critique of Eurocentrism and the Practice of African Philosophy," in *Postcolonial African Philosophy: A Critical Reader*, ed. Emmanuel Chukwudi Eze (Cambridge, MA: Blackwell, 1997), 64.
29 Marimba Ani, *Yurugu: An African-Centered Critique of European Cultural Thought and Behaviour* (Trenton, NJ: Africa World Press, 1994), 1.
30 Ani, *Yurugu*, 7–8.

31 Ibid.
32 Ibid.
33 Ibid.
34 Kincheloe and Steinberg, *Addressing the Crisis of Whiteness*, 5.
35 Ibid.
36 Paulin Hountondji, "Producing Knowledge in Africa Today the Second Bashorun M.K.O. Abiola Distinguished Lecture," *African Studies Review* 38, no. 3 (1995): 2.
37 Ngugi Wa Thiongo, "Europhone or African Memory: The Challenge of the Pan-Africanist Intellectual in the Era of Globalisation," in *African intellectuals: Rethinking Politics, Language Gender and Development*, ed. Thandika Mkwandawire (South Africa: UNISA Press, 2005), 158.
38 Neil Smelser, "Psychological and Cultural Trauma," in *Cultural Trauma Collective Identity* ed. Alexander, Jefferey, Ron Eyerman, Bernhard Giesen, Neil J. Smelser, and Piotr Sztompka (Los Angeles: University of California Press, 2004), 38.
39 Edward W. Said, *Orientalism* (London: Penguin, 1977), 2.
Following, Stuart Hall, our understanding of the concept "discourse" is taken to mean a particular way of representing 'the West,' 'the Rest' and the relations between them. Furthermore, a discourse is a group of statements which that provide a language for talking about (i.e., a way of representing) a particular kind of knowledge about a topic. See Stuart Hall, "The West and the Rest: Discourse and Power," in *Formations of Modernity*, ed. Stuart Hall and Bram Gieben (Cambridge, UK: Blackwell, 1992), 291.
40 Hall, *The West and the Rest*, 3.
41 Ibid., 294.
42 Frantz Fanon, *Black Skin, White Masks* (France. Editions de Seuil, 1952), 7.
43 Bame Nsamenang. "Eurocentric Image of Childhood in the Context of the World's Cultures," *Human Development* 42, no. 3 (1999a):160, downloaded July 9, 2014, http://www.unige.ch/fapse/SSE/teachers/dasen/Nsamenang1999.pdf.
44 Alan Pence and Kofi Marfo, "Early Childhood Development in Africa: Interrogating Constraints of Prevailing Knowledge Bases," *International Journal of Psychology* 43, no. 2 (2008): 80, downloaded July 9, 2014, http://www.tandfonline.com/doi/pdf/10.1080/00207590701859143.pdf.
45 Camilo Soares, "Aspects of Youth, Transitions, and the End of Certainties," *International Social Science Journal* 52, no. 164 (2000): 209, downloaded July 9, 2014, http://onlinelibrary.wiley.com/doi/10.1111/1468-2451.00252/abstract.pdf.
46 Oxford University Press, "Youth," in *Oxford English Dictionary* (2014). Accessed July 12, 2014. http://www.oed.com/view/Entry/232184?redirectedFrom=youth#eid.
47 Ibid.
48 Gill Jones, *Youth* (Cambridge, UK: Polity Press, 2009), 3.
49 Deborah Durham, "Disappearing Youth: Youth as a Social Shifter in Botswana," *American Anthropological Association* 31, no. 4 (2004): 591, downloaded July 9, 2014, http://www.jstor.org/stable/pdf/4098870.pdf?acceptTC=true.pdf.
50 Durham, "Disappearing Youth: Youth as a Social Shifter in Botswana," 291.
51 Wilma King, *Stolen Childhood: Slave Youth in Nineteenth-Century America*, 2nd edition (Indiana: Indiana University Press, 2011), XX.
52 Ibid.
53 Durham, "Disappearing Youth," 591–592.
54 Nsamenang, "Eurocentric Image of Childhood in the Context of the World's Cultures," 160.

55 Mwenda Ntarangwi, *Children and Youth in Africa: Annotated Bibliography 2001–2011* (Dakar: Codesria, 2014), 3.
56 Ibid.
57 Kofi Marfo, "Envisioning an African Child Development Field," *Child Development Perspectives* 5, no. 2 (2011): 143, downloaded July 9, 2014, http://onlinelibrary.wiley.com/doi/10.1111/j.1750-8606.2011.00169.x/pdf.
58 Ibid.
59 Jegede, Olugbeniro and Peter Akinsola Okebukola, "The Relationship between African Traditional Cosmology and Students' Acquisition of a Science Process Skill," *International Journal of Science Education* 13, no. 1 (1991): 38, downloaded July 9, 2014, http://www.tandfonline.com/doi/abs/10.1080/0950069910130104#.VZ5hU_mqpBc.pdf. 38.
See also Bame Nsamenang, "Conceptualizing Human Development and Education in Sub-Saharan Africa at the Interface of Indigenous and Exogenous Influences," in *Cross-Cultural Perspectives in Human Development: Theory, Research, and Applications*, ed. T S. Saraswathi (India: Sage, 2003b), 215.
60 Jedgede and Okebukola, "The Relationship between African Traditional Cosmology," 38.
61 Ibid., 38–39.
62 Nsamenang, "Conceptualizing Human Development," 216.
63 Ibid.
64 Ramose, *African Philosophy through Ubuntu*, 35.
65 Ibid., 36.
66 Ibid.
According to Ramose, Ubu- evokes the idea of being in general. It is enfolded being before it manifests itself in the concrete form or mode of existence of a particular entity. Ubu- as enfolded being is always orientated towards unfoldment . . ." Ubu- therefore expresses the ontological (p. 36).
Additionally, he argues that ntu- becomes the nodal point at which being assumes concrete form or a mode of being in the process of continual unfoldment." Therefore, ntu- according to, Ramose expresses the epistemological (p. 36).
67 Nsamenang, "Conceptualizing Human Development," 216.
68 Bodil Folke Frederiksen and J. Jairo Munive, "Young Men and Women in Africa: Conflicts, Enterprise and Aspiration," *Young* 18, no. 3 (2010): 251, downloaded July 9, 2014, http://www.maths.manchester.ac.uk/~mrm/Download/Mattia/FrederiksenMunive_Young18.pdf.
69 Ibid.
70 Nsamenang, "Conceptualizing Human Development," 217.
71 Ibid.
72 Durham, "Disappearing Youth," 591–592.
73 Frederikson and Munive, "Young Men and Women in Africa," 250.
74 Mamadou Diouf, "Engaging Postcolonial Cultures: African Youth and Public Space," *African Studies Association* 46, no. 2 (2003): 4, downloaded, July 9, 2014, http://www.jstor.org/stable/pdf/1514823.pdf?acceptTC=true.pdf.
See also, Frederikson and Munive, "Young Men and Women in Africa," 251.
75 Diouf, "Engaging Postcolonial Cultures," 4.

76 John O. Igue, "A New Generation of Leaders in Africa: What Issues Do They Face," Tr by Sarah Jordan, International Development Policy | Revue internationale de politique de développement [Online], 1 | 2010, Online since March 11, 2010, connection on May 03, 2019. URL: http://journals.openedition.org/poldev/139; DOI: 10.4000/poldev.131.
77 Josepha Campinha-Bacote, "Cultural Competence: A Critical Factor in Child Health Policy," *Journal of Pediatirc Nursing* 12, no. 4 (1997): 260–262, downloaded July 16, 2014, https://www.pediatricnursing.org/article/S0882-5963(97)80013-9/pdf.
78 Josepha Campinha-Bacote, "A Culturally Competent Model of Care for African Americans," *Urologic Nursing* 29, no. 1 (2009): 49–54, downloaded July 16, 2014, https://www.suna.org/download/members/unjarticles/2009/09feb/49.pdf.
79 Josepha Campinha-Bacote, "The Process of Cultural Competence in Delivery of Healthcare Services: A Model of Care," *Journal of Transactional Nursing* 13, no. 3 (2002): 181, accessed July 17, 2014, https://journals.sagepub.com/doi/pdf/10.1177/10459602013003003.
80 Ibid.
81 Campinha-Bacote, "The Process of Cultural Competence," 182.

5. *A Psychologist's Perspective on Becoming Agents of an Unruly Transformation*

MELINDA CONTRERAS-BYRD

I am the product of the urban, U.S. ghetto of Newark, NJ. My family is African-American and Cuban. I became a Christian at the age of 12 and have continued this spiritual path throughout my life. I am a licensed psychologist, an ordained African Methodist Episcopal Church Elder, a Womanist theologian and poet, and a Cognitive Behavioral, Multimodal, Psycho-spiritual psychotherapist.

I have included this biographical sketch as a way to "practice what I preach." You see, in this essay, I warn against accepting the validity of a universal norm; and furthermore, challenge readers to determine if they have inadvertently done so. With respect to norms, I believe that the particular stories or biographies of those who teach, or hold the power to name, is of critical importance in forming an educated opinion about the usefulness and legitimacy of any wisdom taught, and any norm being proposed. Our ideas about what is acceptable, needful or axiomatic vary as a function of who is making the judgment. The conscious or unconscious use of concepts of the universal norm is the bedrock upon which much of the thinking and behavior toward Black people is based. Improperly applied, concepts of universal norms can be destructive. So it is my intention to challenge readers to assume the responsibility to do a background search of all those seeking to serve as agents of transformation within our communities. In this way, we will protect our communities from the negative consequences of embracing both false norms, and from those self-proclaimed and illegitimate transformers that wreak havoc upon our ability to have positive identity development, increased expectations and positive self-assessment. I have told you who I am so that you can make your own determination about the relevancy and legitimacy of my ideas as they apply to whomever you advocate for.

I have also included the information about myself because a second factor that I explore in this chapter is the importance that ethnic culture plays in every aspect of the lives of Black people. Although hardly acknowledged in graduate pedagogy (in the pedagogy of graduate level courses), the ethnic culture of the speaker and hearer serves to profoundly influence the information being taught as well as the decision-making processes that occur as a result of the teaching. Therefore, I want to encourage readers to make a choice to be very careful about all life-influencing judgments that we as (both formal and informal) teachers, preachers, therapists or activists make, for we constitute a portion of those from our communities who are gifted with the responsibility to serve as agents of transformation.

As a practicing Black psychologist and clergy, it is my intention to offer a discussion that demonstrates ways in which faith and psychology can merge with Black culture to create new thinking and behavior that will instruct, reorient, challenge and empower people in our communities. If we wish to assess the needs of Black communities, if we wish to be agents of transformation, then we must begin by reexamining our foundational ideas about what is "normal," what is needful and what is relevant. The ideas that I have developed regarding norms and culture, serve as foundational truths that undergird both my clinical approach to therapy and my hermeneutical approach to praxis. Those seeking to serve as change agents must realize that our actions are based upon some foundational thinking. Whether we realize it or not, this thinking involves acceptance of a theory related to normalcy and the relevance of culture in personal and community transformation.

Acceptance of Universal Norms

In both ministry and psychotherapy, professionals deliberately or unconsciously assume to know and teach ideas of that which is "normal," "acceptable" or "needful." Ministers and teachers often do so based on a platform of foundational beliefs that presume some level of universality and potential for the betterment of those who lay claim to these approaches. The thing to be aware of is this: there is an insidious aspect to the foundations upon which classical psychological theories and interventions as well as biblical exegeses and praxis are based. Sadly, often we are not aware of this reality. By failing to act in accordance with the ramifications of this truth we do a disservice to our clients, students, and parishioners. It is imperative that we begin to hold ourselves accountable to the cultural, socio-political, spiritual, and moral outcomes of the approaches we espouse.

As an example of this insidious effect, typically the Christian Bible is used without regard for the many implications that culture holds for how its words are interpreted and lived out. In our interpretation and teaching of the Bible, we do what we were taught because it seems to be the norm. But what we fail to realize is that in so doing, we have embraced the Bible as a culture-free book. We then go on to determine what qualifies as "the church," who qualifies as a "Christian" and even define transformation in accord with cultural norms that do not fit our situation. I am suggesting that it will take more than what theological institutions offer in order for Black people to take a Jewish-based Bible and create from it a spirit-empowered community that will engage, educate and empower members of the African diaspora.

We, theologians and clergy, must engage in a conscious struggle to create our own cultural-personal hermeneutic—holding both ourselves and our colleagues of color responsible to offer a whole God and Jesus—that is relevant, and balanced by love and justice. As academics, clerics and psychotherapists, we achieve this by finding or creating theoretical frameworks that account for the history, culture and legitimacies of difference inherent in our life experience.[1]

As agents of transformation, we all must accept the responsibility to step outside of the box and perhaps be the few who are shaking our heads no, when the majority of our colleagues are shaking their heads yes. I would like to use a brief history of Black psychologists in the United States as an example of what I am saying.

The 1960s and 1970s were notably turbulent times in the United States. These were times of "agonizing reappraisal," social and political change, and at least the intellectual dismantling of many U.S. institutions.[2] The Vietnam War, the hippie and Flower Power movements, the nascent Civil Rights Movement, Women's Liberation, Nationalist and Third World coalitions gave rise to an unprecedented time of questioning, challenging and redeeming upheaval. The energy expended during these decades resulted in the realization that theories, textbooks, and advanced academic studies offered within the United States were woefully lacking as tools for accurate assessment of "minority" populations.[3] Worse, it was becoming clear that because it lacked any Afrocentric critique, academic scholarship across a broad spectrum was culturally insensitive, counter-revolutionary, and arguably—by the assessment of some Black church members—a "tool of the devil." As the implications of this truth began to unfold, new things began to happen.

On September 2, 1968, an annual conference of the American Psychological Association (APA) was thrown into uproar when a group of Black psychologists made a scathing and well-organized presentation of the cultural and political shortcomings of this organization—the sole voice for the practice of psychology in the United States.[4] From this act of unified self-determination, the Association of Black Psychologists (ABPsi) was born.[5] In its effort to highlight and dismantle inherently racist thoughts and protocol within American professional health and education communities, ABPsi went on to declare a moratorium on the psychological testing of all Black children.[6] The issues at this and other conferences became the growing revelation: Black people were being labeled, stereotyped, weighed in every form of balance and found desperately wanting.[7]

Psychologists of color began to create textbooks on cultural sensitivity and relativity, arguing against the unspoken norms used. These textbooks raised questions about unspoken norms and revealed "that something" was racist, classist, and sexist.[8] Meanwhile, theologians in the United States began to look at Christian seminary curriculum and classic theological writings with suspicion and a new curiosity.[9] The questions for us were these: Where are my people in the church and theological history with which we are presented? What truth or relevance does this teaching or interpretation hold within the context of my life experience and culture? Do they presume any unspoken racist assumptions about Black people? Clearly, there are several important negative implications of the insidious application of a belief in a universal norm. Psychological theories and Christain theologies of past and present Western societies are based upon accepted norms—norms that are inaccurate and exclusive of Black cultures.[10]

When we begin to honor the cultural gift that God has given us—then we will begin to see the need to step outside of the norm. And when we step outside of the norm, when we seize the audacity of self-determination within whatever sphere of society we have been placed, ***then*** we become people seen as renegades, and labeled as unruly.

Every faction of would-be agents of this transformation must begin to ask the questions that will uncover the answers that will aid in transformation. To continue the struggle to address and rectify this problem within the clinical context, Black therapists must pose a series of ongoing questions:[11] Do the textbook-informed clinical goals and interventions that we set for *our* at-risk youth really support that we are in fact acting as agents of change in our communities? Can we entrust our children's academic futures solely to school districts as though these institutions' explicit and implicit, conscious and unconscious goals for our children are the same as those for white children? Can we assume that all school districts have an equal investment in bringing all children to their highest potential? Should the oppositional behavior of some angry and aggressive Black clients *only* be interpreted as personal mental health issues, labeled and medicated away; or do our ethical responsibilities as Black clinicians extend outside the therapy office and into the hegemonic systems of power in our societies? What if the *true* client is the society and *not* the person sitting in our office? Is our goal to mold oppositional students into the type of student that will pose no problem in the school; or can we use our knowledge of human development and behavior to help them learn the tools to maintain their righteous outrage over the injustice of their daily lives and the savvy to navigate the system with their integrity and leadership skills still intact? Do our foundational presumptions regarding what constitutes a healthy marriage or a functional-family correspond to the presence of what we know to be the strengths of our culture?

With regard to issues of faith, Black theologians and clergy must engage in an ongoing dialogue that raises critical questions. Do we as pastors see our roles as using God's word to mold parishioners into keeping the peace and maintaining the status quo? Do we preach a colorless, otherworldly gospel in which there is nothing of Africa, no legitimacy for civil disobedience, no questioning of authority, or coloring outside the lines? Does our preaching ignore the harshness of life in favor of a word that promises prosperity; or do we raise all the hard issues of life and struggle with our people to find a word of God in them? Are we as theologians determined to bring a Black hermeneutic to bear upon our understanding of the scriptures? Does it occur to us to translate our writings from the words of the academy into words that will benefit the community from which we were nurtured and sent?

The Significance of Ethnic Culture

Ethnic culture is at the center of who we are and informs many aspects of our thinking and behavior. Although I explore here the idea of culture, you will see that it is intertwined with concepts of "the norm." The ramification of being a "minority" within a given culture is a critical factor that must be considered when making decisions about the meaning of "self," God, or justice.[12] The issue here is that when Western societies have espoused theological and theoretical approaches that attempt to account for the presence of culture and ethnicity, these approaches have been based upon the unspoken idea that difference equaled deficit.[13] Whenever the assessment results of Black people differs from those of whites, the difference is assumed to be a demonstration of a problem and evidence of a perceived genetic deficit.[14] As a consequence, this data is used to determine the target area for an intervention to address a now confirmed deficit. We learned from the classic text, *Black English*, by J.L. Dillard that even the unconscious syntactical structuring African Americans created was attached to our African language ancestry.[15] We learned from the classic psychological theories in Reginald L. Jones's, *Black Psychology* that culture informs attribution, resilience, concepts of family, and the building of adequate support systems.[16] Although African Americans live in a society and culture that is Eurocentric, Black behavior and thinking are Afrocentric and therefore legitimately different.[17] From the classic research of Black psychiatrists, William Grier and Price Cobbs, came the important fact that one cannot detach cultural experience from any accurate understanding of "anger."[18] We also learned that the accuracy of clinical understanding and diagnosis are clearly related to ethnicity and cultural experience. Donald K. Cheeks' work asserted that even the attribute of "assertiveness" is culture bound.[19] According to his studies, assertive Black men were often characterized by white assessors as threatening and haughty.

The results of a recent study I completed supports my theory that even the self-care choices Black clergy make are influenced by our culture.[20] We take on increased levels of responsibility and sacrifice for our parishioners based on certain cultural imperatives that inform what we deem as good pastoring. We pastor in accord with a hermeneutic that is culturally and historically influenced.[21] Likewise, the liturgies that we create and the focus of the gospel that we preach are all a reflection of both our ethnicity and our culture.[22]

I believe that therapy can be a tool of liberation. In the right hands, psychological theory and practice can aid in releasing from guilt, empowering the abused, and giving voice to the voiceless.[23] Therapists can encourage their clients to ask questions in all areas of life with the expectation of being heard and respected. This can be practiced and reinforced in their interactions with us. Both therapists and clergy can assume the responsibility to ask questions, challenge what is taken for granted, and motivate clients toward a vision that is beyond what they had initially imagined. Therapeutic approaches can be used to put the client in the driver's seat and acknowledge the truth—that they are their own experts, and we are but fallible helpers.[24]

Beginning with Moses and the prophets of the Old Testament to Jesus and the latter prophets—Denmark Vesey, Nat Turner, Martin Luther King, Jr., Malcolm X, Nelson Mandela, and the hip-hop voices of this present age—the word of God has always caused discomfort, conflict, upheaval, and renewal.[25] As theologians and clergy we are called to be prophets of an ongoing, holy unrest. Perhaps that is why we were blessed with Blackness.

But how do we handle the gift of teaching or ministry when it comes to Black individual and communal identity? In answer to this question, I will end where I began. It all starts with who we are, and our willingness to rise to the occasion of asking the questions that will give us the accurate and transforming answers. In the questions, are the challenges that will set us apart in ways that will mark us as unruly. So, ask yourself, do our parishioners see themselves when they enter our churches? Do they believe that their Blackness is significant, and our people are worthwhile; or do we adorn our churches with images that do not reflect our reality, our experiences, or our beauty? Can we accept a theology of revelation with a hidden presumption that some cultures are more naturally inclined to receive a word from God than others? Do we struggle with the biblical God of the Old Testament and thus pass on to our church members the skill and right to challenge and reinterpret scriptures such as to uncover a "liberating word"?[26] Do we highlight the "texts of terror" or do we deftly skip over them, leaving our people, one day, to uncover a God they can only understand as racist, jingoistic, and repulsed by human disability?[27]

Will it make any significant difference if we neglect to point out the Black presence in the scripture, or make note of the key church Fathers and Mothers who were of African heritage?[28]

Does our understanding and preaching of the gospel aid in the production of cognitive dissonance in our members who struggle to resolve questions of allegiance with respect to where their culture stands in relationship to their faith?

I believe our present call is to determine the specific theological views and psychotherapeutic theories and practices that are culturally syntonic and life-affirming. I believe our call today is to begin the ministry of creating viable vehicles of transformation that result in holy socio-political visions and the cultural-spiritual empowerment of all of God's people.

Notes

1 Cain Hope Felder, *Troubling Biblical Waters* (Maryknoll: Orbis Books, 1990), 25.

2 I use the phrase, "agonizing reappraisal," to illustrate the radical nature of the shift in the social and cultural climate in the United States during this time. This term was first used by Secretary of State John Foster Dulles in 1953 in relation to France and the action the United States should take if it failed to ratify the European Defense Community. Thereafter the term became a popular phrase used to denote a reassessment of a policy forced on one by a radical change in circumstance. See Edward Weintal, "John Foster Dulles," *Encyclopedia Britannica*, June 7, 2014. http://www.britannica.com/EBchecked/topic/173368/John-Foster-Dulles.

3 Robert L. Williams, William Dotson, Patricia Don, and Willie S. Williams, "Critical Issues in Testing and Achievement of Black Americans," *Journal of Negro Education* 49, no. 3 (Summer 1980): 263–269.

4 James L. Meyers, "Gone Too Far to Turn Back Now: Which Way ABPsi," *Psychological Discourse*, 22 (1991): 6–7.

5 M. B. H. Bennett, "The Second Time Around," *Psychological Discourse* 23, no. 7 (1992): 4–7.
6 R. E. G. King, "Highlights in the Development of ABPsi," *Journal of Black Psychology* 4, no. 1&2 (1977–1978): 9–12.
7 Ibid., 13–24.
8 Reginald Lanier Jones, *Black Psychology* (New York: HarperCollins Publishers, 1980), 22–23.
9 Cain Hope Felder, *Troubling Biblical Waters*, 26.
10 A. Jackson, "Healing and Liberation: Critical Challenges," *Psychological Discourse* 24, no. 9 (1993): 4–6.
11 Thomas A. Parham, "President's Message: The Year in Review," *Psychological Discourse* 27 (1996): 4–10.
12 A. Wilson, "Redefining Psychology: From Alienation to Liberation," *Psychological Discourse* 24 (1993): 3–7.
13 N. Boyd-Franklin, "The Past, Present and Future of Research in Family Therapy," *Psychological Discourse* 26, no. 6, (1995): 4–7.
14 Williams, Dotson, Don, and, Williams, "Critical Issues in Testing," 270–273.
15 Joey Lee Dillard, *Black English* (New York: Random House, 1972), 29–30.
16 Reginald Lanier Jones, *Black Psychology*, 24–25.
17 Wade W. Nobles, "Implementing Our International Agenda: Step 1," *Psychological Discourse* 25 (1994): 4–5.
18 William H. Grier and Price M. Cobbs, *Black Rage* (New York: Basic Books, 1968), 18–19.
19 Donald K. Cheek, *Assertive Black, Puzzled White* (Atascadero: Impact Publishers, Inc., 1976), 15–17.
20 Melinda Contreras-Byrd, *Factors in the Development of Successful Strategies for Engaging Black and Latino Pastors in Self-Care*, Pastoral Study Project, Louisville Institute, May 2013.
21 S. Abdullah, "Cultural Healing: Sankofa to Maat," *Psychological Discourse* 30 (1999): 4–6.
22 James H. Cone, *Black Spirituals and the Blues* (Maryknoll: Orbis Books, 1992), 19.
23 J. White, "Recurring Psychological Themes in the Black Experience," *Psychological Discourse* 26 (1995): 4–6.
24 William S. Williams, "Autobiography of Williams S. Williams," in *The History of Black Psychologists: Profiles of Outstanding Psychologists*, ed. Robert L. Williams (Bloomington: AuthorHouse, 2008), 35.
25 Herbert Aptheker, *American Negro Slave Revolts* (New York: International Publishers, 1983), 115–116.
26 Phyllis Trible, *Texts of Terror: Literary Feminist Readings of Biblical Narratives* (Minneapolis: Fortress Press, 1984), 55–56.
27 Ibid., 64–65.
28 S. Abdullah, "Cultural Healing," 7–8.

6. *Affirmative Action*[1] *and the New Jim Crow: Listening for and Living from the "Sound of the Genuine"*

KAREN D. CROZIER

Introduction

Howard Thurman, one of the world's greatest theologians and pastors of African American descent, stated "you must wait and listen for the sound of the genuine that is within you. When you hear it, that will be your voice and the voice of God."[2] Thurman's insight is instructive for developing and sustaining one's prophetic, redemptive voice in the midst of various forms of oppression based on race, religion, and gender within institutional and social structures. He offers a different way of being and leading by discerning and submitting to the "sound of the genuine." In the process, one becomes awakened to the self and the divine.

This way of being and leading, as listening to and living from the sound of the genuine, is articulated in a leadership and social activism experience. This leadership orientation, I contend, broadens socio-political notions of affirmative action in responding to contemporary manifestations of racial violence and injustice such as the New Jim Crow.[3] In addition, Thurman's thought invites and provokes people to honor their respective voices while creating space to hear and honor the sound of the genuine in another person in which all voices can be experienced as unique expressions of the divine. In this vein, leadership is about, in large part, creating and occupying spaces that allow for deep listening of self, others, and the divine towards affirmative action(s) in living from "the sound of the genuine."

In this chapter, I presuppose that affirmative action must transcend practices of developing, and protecting, federal and state policies to include a socio-political and theological ethic within and beyond socially constructed identities, and institutional systems of oppression. In this vein as a Christian, female of Afrikan[4] descent who resides in the United States, affirmative action does not merely aim to legislate behavior regarding historical and contemporary injustices perpetrated against United States enslaved and emancipated descendants of Afrikan origin. In a more wholistic, existential, and redemptive way, affirmative action is, also, about being and becoming human, and of being ready for "the creative encounter"[5] of the divine in creation, individuals, and various racial, ethnic, tribal, and national groups. In the spirit of the U.S. 21st Century Black Lives Matter national and international movement, affirmation action includes participating in and bearing witness to divine justice, righteousness, and transformation of oppressive relations and conditions. Hence, I argue, this alternative rendering of affirmative action entails creating, discerning, participating in, and sustaining space for self and others to become more fully human in ways that debunk and redefine white male supremacist notions of human identity, liberation, and dignity. Moreover, affirmative action also entails cultivating an interiority of living from and listening to "the sound of the genuine" that necessitates a mystical orientation in and with the world and the divine, to access the breadth and depth of wisdom within and beyond one's particularity towards justice and wholeness in both the church and world.

Below, a more comprehensive expression of affirmative action is presented by first briefly discussing the limitations of affirmative action at the federal level. Next, I define, discuss, and then later integrate Thurman's notion of "the sound of the genuine" to convey a theological ethic of affirmative action. Then, Alexander's major claims in *The New Jim Crow* are presented to understand the legal scholarly content and analysis that, in my mind, require an innovative affirmation action response in order to move beyond the limitations of federal legislation. After discussing Alexander, I describe and discuss an affirmative action practice and experience which integrates experiencing Thurman's "the sound of the genuine" and responding to aspects of the New Jim Crow. Finally, I conclude with the significance of affirmative action as listening to and living from "the sound of the genuine" in one's leadership and social activism in hope that it will help us as humans access divine, material, and interior resources to advance, and bear witness to, racial healing and justice.

Affirmative Action: Policy Limitations

Historically, civil rights federal policies in the United States have attempted to address the political disenfranchisement, economic exploitation, and social denigration of black lives. For example, the U.S. executive order issued by Abraham Lincoln's Emancipation Proclamation of 1863,[6] and John F. Kennedy's civil rights statement in 1961 and televised address in 1963[7] were monumental though socially and morally inadequate. President Kennedy, in his televised address on civil rights on June 11, 1963 just five months prior to his assassination, asserts: "One hundred years of delay have passed since President Lincoln freed the slaves, yet their heirs, their grandsons, are not fully free. They are not yet freed from the bonds of injustice. They are not yet freed from social and economic injustice. And this Nation, for all its hopes and all its boasts, will not be fully free until all its citizens are free."[8] Kennedy, in this same speech, outlines particular legislative actions that he would initiate including voter registration protection, access to public facilities such as hotels, restaurants, and retail stores, and legal support to end segregation in public education. In his affirmative action policies as President of the United States, Kennedy, nevertheless, was aware of the severe limitations of legislation and policy. Towards the end of his address, he states, "But legislation, I repeat, cannot solve this problem alone. It must be solved in the homes of every American in every community across our country."[9] Apparently, Kennedy was painfully aware of the shortcomings of Lincoln's Emancipation Proclamation of 1863 though he (Kennedy) did not shrink back from asserting the U.S. government's responsibility in caring for all lives, especially black lives. The pressure of the civil rights action of Rev. Dr. Martin Luther King, Jr. of the Southern Christian Leadership Conference (SCLC), John Lewis and Ella Josephine Baker of the Student Nonviolent Coordinating Committee (SNCC), and countless others sung and unsung sheroes and heroes pushed Kennedy to act responsibly even though he realized the limitations of his office.

In the twenty-first century, legal scholar and professor, Michelle Alexander in *The New Jim Crow: Mass Incarceration in the Age of Colorblindness*[10] calls for a grassroots multicultural movement to address the mass incarceration rates, especially among low-income black males, through an ethic of care and compassion. She, too, invokes something more than mere legislative and policy engagement by including morality and the need for social change. In citing historian Lerone Bennett Jr., Alexander lays before the American people[11] a choice, an option of not blaming the black males as causing their own problem. More specifically, she notes Bennett Jr. saying "a nation is a choice"[12] and then Alexander expounds on Bennett Jr.'s statement when she asserts "we could choose to be a nation that extends care, compassion, and concern to those who are locked up and locked out or headed for prison before they are old enough to vote."[13] In a creative and provocative way,

Alexander, as a legal scholar, invites those who are listening to her case against the systemic, state sanctioned mass incarceration of black low-income males to act with a new socio-political vision and interiority. Although she never explains how one can arrive at a place of care, compassion, and concern, the affirmative action practice as articulated below is presented as an option to build a nation, a people that chooses to care about black lives and advance racial justice.[14]

"The Sound of the Genuine"

On May 4, 1980, Howard Thurman delivered the Baccalaureate Address entitled *The Sound of the Genuine* at Spelman College, an historically black college for women[15] (14). In addition, he received an honorary doctorate from Spelman (an institution he had served, briefly, in the 1930s) during this occasion. In Thurman's transcribed address,[16] he never clearly states "the sound of the genuine" is this or that. However, in the quote, as cited in the introduction, he clearly asserts that it is one's voice and the Voice of God. To know one's self and deep interiority is to become acquainted with a universal, transcendent reality as well. Moreover, as in the quote, and the transcribed address, Thurman exhorts the audience to cultivate an increasing ability and capacity to listen for that which is always, already there, "the sound of the genuine." The gravity Thurman placed on "the sound of the genuine" in his address is cited below:

> There is something in every one of you that waits, listens for the genuine in yourself—and if you can not hear it, you will never find whatever it is for which you are searching and if you hear it and then do not follow it, it was better that you had never been born. You are the only you that has ever lived; your idiom is the only idiom of its kind in all the existences, and if you cannot hear the sound of the genuine in you, you will all of your life spend your days on the ends of strings that somebody else pulls.[17]

There are several of Thurman's points on which I would like to briefly comment. First, he presupposes everyone has a core, essential self that is to be, and can be, known. While this presupposition may not align with contemporary postmodern notions of the self, nonetheless, Thurman offers a way of knowing and experiencing one's self amidst other competing noises, voices, and forces. For a person of a disinherited people group or class, Thurman's insight and exhortative practice of listening is revolutionary. Those voices which have been unjustly inscribed, encoded, and/or internalized do not necessarily constitute "the sound of the genuine" for Thurman. Yet, the competing, unexamined voices are part of the fodder that must be examined as one comes to know and be known in time, place, and space. That which has originated from outside of oneself should not have the final authority in prescribing one's inner reality and external response.

Second, in its most basic sense, waiting and listening for "the sound of the genuine" is an affirmative act. It affirms an anticipation of an alternative reality and way of being in the world. Moreover, in a subtle, inconspicuous way, the process of waiting and listening can be practiced anywhere at any time regardless of what is, or is not, going on externally. Although Thurman is not instructive on how to wait and listen in his address, it is in *The Creative Encounter* where he expounds on how one prepares to encounter self, creation, and the divine through prayer. In the Baccalaureate Address, Thurman merely emphasizes the necessity and inherency of the practice.

Third, Thurman declares that to not follow, or respond to, "the sound of the genuine" once it is heard is to deny the unique, particular gift of one's self. Here, Thurman may sound condemning in his assertion. However, in the context of black women who are about to receive their undergraduate degrees, Thurman's wisdom and love are life-giving. Wherever they went, and whatever vocation they entered, and existed, they were encouraged and reminded to pursue a higher call of knowing one's self as gift, and as a responsible self while yet being part of a universal, transcendent reality. As will be seen below in the discussion on Alexander's *The New Jim Crow*, Thurman's exhortation is instructive for today to combat contemporary voices and forces that compete with "the sound of the genuine."

The New Jim Crow

In a nutshell, Alexander's major claim is that the U.S. domestic war on drugs is the *New Jim Crow* because unjust drug policies, drug policing, racial profiling, drug sentencing, and police brutality leave far too many low-income black males locked up and locked out of the U.S. society. Her analysis opens up new avenues to understanding contemporary manifestations of race-based and class-based violence and injustice by connecting the historical Jim Crow South policies and practices of black disenfranchisement to contemporary policies and practices of exclusion and dehumanization of black lives. Within the vicious system of the New Jim Crow, according to Alexander, African American males[18] become locked up and locked out of American society, and their families and communities become secondary and tertiary victims.

The practice and prevalence of the New Jim Crow is occurring in what many consider to be a post-racial, color-blind U.S. society. In this context, Alexander exposes how supposedly race-neutral or color-blind policies lead to negative race-based outcomes particularly for African American males and their respective kinship connections. Her analysis of the criminal justice system documents the ever increasing racial disparities in light of this nation's war on drugs in the era of color blindness. Hence, her work discounts those who contend that race-neutral or color-blind policies are effective measures for ridding the country of its deep-seated racial history and present.

More specifically, Alexander asserts that the "War on Drugs" is "the New Jim Crow." This updated, sophisticated system of social and political disenfranchisement has led to a disproportionate number of African American males being channeled into the criminal justice system for drug crimes including distribution as well as mere possession. Then, upon their release, depending on their state of residence, they continue to experience discrimination in, and exclusion from voting, jury duty, housing, jobs, and educational opportunities, and thereby become relegated to an invisible racial caste, the perpetual racially controlled, underprivileged, and marginalized.[19]

Alexander ties the national "War on Drugs" to Ronald Reagan's presidential administration in the 1980s. This "war" is believed to have been fabricated because when Ronald Reagan declared a federal war on drugs in 1982, fewer "than 2 percent of the American public viewed drugs as the most important issue facing the nation."[20] Today, it has blossomed into the well-disguised, comprehensive and intentional system she calls "The New Jim Crow" because Reagan's agenda was never about addressing a drug problem, but more about how race could be used for political gain without being perceived as racism.[21] She describes Reagan's political maneuver as fulfilling Nixon's "Southern Strategy"—the political endeavor to lure disaffected southern whites from their loyalty to the Democratic Party—thereby exacerbating the fears of Southern whites, resulting in the criminalizing of black people.[22] In the end, Reagan broadened the scope of the federal government's law enforcement reach to the streets of urban centers, and provided state and local law enforcements with federal resources to fight the manufactured "War on Drugs." Through the guise of getting "tough on crime" towards creating "law and order" Reagan espoused a color-blind rhetoric with devastating race-based outcomes.

According to Alexander, the federal government's criminalizing of African Americans alongside pejorative media images of black people as drug dealers and users make it unnecessary to speak directly of race today because speaking about crime is talking about race.[23] The media and political discourse left no doubt that only African Americans are guilty of such drug crimes. Alexander notes that epithets like " 'welfare queen' became a not-so-subtle code for lazy, greedy, black ghetto mother," for black females.[24] For the criminalized black male, Reagan is noted as saying "a staring face—a face that belongs to a frightening reality of our time: the face of a human predator."[25] However, when one makes a closer examination of the statistics concerning drug use, Alexander notes, "people of all races use and sell illegal drugs at remarkably similar rates."[26] More specifically, according to a study conducted, in 2000, by the National Institute on Drug Abuse, white students use cocaine seven times the rate of black students, use crack cocaine eight times the rate of black students, and use heroin at seven times the rate of black students."[27] Another study in 2000, conducted by the National Household Survey on Drug Abuse reported that "white youth aged 12–17 are more than a third more likely to have sold illegal drugs than African American youth."[28]

Unfortunately, it is difficult to pay attention to hard data when the media images seem to dictate another narrative that is inconsistent with what researchers have uncovered empirically. Furthermore, although the data does not refer to adult drug traffickers and users, it reveals yet a deeper and broader picture of the power of deception that is often delivered through the media. The data referring specifically to adults indicates a similar racial disparity. For example, "black men have been admitted to state prison on drug charges at a rate that is more than thirteen times higher than white men, . . . and 1 in every 14 black men was behind bars in 2006, compared with 1 in 106 white men."[29] When black people or African Americans only constitute 12.6% of the national population,[30] the danger of black males becoming extinct or removed from plain sight due to incarceration is highly likely.

By design, according to Alexander, the "War on Drugs" in the United States has not led to the decrease of the trafficking or use of illegal drugs but has increased the number of African American males who are behind bars in prisons and jails, or on probation and parole. Moreover, Alexander contends that the supposedly color-blind system plays out in the following two step process:

> The first step is to grant law enforcement officials extraordinary discretion regarding whom to stop, search, arrest, and charge for drug offenses, thus ensuring that conscious and unconscious racial beliefs and stereotypes will be given free reign. Unbridled discretion inevitably creates huge racial disparities. Then, the damning step: close the courthouse doors to all claims by defendants and private litigants that the criminal justice system operates in racially discriminatory fashion. Demand that anyone who wants to challenge racial bias in the system offer, clear proof that the racial disparities are the product of intentional racial discrimination—i.e., the work of a bigot .... This simple design has helped to produce one of the most extraordinary systems of racialized control the world has ever seen.[31]

This scathing critique of the supposedly race-neutral or color-blind criminal justice system exposes how race really does matter in the "War on Drugs." Race becomes silenced in the courts as if both law enforcement and the courts are free of racism and racists.

By race-ing the criminal justice system, Alexander demonstrates how race still matters in the age of color blindness and a supposedly post-racial society. Because it is no longer "politically correct" or socially permissible for many white people to be openly racist, those who have political and economic power have ceased using explicit race-based language to advance their agenda of political control through the use of race. Alexander encourages her audience to move to a place of care and compassion regarding race matters; she posits that in the era of color blindness, racial indifference, the lack of compassion and care about race and racial groups, is fortifying the systematic exclusion and control of African Americans with drug offenses.[32]

In her ethic of care and compassion, Alexander instructs two specific groups. In a creative and constructive way, she thoroughly engages racial justice advocates, like herself, while simultaneously speaking to many white Americans who revere color blindness as a virtue instead of disowning it as another form of racism.[33] In her intense and rather extensive dialogue with racial justice advocates, she is pushing them to see the immensity of the New Jim Crow that requires all of their resources and creativity above and beyond what many have given to fighting for affirmative action.[34] She argues that in light of the new racial undercaste, affirmative action policies do not engender hope, jobs, housing, or a political voice for the incarcerated and released drug felon. Hence, new priorities and ways of engagement must emerge that move beyond mere career advancement as racial justice advocates to more of a grassroots movement.[35] In the end, the advancement of legal careers merely perpetuates "the New Jim Crow," and leaves the people who are the most vulnerable, in the system, exploited. "The New Jim Crow" is a different beast that cannot be engaged as if it is the same as Jim Crow racism of old.

Alexander's assessment of the war on drugs in the United States and the adverse impact on low-income African Americans clearly indicates that the country is far from being post-racial. Moreover, the interconnecting roles of the political and economic elite along with the media dictate what is perceived as real concerning race and race matters. Wahneema Lubiano, a scholar of Literature and African and African American studies, asserts:

> The idea of race and the operation of racism are the best friends that the economic and political elite have in the United States. They are the means by which a state and a political economy largely inimical to most of the U.S. citizenry achieve the consent of the governed. They act as a distorting prism that allows

> that citizenry to imagine itself functioning as a moral and just people while ignoring the widespread devastation directed at black Americans particularly, but at a much larger number of people generally. Poverty has a black face—not in reality, but in the public imagination. Crime has a black face—again, not in reality but in the public imagination.[36]

Black people in the United States have been criminalized and dehumanized, again, in the public imagination in light of the New Jim Crow. Therefore, a public, socio-political response is necessary to educate the masses of the misrepresentation of black lives while affirming the humanity of black people. Furthermore, deepening one's connection within and beyond the U.S. borders is paramount; black people in the Afrikan diaspora are in a similar struggle for freedom.

Womanist ethicist Barbara A. Holmes in *Liberation and the Cosmos: Conversations with the Elders*, cites Vincent Harding, historian, theologian, activist, and coauthor of Martin Luther King's Vietnam speech, stating, "The black struggle for freedom is at its heart a profoundly human quest for transformation, a constantly evolving movement toward personal integrity and toward new social structures filled with justice, equity and compassion."[37] Harding's declaration highlights at least two significant interconnections. First, the struggle for black freedom constitutes a human endeavor for change in self and society, a denouncing of oppressive and repressive regimes, practices, and ideologies that negate one's humanity. Second, the human self and social, institutional structures are never to be seen as fixed, permanent realities. Rather, both the human self and social, institutional structures have the capacity to be healed, redeemed, and transformed as black people refuse to participate in the denial of their freedom, and non-black people refuse to benefit from and/or be silent about anti-black policies, ideologies, and practices. In short, Harding seems to be saying that the black struggle for freedom implicates everyone regardless of one's race, ethnicity, gender, sexual orientation, class, age, or religion. Anyone and everyone who participates in the black struggle for freedom is joining the movement to create a new self and society such as Martin Luther King's notion of the Beloved Community[38] or Jesus of Nazareth's vision and proclamation of God's reign of transnational kinship[39] that exemplifies just relations, righteous distribution of goods, interdependency, human flourishing, access to basic needs, intentional care and provision for the most vulnerable individuals and people groups, and the resolving of intrapersonal, interpersonal, institutional, and international conflict through nonviolent, compassionate means. Although Harding does not employ the language of affirmative action, his thought reflects a transformative practice and ethic that unequivocally invites the masses to pursue black freedom for self and the common good. In short, I contend, it is commensurate with my construction of affirmative action or Thurman's exhortation to wait and listen for, and follow, "the sound of the genuine."

King, as well, knew the limitations of legislation in the black struggle for freedom, and his vision and practice of the Beloved Community was his affirmative action response to address the need for the change of heart and mind, too, in conjunction with the regulation of behavior through legislation.[40]

For Harding a key component of what it means to be human is open, yet to be fully understood and realized especially in light of the injustice, inequity, and hostility experienced by people of Afrikan descent in the United States primarily at the hands of Euro-Americans. Moreover, explicitly, Harding focuses on the eternal pursuit of wholeness and integration personally and socially, and implicitly on not being consumed or consoled by what one acquires access to or possession of as the fulfillment of one's humanity. Holmes argues that human liberation is not a goal or fixed end, and this is part of the failure of black freedom struggle.[41] She points to the need to include a spiritual interiority because "Liberation is a wisp of self-reflection, the refusal to surrender self-respect for survival. It is a framework that is open enough to construct temporary dwelling places, but ultimately liberation is a goal that hastens ahead of us."[42] This sense of deep reflection and insight occurred for Fannie Lou Hamer, a U.S. civil and human rights leader, when she announced that she did not desire to be equal to white men who terrorized and tortured her and other affirmative action freedom fighters as they were exercising their right to vote. During the investigation she was interrogated as if she was the alleged perpetrator of such violent, unjust crimes. When the white law enforcement officers were not found guilty, Mrs. Hamer saw the degenerate hearts of a people and a nation so much so until she refused to accept "whiteness" as the norm for human liberation and equality.[43]

Holmes, King, Harding, and Hamer remind and admonish us that affirmative action in the context of racial injustice and oppression is a human endeavor of recovery and redefining of one's humanity for justice and redemption of all people groups and requires the cultivation and integration of a spiritual interiority. The cultivation of a spiritual interiority as expressed by Hamer, Holmes, and Harding can be seen as akin to Thurman's exhortation to listening, and responding, to "the sound of the genuine."

Affirmative Action for The New Jim Crow

Alexander critiques the civil rights community, racial justice advocates, and various laywers' organizations for their weak response to increasing incarceration rates of African Americans.[44] The current efforts are inadequate to address the enormity of the problem in her assessment. More specifically, she contends "There is no broad-based movement brewing to end mass incarceration and no advocacy effort that approaches in scale the fight to preserve affirmative action."[45] Here, Alexander points to the fact that while affirmative action legislation may not be sufficient, it should not be allowed to be eliminated by those who claim to be racial justice advocates. Moreover, she cries for a multicultural, diverse response by the people, racial justice and civil rights professionals, and the politicians to work at saving affirmative action and dismantling the contemporary manifestation of Jim Crow in the form of mass incarceration.

Alexander's call to engage across racial, ethnic, cultural, class, religious, denominational, and political lines to advocate for affirmative action and seek to dismantle the disenfranchisement of black lives was heeded. On June 16, 2011, I facilitated a peacemaking circle process, in the academy, of 18 participants who engaged Alexander's text and claims. In short, the peacemaking circle process is a restorative justice practice and process that I employ to deal with sensitive topics and issues so all who are present can speak their truth, narrative, and experience on the topic at hand in a more safe and sacred space.[46] It is a constitutive part of my affirmative action practice in listening for and to the sound of the genuine within me and others.

At this particular peacemaking circle , there were black, brown, yellow, and white people who were students in high school, college, and graduate school, as well as people from k-12 education, political and community organizing, pastoral ministry, higher education as faculty and administrators, law enforcement, the legal profession, the penitentiary, and retirees. There was diversity in gender, sexuality, class, ability, and region of origin. In this space, there was a relinquishing of control demonstrated by white males and females, coupled with a posture of listening as nonwhite people spoke their truth and pain regarding Alexander's claims. The nonwhite participants did not shrink or stutter in the presence of the white participants. In fact, many claimed it was their first time ever speaking of racial harm and injustice in the company of white people. As they unearthed what had been hidden to the eyes and ears of white strangers, and their oppressors, black participants accessed their voice and agency to affirm and concretize aspects of Alexander's claim and analysis.

My invitation to one and all to be fully present, including myself as the facilitator who is mindful of listening for and living from the sound of the genuine, was risky. Who would be ready to share, and hear, such difficult truths? How would I respond as the facilitator to tensions, apparent contradictions, and glaring disagreements within such a rich diverse space? From my observation and experience, personal narratives from the past and the present were reconstructed and yielded new meaning. Tears flowed from the eyes of some of the white participants as they recalled discrimination and degradation inflicted on the black people they knew from their childhood and family experiences. Knowing black people as only maids and servants they expressed consciousness of their guilt and shame in the peacemaking circle process. Fortunately, white fragility did not overwhelm the space, and neither did black rage. Although there were times when black rage filled the air because of the deep pain within, the sorrow and suffering were being released as the silence no longer dominated. Moreover, what one white female participant had yet to experience from me, she was able to experience from another nonwhite (Asian) female participant. Although she (the white female) and I had been working on developing a plan of engagement in response to Alexander's text, we were not able to give each other what was needed to advance the work. I experienced her as being unable to grasp how white systemic, state sanctioned discrimination and injustice against black people was not synonymous with an individual black person refusing to hold her hand at an event—a concern that had remained with her for years. In addition, she saw hatred and racial injustice in the Nation of Islam as if they had created systemic policies and processes to subjugate and dehumanize white people. At the core of it, she wanted me to acknowledge her humanity while exonerating her from being a participant in a racist culture, and I was working to acknowledge her humanity as well as the black person's humanity who refused to hold her hand and the humanity of the Nation of Islam. In our relationship, she did not feel loved by me, and was healed during the peacemaking circle process when the Asian woman explicitly said to her, "I love you."[47]

Vulnerability was on full display by those who yearned for a brand new day in which we all experience the erasure of the biological fallacy and ideology of white supremacy and black inferiority. Race was engaged not as an abstract, intellectual category nor as something that is to be merely forgotten, but as a way of meaning-making of diverse histories and current realities. Racism was being redeemed from those who claimed the United States was in an age of color blindness. Those who wanted to use euphemisms and coded language to speak derogatorily of the darker human race did not have linguistic power in this peacemaking circle space. The ongoing impact of such an experience can only be told as each person continues to show up in each existential moment to declare their humanity even in the face of threats and calamity. In my attempt to listen for and live from the sound of the genuine,

I was able to co-create a space in which we were held, and some even healed, in the place known as the academy.

Building the capacity to heal and renew from within allowed me to externalize a new way of being. No, a broad-based movement was not realized from the peacemaking circle process. However, what did emerge was of significance. In the 2011–2012 academic year, I developed a peacemaking circle process series on Alexander's *The New Jim Crow*. Local politicians came to speak on panels with law enforcement officers and community activists regarding my perspective as a Christian black female academic. A scholarship in honor of Martin Luther King, Jr. and Fannie Lou Hamer was developed for students of Afrikan descent born in the United States. This scholarship was broad in scope as it partnered with churches, community agencies, and community colleges. In the local church, a minister colleague and I developed sermons, services, and public actions to protest and raise awareness. The SPIRIT was experienced in each endeavor in my intentionality of listening for and living from the sound of the genuine.

In my facilitation of the peacemaking circle process or affirmative action practice, there was breathing space and the ability to transgress various borders and structures to encounter self and others. A different table was prepared, one that was not controlled or owned by white males. Possibly, the way we engaged and shared from such a deep place, we were at God's banquet table. Various emotions including fear were held by each other and a force, a presence, bigger than all of us. Black people who had never spoken their story of racial degradation in the presence of white people found their voice to speak their truth. White people who listened and cried remained present in the space when they could have easily suppressed the tears, or left the space to hide from the shame. On another level, they could have been silent as a way of maintaining and perpetuating white privilege, and racist structures of violence and injustice.

God's banquet table emerged as a dwelling space that Holmes spoke of that occurs when we take seriously the cultivation of our spiritual interiority through expression of vulnerability. The divine is the host, and we are co-hosts in the denouncing and transforming of the white male master's table into a space of healing from false identities, fears, and fragmentation. At this table, diversity becomes more than a place at the table, and equity becomes something other than voice or power given at the table. At this table, diversity is inherent, normative, valued, and embraced, and all are invited to share from their particularity as they grow in hearing, receiving from those who transcend their respective social location. At this table, for a moment in time, space, and place, we recover and retrieve our sense of shared humanity.

Now, Psalms 23:5–6 is instructive on a deeper level as we grow in our ability to trust God's providential care while traveling through and beyond the valley and shadow of death; God's table has been prepared for us as we respond to people who have policies and practices of exclusion and dismissal. God's table has been prepared for us to experience our respective and collective humanity as we participate in life abundantly instead of clamoring at the proverbial white male's table of exclusion to be seen and heard. God's table has been prepared for us, and we must continue to seek and discern that table, and no other table in order to express affirmative action in public spaces.

Conclusion

Thurman's notion of waiting and listening for the sound of the genuine is an inside-out practice that enables me to heal from the social barriers and constructed identities that negate life and human flourishing. In the sacred spaces like the one described above, I am able to intentionally listen for and live from the sound of the genuine. This aspect of affirmative action of an inside-out practice allows for the development of moral and spiritual authority to stand, and sit when necessary like Rosa Parks, against the internalized forms of racial violence that need to be healed. In the standing and/or sitting, I assume responsibility for both the personal and social forms of racial violence and injustice that have been perpetrated yet unresolved throughout history. In other words, my affirmative action includes the necessity of intrapsychic or intrapersonal healing and transformation alongside social healing and transformation as articulated by Harding. Unfortunately, the problem does not merely exist in society.

In conclusion, Jesus of Nazareth in the Gospel of Matthew is called Immanuel, God with us. It is my hope and prayer that in my expression of affirmative action, I will constantly deepen my capacity, and invite others to do the same, to experience and encounter Immanuel in self, others, and creation that bears witness to a new and just order. As I listen to and live from the sound of the genuine, I become more fully human and responsive to injustices and inequities. In this expression of affirmative action, I become more immersed in and with the world out of love of self, neighbor, and the divine. Ashe.

Notes

1 While the author recognizes the legal and institutional significance of "affirmative action" she is speaking in theological terms and uses the term "affirmative action" to propose a communal praxis of transformation.

2 Howard Thurman, *The Papers of Howard Washington Thurman: Volume 1 My People Need Me, June 1913–March 1936*, ed. Walter Earl Fluker (Columbia, SC: University of South Carolina Press, 2009), xiii.
3 The "New Jim Crow" is a term that was made popular by legal professor and scholar, Michelle Alexander. Since Alexander's 2010 publication, many white people in the U.S. have moved from colorblindness to racial reckoning and the multicultural grassroots compassionate movement she argued for is happening as a result of protests and resistance movements for Black lives.
4 The term "Afrikan" is spelled with the letter "k" instead of the letter "c" to denote my connection to the Afrikan diáspora with Kemetic beginnings. See Kimani K.S. Nehusi "From (Medew Netjer) to Ebonics," in *Ebonics and Language Education*, ed. Clinton Crawford (Brooklyn, NY: Sankofa World Publishers, 2001), 56–122.
5 In Howard Thurman's *The Creative Encounter: An Interpretation of Religion and the Social Witness*, 1954, "the creative encounter" is described as a prayerful, contemplative way of being in the world that assists one openness and readiness to encounter and experience the divine, the source of LIFE in life that grounds one's being to self and the cosmos.
6 Christopher Waldrep, *Race and National Power: A Sourcebook of Black Civil Rights from 1862–1954* (New York: Routledge, Taylor & Francis, 2011), 21–23.
7 See Borgna Brunner and Beth Roven, *Affirmative Action History: A History and Timeline of Affirmative Action*, http://www.infoplease.com/spot/affirmative1.html accessed on November 30, 2015 and Jonathan Birnbaum and Clarence Taylor (eds.), *Civil Rights Since 1787: A Reader on the Black Struggle* (New York: New York University Press, 2000), 490–492.
8 John F. Kennedy, "Television Address on Civil Rights," in *Civil Rights Since 1787: A Reader on the Black Struggle*, ed. Jonathan Birnbaum and Clarence Taylor (New York: New York University Press, 2000), 491.
9 Ibid., 492.
10 The text by Alexander was chosen because as a former employee of the Center for Peacemaking and Conflict Studies (CPACS) and the Victim-Offender Reconciliation Program (VORP) at Fresno Pacific University, I came across Alexander's book at a time that offered me a systemic legal analysis, and socio-political rationale in response to interpersonal, institutional, and social racial violence, crime, harm, and injustice from a female of Afrikan descent. Through peacemaking circles, I employed Alexander's book to inform and engage institutional members from the academy (students, staff, faculty, and administrators), law enforcement, judicial system, pre-k-12 education, religious community, community college, community/civic organizations, and municipal public servants.
11 In my opinion, Alexander never explicitly defines who constitutes the "American people." However, I think the following conception of who she is referring to can be deduced as the white enfranchised voting and economically elite classes, and non-white racial justice advocates regardless of race, ethnicity, gender, sexuality, socioeconomic status, or profession.
12 Alexander, 206.
13 Ibid.
14 At Fresno Pacific University's 6th Annual Martin Luther King, Jr. Celebration (January 22, 2016), Rev. Dr. Iva E. Carruthers, General Secretary of the Samuel Dewitt Proctor Conference was the keynote speaker. During this speech,

Dr. Carruthers mentioned that Michelle Alexander had contacted Proctor because Alexander believed that she had to partner with a strong African American faith-based organization in order to get her message out. Hence, after publishing her legal scholarship, Alexander turned to those who had social and moral authority in their engagement of political issues.

15 Howard Thurman, "The Sound of the Genuine," *Crossings Reflection #4*, University of Indianapolis, http://eip.uindy.edu/crossings/publications/reflection4.pdf, accessed April 28, 2016.

16 Ibid. The Baccalaureate Address is transcribed from an audio recording, and it is an excerpt of the audio recording.

17 Ibid.

18 Alexander only focuses on African American males though she acknowledges that much could be said about the experiences of women, Latinos, and immigrants in and with the criminal justice system, 15–16.

19 Alexander, 1–4. See also Angela Y. Davis, *Are Prisons Obsolete?* (New York: Seven Stories Press, 2003) and *Abolition Democracy: Beyond Empire, Prisons, and Torture* (New York: Seven Stories Press, 2005); Douglas Blackmon, *Slavery by Another Name: The Re-Enslavement of Black Americans from the Civil War to World War II* (New York: Anchor Books, 2008). Davis has been an arch proponent, for decades, of abolishing what she calls the Prison Industrial Complex, and the way the system has disproportionately affected African Americans in the U.S., and other nonwhite people groups in foreign lands through the U.S. imperialist practices. Blackmon documents how slavery persisted in a different form after the Civil War and Lincoln's Emancipation Proclamation. Alexander focuses specifically on the U.S. war on drugs with a goal of dismantling the war on drugs because it is increasing the African American prison population and creating a permanent racial caste. Davis focuses on prison abolition, and has been championing this cause before the emergence of the U.S. war on drugs as documented by Alexander.

20 Alexander, 49.

21 Ibid., 4, 49.

22 Ibid., 48–53.

23 Ibid., 103.

24 Ibid., 48.

25 Ibid., 48.

26 Ibid., 97.

27 Ibid., 97.

28 Ibid., 97.

29 Ibid., 98.

30 Sonya Rastogi, Tallese D. Johnson, Elizabeth M. Hoeffel, and Malcolm P. Drewey, Jr.,*The Black Population: 2010 Census*, Accessed on July 15, 2012, http://www.census.gov/prod/cen2010/briefs/c2010br-06.pdf.

31 Alexander, 100–101.

32 Ibid., 198.

33 Ibid., 224–243.

34 Ibid., 224–243.

35 Ibid., 224–243.

36 Wahneema Lubiano, "Introduction," in *The House that Race Built: Black Americans, U.S. Terrain*, ed. Wahneema Lubiano (New York: Pantheon Books, 1997), vii.
37 Barbara A. Holmes, *Liberation and the Cosmos: A Conversation with the Elders* (Minneapolis, MN: Fortress Press, 2008), 59.
38 See Richard Wayne Wills, Sr. *Martin Luther King, Jr. and the Image of God* (Oxford: Oxford University Press, 2009), chapter 6.
39 See Richard Horsely, "The Kingdom of God and the Renewal of Israel," in *The Bible and Liberation: Political and Social Hermeneutics*, ed. Norman K. Gottwald and Richard A. Horsley, rev. ed. (Maryknoll, NY: Orbis Books, 1993), 408–413.
40 Wills, Sr., *Martin Luther King, Jr. and the Image of God.*
41 Holmes, 62.
42 Ibid.
43 See "To Praise Our Bridges: Fannie Lou Hamer" in *Mississippi Writers: Reflections of Childhood and Youth, Volume II: Nonfiction*, ed. Dorothy Abbott (Jackson, MS and London: University Press of Mississippi, 1985), 326.
44 Alexander, 9–11.
45 Ibid., 11.
46 See Kay Pranis, *The Little Book of Circle Processes: A New/Old Approach to Peacemaking* (Intercourse, PA: Good Books, 2005). A component of the peacemaking circle process is establishing guidelines of respect and needs that is discussed and agreed on by all participants. In the peacemaking circle process on June 16, 2011, basic guidelines were presented such as listening to others when you do not have the talking piece, using "I" statements to express feelings and reactions to what is being shared, and the freedom to hold the talking piece until one is ready to share or to pass it if one does not have anything to share or do not want to hold it until thoughts become words. These basic guidelines and agreement of mutual respect were developed for this session because there was not sufficient time for an extended process in which each circle participant would identify what is desired or needed for respect and safety and then discussion around what is generated from the group.
47 I approached my white female colleague at the end of the peacemaking circle about her experience. She informed me of the comfort she experienced when the Asian woman spoke the words of love and that she had not heard that from me. I paused and was grateful for her truth. I had to consent to the fact that I had not spoken those words although they were in my heart. She admitted that she knew I loved her though had never said it. Also, I thought that, possibly, I did not express the compassion in words because I did not know how to do so without affirming her sense of being innocent and blameless regarding white racism and privilege. This is another burden black racial justice advocates bear in the company and companionship of many of those who profess to be white progressives and/or do-gooders.

Part II: Sites of Religious Landscaping: Black Churches and African Independent Churches

7. "To Be Relevant": Black Churches, Education and Productive Engagement

DONN WORGS

During the late 1990s a colleague and I traveled to Hampton, Virginia to learn more about the city's recent government reforms. Hampton had been widely recognized as an innovator because of the way they had reorganized the local government and because of some new initiatives that incorporated community organizations and the citizenry into decision making processes and the delivery of important public services.[1] While studying the city, we paid special attention to the government's collaboration with community groups to support youth development and education. As we learned more about these efforts, we soon realized that at the center of much of this activity was a black church, Queen Street Baptist Church.

Queen Street Baptist Church, one of the oldest African American churches in the city, was led by an activist pastor with a background in community development. At the time, the church was engaged in a variety of outreach activities, but their work in education was perhaps the most extensive. The church partnered with the city government and the school system in a number of ways. The church provided almost two dozen volunteer coordinators for tutoring programs in city schools, operated after-school programs in a dozen schools, ran one of the city's neighborhood learning centers, and organized parents. At a time when the school system was coming under increasing pressure to improve test scores, the supplemental tutoring provided through these partnerships was heralded as a key strategy for improving student achievement. The church leadership felt that they were doing work that the city's government could not do.[2]

Some years later, I spoke with a leader of the Community Anti-Violence Project (CAVP) in Washington, DC. The CAVP was founded by a Howard University professor working with churches in a Washington neighborhood that had been impacted by violence and despair. In response, community members mobilized through local churches to try to do something about what was happening. They decided to establish an educational program to tutor youth in the neighborhood. Church members would contribute their effort and modest resources (along with the support from allies and volunteers from local colleges) to help educate youth in the community. The church members' contributions varied; some gave donations, some tutored, some cooked food for the youth. Regardless of the modesty of their contributions, they understood the project as an attempt at community empowerment.[3]

The efforts of Queen Street Baptist Church and the CAVP are laudable, yet they are not unique. Across the United States, one can find examples of black churches supporting public education in their communities in various ways. These efforts range from contributing school supplies to contributing hundreds of thousands of dollars. They help pay salaries for staff members, provide volunteers, administer supplementary programs, sponsor public charter schools, and the list goes on. These kinds of contributions from black churches to the education of their communities are not new. From the days of enslavement to the present, we find black churches as key actors in the provision and promotion of education among African Americans, and key vehicles through which African Americans have engaged in public life through attempts to enhance the public good of education. These activities offer compelling examples of the impulse to shape and reshape the landscape of social institutions which help to determine the life chances of African Americans and stand in contrast to the images and discourses portraying a retreat from public life and civic engagement.

Public administration scholars refer to efforts like those of Queen Street, where community members or groups contribute their own resources and efforts to help produce public goods and services—in this case education—as coproduction.[4] Coproduction is an area of public engagement that is widespread, yet the impacts and democratic implications are under appreciated.[5] Black churches in particular have a long tradition of these kinds of activities which continue today—especially in the area of education. Examining this tradition reveals a persistent willingness to contribute to a public good, a willingness which is at the heart of democratic citizenship. Moreover, this sentiment can potentially be tapped to address some of the shortcomings of the state. This chapter will explore this phenomenon and suggest the potential democratic implications for this realm of engagement.

Productive Engagement

In recent years there has been a steady stream of critics decrying the decline of civic engagement in the United States. This supposed retreat from public life spawned much academic attention.[6] Yet, those who make these claims do not spend much time looking at programs like the CAVP or the work of churches like Queen Street. This reflects a lack of attention to what I call "productive engagement." Productive engagement entails efforts where individuals pool resources and coordinate their work to provide a public good or solve a collective challenge—either independent of government, or through activities that seek to complement or supplement the work of government (coproduction). Exploring examples of productive engagement reveals a variety of ways in which ordinary people engage in public life and suggests the productive potential of civil society. Understanding productive engagement may allow us to tap this arena of engagement as a means of improving conditions for disadvantaged communities.

Black churches have long been key actors (or vehicles for action) in this realm—especially with regard to education. Efforts aimed at transforming schools and education are ultimately aimed at constructing or transforming the social, political and physical landscapes which shape the life chances of African Americans. Thus, productive engagement around education is a particularly powerful manifestation of the impulse to shape or reshape landscapes which this volume explores from various angles. I turn now to a brief discussion of the tradition of black churches coproducing education in the United States followed by a discussion of the extent and potential implications of this phenomenon in the contemporary context.

African Americans and the Coproduction of Education

Finding examples of the tradition of African American productive engagement is a fairly easy task. Students of African American history will readily recognize the frequency with which African Americans have practiced productive engagement. The discourse on the self-help tradition for example is largely about productive engagement.[7] There are countless examples of collectives collaborating to address common problems in contexts where the state was absent or hostile.

An especially active arena for this activity has been the realm of education. From the period before the Civil War, through the present there have been countless *clear* examples of African Americans and their allies mobilizing their resources in order to provide or transform educational opportunities for African Americans.[8] Three historical examples highlight this tradition and offer some perspective on the democratic implications of this work. The expansion of black education during the years immediately following the Civil War, the establishment of the Rosenwald schools, and the education activities during the Civil Rights Movement are fascinating examples of coproduction—with black churches often at the center of these efforts. Moreover, each display phenomena which we see repeated in contemporary efforts.

African American Education in the Post-bellum South

At the conclusion of the Civil War in 1865, the United States witnessed the phenomenal growth of educational institutions for African Americans in the South. This was the result of extraordinary efforts by the newly emancipated, their already free brethren, white missionaries from the North, the federal government (through the Bureau of Refugees, Freedmen and Abandoned Lands, or the "Freedmen's Bureau") and a few Southern whites. Although they received much help from their allies, it was the actions of the newly freed men and women themselves that was "the primary force that brought schools to [their] children."[9] Studies of black education have uncovered countless examples of black communities pooling their meager resources to establish their own schools. A Freedmen's Bureau official traveling throughout the South found numerous cases of blacks teaching one another in what he called "native schools" and estimated that by 1866 there were 500 such schools throughout the South.[10] These newly freed people would often go through extreme lengths to create, maintain and attend schools, in an environment hostile to black education.[11]

Over time, federal money would supplement the efforts of black communities and their missionary allies and, eventually, state governments would begin to support black public schools.[12] Yet, throughout this period, the schooling of African Americans was primarily the result of black communities and their allies outside of government. Much of the black community contribution came through (or was organized through) black churches. The churches were typically the site for gathering and mobilizing communities and coordinating the efforts to establish schools. Oftentimes school was held in the church building or on the church's property. This was the case in Baltimore County, Maryland for example. There, even after the local and state governments began to allocate funds for black education, the county limited support to teacher salaries and some supplies. The community was responsible for the buildings and thus the school was usually in a church or on church property. This entailed substantial costs and risk. Maintaining the facilities strained the modest resources of black communities, and in the early years, schoolhouses and churches that housed schools proved to be popular targets for white arsonists opposed to black education.[13] This was the case throughout the Southern states.[14] Yet, despite the costs and risks, this was a case of coproduction by necessity.

Thus, this moment in the establishment of education for African Americans in the years following the Civil War entailed extensive contributions from the community members themselves—usually through their churches. Within these extreme conditions—racial hostility, extreme need, and limited state support—the people responded through productive engagement. They were willing to contribute what little they had to produce a collective good.

Rosenwald Schools

As the nineteenth century ended, and the twentieth century began, public education in the Southern states expanded significantly for Whites, while education for Blacks progressed much more slowly. With the turn of the century disparities and inequities in education grew. Although black education had come to be accepted as a "concept," Southern states limited their support to as little as one-fifth of what they contributed to white education.[15] However, in the ensuing decades, there would be growth and expansion of black schooling largely due to the ability of black communities to mobilize to bring pressure on local and state governments, or to mobilize the resources to build and maintain schools with the help of allies. One source of this growth was the Rosenwald program.

Beginning in 1913, the wealthy philanthropist, Julius Rosenwald began to support the construction of schools for African Americans in the South. The Rosenwald program, initially administered through Tuskegee Institute, and later through the Rosenwald Fund, provided funding to build schools until 1932. Importantly, Rosenwald did not cover the total cost of the facilities. The program required local school districts and the local black communities to contribute as well. The communities had to contribute labor, land and/or money for construction of the schools. Varying amounts were contributed—in many cases though, the largest contributions came from the black communities themselves. In fact, the black communities ultimately contributed more than the Rosenwald Fund in the construction of over 5,000 school buildings.[16]

The Rosenwald program was a remarkable example of widespread community contributions to the public good of education. African Americans used a variety of techniques to raise funds and contribute to the building of these schools. And again, black churches were often at the center of these efforts. Churches were often the sites for mobilizing the community and served as hubs for aggregating contributions. Church leaders led campaigns, held rallies, gave donations, took up collections, and contributed land for construction.[17] These contributions are especially noteworthy given that they amounted to these communities being double-taxed.[18] They paid their taxes, yet the state refused to provide equitable allocations for education in their communities. Thus, these people, already strapped, had to pay a significant additional cost on their own. In all, the Rosenwald program illustrates how institutional forms can tap a widespread willingness to contribute. Though it was unfair—the need sparked contributions to the collective good, despite the reality of a double taxation.

Civil Rights Movement

When the Civil Rights Movement exploded at mid-century, education was central. The litigation that resulted in the Brown v. Board of Education decision was ultimately one of the key catalysts of the movement and the subsequent efforts to integrate schools of the South and the North were some of the most important mobilizations for expanding rights. Interestingly, within these battles to integrate schools, there were also moments and examples of collaborative productive efforts to provide education for black children and black churches that were typically key. For example, when local officials closed the public schools of Prince Edward County, Virginia in order to resist integration, black community members organized alternative schools and training centers for their children.[19] This was also the case in the North as well. Boston and Cleveland provide two examples where blacks organized school boycotts to oppose de facto segregation and organized alternative schools for students to attend instead. In both cities thousands of students attended.[20] In all three of these cases, black churches were the most common sites for these alternative schools.

Perhaps the most interesting examples of the provision of education during the Civil Rights Movement were the Citizenship Education Program (CEP) organized by the Highlander Folk School and the Freedom Schools organized by the Student Nonviolent Coordinating Committee (SNCC). In both cases, activists mobilized resources to provide educational experiences to address educational deficiencies, but also to socialize and politicize students in an attempt to spark broader democratic participation and enhance the political power of the communities. Again, black churches were the most likely location for these schools.

The CEP (or citizenship schools) grew out of the efforts of Esau Jenkins, a South Carolina activist and Septima Clark and Myles Horton of the Highlander Folk school.[21] Together, Jenkins, Clark and Horton shaped the citizenship school program with the input of the students. Their objective was not only to spread literacy amongst people who had had limited access to formal education, but also to mobilize them politically. Horton noted that the students did not view themselves as a literacy class, but rather, understood themselves as part of a community mobilization for political power.[22]

Under Clark's leadership, between the program's start in January 1957 and 1961, 400 teachers were trained, and over 4,000 students were taught.[23] The program was eventually turned over to the Southern Christian Leadership Conference (SCLC). The program was a natural fit for the SCLC as the organization's network of black churches and church leaders served to extend the program even further.[24]

The citizenship schools served as a model for SNCC in its own voter registration efforts and for the freedom schools SNCC established during the "Freedom Summer" activities in Mississippi in 1964.[25] Freedom schools sought to provide an educational experience that would counter some of the shortcomings of the segregated school system. As Charlie Cobb wrote in the prospectus for the program, the objectives were to

1. supplement what [the students] aren't learning in high schools around the state.
2. give them a broad intellectual and academic experience during the summer to bring back to fellow students in classrooms in the state, and
3. form the basis for statewide student action such as school boycotts, based on their increased awareness.[26]

In all, 175 full-time teachers in 40 sites taught some 2,000 students during the 1964 campaign.[27] While the instruction was largely the product of the Freedom Summer volunteers who came from outside of the state, the communities had to provide the facilities as well as house and feed these volunteers. Again, much of this was done through local black churches. The churches were common sites for both the Freedom Schools and the Citizenship Schools. As had been the case in earlier years, this was not without risk. Churches that engaged in these activities again became targets for arsonists who opposed the civil rights agenda.[28]

Beyond the provision of facilities and the material support for the programs that came through the black church, religion played a major role. Septima Clark, for example, explained that these projects were carried out within the context of a particular theological perspective. In her essay, "Citizenship and the Gospel," Clark connected the work of the citizenship schools to a particular theological outlook and expressed a link between the education activities (with their political objectives) and religious ideas that supported this work. She noted that "throughout the New Testament, the concern for the poor and underprivileged is expressed as one of the fruits of grace. Where there is obedience to the gospel, there will be concern for the less fortunate."[29] While acknowledging that the missionary tradition recognized the need to meet the practical needs of the people ("Our missionaries could not be content preaching the gospel to hungry folk"), she claimed, "still another step is necessary . . . If we really are to contribute to the 'deliverance of the captives' it is necessary to do something to redeem the system which keeps them in captivity."[30] "The Citizenship Education Program is attempting to provide an opportunity for these people to help themselves and their neighbors."[31]

The Civil Rights Movement provides striking examples of productive engagement around education. These were conscious attempts to use education for collective empowerment. This is important in terms of implications and possibilities for these kinds of actions. In such a context, the contributions came not only from the teachers and providers of the facilities, but also from the students. The notion of individual participation in an education program as a contribution to the collective is a powerful idea with potential implications for the contemporary context.

Taken together, these examples reveal the centrality of black churches and religion in community efforts to use education as a means of building community power and political capacity. In the context of the Civil Rights Movement, churches provided both material and spiritual resources in that they were physical locations for these activities, but also served as vehicles for the transmission of the ideas that undergird the activities. This, of course, was not new. In the post-Civil War South, churches were at the center of establishing schools for black people. That role continued into the twentieth century, as exemplified by the role churches often played in local efforts to build Rosenwald schools. Thus, the activities of the Civil Rights Movement were built upon a legacy that could be traced back for over a century. Over 50 years later, we see this legacy continues. Education remains an arena which African Americans seek to transform through activities emanating from their churches in order to improve the life chances of African Americans in communities across the United States.

The Black Church and the Contemporary Coproduction of Education

In the decades following the legislative victories of the Civil Rights Movement, education has remained a key area of concern for African Americans. Despite some gains, significant disparities between African Americans and whites still exist. Data on test scores, graduation rates, access to challenging curricula, access to "highly qualified teachers," and even school discipline consistently reveal African Americans having significantly worse experiences and outcomes than whites.[32] The disparities are visible whether one looks at national data, state data or even within particular schools. Beyond that, there are even disparate experiences among African Americans. There are some communities that are even more disadvantaged than others. In Maryland for example, blacks in Baltimore City have significantly worse outcomes than blacks in suburban Baltimore County. This goes beyond differences in income, as low-income black students in Baltimore County are more likely to pass standardized tests and more likely to graduate from high schoolthan low-income blacks in Baltimore City.[33]

There may be a number of explanations for these disparities, but the ultimate impact is that students in some communities have significantly worse outcomes than similar students in different settings. Such communities have greater educational challenges than others. Further complicating the politics of the challenge is the fact that in many cities (like Baltimore) public school systems are led by black elected and/or appointed officials.

It is in this context that we find black churches of all sizes seeking to contribute to improved education outcomes for their communities. Black churches around the country attempt to support public education in a variety ways: from donating school supplies as many churches do at the start of the school year, to tutoring students or providing volunteers for various activities as we saw with Queen Street in Hampton; from providing their own programs to supplement the in-school education, to partnering with a school or even running public schools through affiliated organizations. Two of the most significant ways that we find black churches coproducing education are through supplementary programs and through charter schools.

Supplementary Programs

Supplementary programs (programs which provide some kind of additional academic experiences—from tutoring to enrichment experiences) are extremely common, though they vary in intensity, impact and the extent to which they have formalized relationships with particular schools. Consider the CAVP or the array of programs and activities provided by Queen Street Baptist Church. Tutoring programs targeting neighborhood students and special programs that bring church volunteers into schools to provide instructional support can be found in communities all over the United States. While exploring this phenomenon in Baltimore, I found churches of varying sizes and denominations throughout the city who offer a variety of programs. They conduct Saturday academies, after-school programs, SAT preparation, GED classes and summer camps and other summer programs.[34] Some of the more interesting manifestations of these programs are the self-titled "freedom schools" which consciously seek to model the freedom schools of the 1960s. A number of churches across the United States have partnered with the Children's Defense Fund's Freedom School program. There are also others who independently operate their own freedom schools—seeking to connect to the spirit and tradition of the freedom schools of the 1960s. One can find this model in a small church like Pleasant Hope Baptist Church, in Baltimore or in megachurches like Trinity United Church of Christ in Chicago.

Most common though are a variety of after-school programs. Baltimore's Child First Authority is a particularly interesting example of black churches supporting education through after-school programs. Today Child First is an independent organization running after-school programs and coordinating neighborhood schools in the city, but it is primarily the product of black faith-based organizations seeking to support education. The program was created by Baltimoreans United in Leadership Development (BUILD). BUILD is a local affiliate of the Industrial Areas Foundation (IAF), a well-known network of community organizations which organizes through churches and other faith-based organizations.[35] The IAF has a reputation for grass roots organizing and, at times, confrontational tactics. BUILD, whose membership is comprised primarily of predominantly black churches, has been quite effective using this IAF approach and has a range of accomplishments including a living wage campaign and developing affordable housing since it was formed in 1977.[36]

When BUILD organizers and members turned their attention to education, one of their initiatives was to expand the availability of quality after-school programs. Child First was their attempt to do that. The program was modeled on the work of one of the BUILD churches, Koinonia Baptist Church, which had conducted an after-school program as a way to provide a safe and supportive space for youth in a neighborhood that faced the typical array of inner-city challenges. Child First was formed when BUILD organizers successfully pressured the city and state governments to provide funds to support after-school programming. Today, with continued government funding as well as foundation support, Child First operates after-school programs that provide academic and cultural enrichment experiences in a dozen schools, serving as many as 1,200 students per day. It has also expanded its activities to include supporting seven "community schools," which entails Child First organizers working in the schools to facilitate partnerships with outside organizations.

Initially, the programs relied heavily on BUILD volunteers in addition to the public funding. Today, although the efforts are led and coordinated by paid staff, they still make use of parent and community volunteers. While the academic and cultural instruction is significant, perhaps the most interesting aspect of their work is the organizing component that remains a key focus. From its founding, Child First activists have organized parents and community members to support the schools in which they work—using the BUILD/IAF approach to community organizing. Initially the focus was on building a strong constituency that could advocate for the students and the particular schools—pushing for resources, special programs or facility needs. Interestingly, in recent years they expanded those efforts to move beyond just advocating for their particular schools to push for system-wide reforms. Thus, a program rooted in community organizing efforts among the churches fostered a program that provided supplementary experiences to students, created a support network to enhance the schools, and ultimately became a key actor in efforts to enhance public education citywide. Importantly, much of this work is still coming out of the faith-community as the advocacy work and organizing efforts rely heavily on BUILD churches and their members.

Public Charter Schools

Some of the most extensive contributions individual black churches have made to public education in their communities can be found among the charter schools affiliated with black churches. A public charter school is a publicly funded school that is run by a group or organization under a contract (or charter) with the state or local jurisdiction. The charter exempts the school from certain state or local rules and regulations, giving the charter school autonomy and flexibility in terms of designing curriculum, programs and approach, yet still requires that the school meet certain accountability standards (e.g., student achievement on standardized exams).[37] At present, there are roughly 6,100 charter schools in the United States, about 6.6% of all public schools, which enroll about 5% of all public school students. Charter schools have been controversial since they first emerged. Critics claim that they undermine public education by draining necessary resources that could be going to the traditional public schools, while test scores for charters as a whole tend to be lower than those of the traditional public schools.[38]

A number of black churches have been affiliated with particular charter schools during the roughly 25 years that they have been in existence. Black churches are affiliated with charter schools in a few ways. In some cases, recalling the earliest days of black education, churches provide the physical space for schools either in the church structure or on church property. In other cases, the church serves as a key partner with the school—providing volunteers or donating materials or other support. The most extensive involvement comes when the church essentially creates and manages a school through an affiliated organization. Given the constitutional requirements of separation of church and state, churches that wish to form charter schools do so through a separate organization (e.g., a community development corporation or other separate nonprofit organization).

There is a diverse set of churches that form and run charter schools. There are schools that are the product of large churches with extensive community outreach activities. This is the case with People for People Charter School in Philadelphia which is run by People for People Inc. founded by Rev. Herbert Lusk as the nonprofit development corporation for Greater Exodus Baptist Church. In Houston, Windsor Village United Methodist Church has founded two charter schools through an affiliated organization to go along with an array of community development projects that include the creation of hundreds of units of housing and hundreds of jobs. There are also cases of smaller churches for whom the foray into a charter school is their primary and most substantial project. This is the case with Northwood-Appold United Methodist Church in Baltimore for whom their charter schools constitute their primary community outreach projects. Northwood-Appold, a church with a relatively small congregation, founded the Northwood Appold Community Academies (an elementary and a middle/high school).

Northwood-Appold is one of two black churches in Baltimore that are currently sponsoring charter schools. The other is the Empowerment Temple AME Church which is affiliated with the Empowerment Academy. The churches and their affiliated schools differ, yet there are similarities between these two efforts. The Empowerment Temple is one of the largest black megachurches in the state and for the first fifteen years of the school's existence, the church was pastored by Rev. Jamal Bryant who was not only one of the highest profile black ministers in the city, but in the nation. Northwood-Appold is a small church with an older congregation and is led by Rev. Cecil Gray, who has a much lower profile.

Both efforts have taken creative curricular approaches. The Northwood Appold Community Academies (NACA) are guided by what they refer to as a "freedom and democracy" curriculum inspired by and grounded in the black freedom struggle combined with recent innovative curricula. Rev. Gray, who designed the curriculum, is the son of Victoria Gray, a leader in the Civil Rights Movement, and a key figure during SNCC's Freedom Summer work in Mississippi. Empowerment Academy has a curriculum based on an arts integration model which infuses the arts into the instruction in core academic subjects and incorporates core academic subjects into the teaching of the arts.

Each church makes substantial contributions to their school. Empowerment Temple has contributed between $100,000 and $250,000 annually to support the school—by paying the salaries of key staff members (in particular the faculty in the arts) and providing volunteers, supplies and other resources. Northwood-Appold, has more meager resources, but provides the building for the school (it had housed a private schools some years ago), in addition to having some key members, its pastor and first lady contribute significant amounts of time and effort to running and supporting the school.

The NACA schools and the Empowerment Academy are examples of black churches making a variety of contributions to help create and maintain what appear to be successful schools. The contributions run the gamut from designing the curricula and programs to aggregating resources and building political support; from financial contributions to tutoring and reading to children, to the mundane work that goes into preparing the facilities for students—cleaning, making repairs, putting together furniture etc. These are prototypical examples of coproduction. Notably, both schools appear to be academically successful, typically outperforming the citywide achievement on standardized exams. The Empowerment academy typically outperforms the statewide averages and was recognized as an "opportunity school" because of the high-test scores of its low-income students.[39]

It is important to note however, that not all charter schools that are connected to churches should be heralded as examples of coproduction or productive engagement. The case of a church that rents out space to a charter school in a mutually beneficial arrangement is not necessarily praiseworthy for those who are interested in democracy and community improvement. This is not productive engagement as there is no sacrifice of resources or effort involved with a contribution to the public good. This is merely a commercial relationship. While those kinds of mutually beneficial relationships should not necessarily be frowned upon, there are cases which are worthy of criticism as they reflect opportunism rather than a public spiritedness or a democratic ethos. The public funds available to support charter schools have attracted opportunists—some of them affiliated with black churches—seeking to profit financially in the name of education, or merely seeking to use the opportunity to further their religious agenda devoid of any community mindedness. Some church affiliated charter schools have been cited for religious messages and for questionable financial practices.[40]

In the worst cases, there may be a blatant attempt to profiteer in the name of education. This was the case in Houston, where the Prepared Table Charter School was shut down and the pastor and other members were indicted for embezzling funds amid reports of fraud.[41] In contrast to the Northwood-Appold or the Empowerment Temple, this church's leaders were taking money out of the school rather than adding resources to the education of young people in the community.

Setting aside the examples of opportunism, the important story for those concerned with democracy and public engagement is the frequency with which examples of productive engagement can be found. From the nineteenth century to the present, the tradition of black churches as key actors in the production of education for black people persists. Of course, not all black churches engage in this work, though many have, and many still do. We are left then with the question of why. Why do black churches, church leaders and congregants sacrifice their time and money and effort to contribute to the collective good of education for black communities? I turn now to a brief discussion of why black churches engage in these activities and an exploration of some of the implications of this phenomenon.

Why Coproduce Education?

Reviewing the tradition of black churches coproducing education leads one to the question of why. Why have black churches so often been engaged in these activities? As I have explored this phenomenon, I have asked ministers, program directors and volunteers why they and or their churches engage in this work. Their responses are usually rather simple and typically quite similar. The essence of these responses was captured succinctly by one minister when asked why his church sponsors a charter school. He replied simply, "To be relevant." Others responded to that question with similar comments. They pointed to the fact that there is a need and said almost "matter of factly" that the church should be trying to meet that need. These responses suggest an explanation that is deceptively simple—there is a need to be met. They did not describe their actions as reflective of a grand theology of liberation or nationalist political agenda. Rather, it was taken for granted that where there is an apparent need, the church ought to try to do something about it.

Explaining this phenomenon must at least in part entail a discussion of theology. Despite the apparent simplicity, the above responses reveal a key theological belief. This belief was expressed explicitly by Septima Clark when she discussed the efforts of the citizenship schools during the Civil Rights Movement and was implicit in the efforts in Baltimore County and elsewhere in the earliest period of black public education expansion. It was accepted that the church should be involved in practical worldly activities.

Understanding the theological roots of why black churches engage in support of public education will ultimately require a targeted in-depth analysis. However, the historical examples and my interviews with leaders of some of these efforts suggest two ways in which theology impacts this phenomenon. There may be a theological mandate for practical actions being manifest in the realm of education or, there may be a democratic impulse manifest through churches governed by a theology that permits practical action.

There may be efforts grounded in a theological orientation (e.g., social gospel or black liberation theology) that pushes the church and church leaders to find ways to impact the community that is in need. Thus, it is the theology that drives the effort to impact the community, and what unfolds is the product of the available resources, skills, opportunities etc.

On the other hand, theology may only be a factor in the sense that it permits practical actions, but the impetus comes from a more democratic or political agenda. The church becomes the vehicle for a political sentiment because of the centrality of the church within the community. In such a case, a community may need a school, so community members mobilize through the church because of the resources of the church and the role of the church in the community. This is apparent in the days following the Civil War—a school is needed, and there are few options for establishing a school except a local black church—typically the only structures available for a black community. Today, individuals in black communities may want to do something to impact education—and still churches may be the most viable vehicle available through which to bring their vision together, gather resources and ultimately to implement the vision. To be sure, these two manners in which theology may be at work are not mutually exclusive. A particular effort might reflect both of these dynamics.

It is important to also note that the relationship between engagement and theology is not a one-way street. It is not merely the case that actions are the product of theological orientation. Theology may also be impacted by actions and experiences. One minister who worked with the Child First programs noted that theology impacted their actions, but that the "actions impacted their theology."

Conclusion

African Americans have a strong tradition of collective action and productive engagement in the realm of education. This is due in part to a sense that education is a key means for community uplift. From the days of emancipation to the present, African Americans have expressed a sense that education was critical to freedom and uplift. In a context where there is a sense of a retreat from public life and civic engagement, it is significant that this is a realm where we find so many examples of individuals and collectives like churches contributing resources—time, work and money to help provide education in their communities. That has to be understood as reflective of the vitality of democratic participation. There are people who may not vote, go to a protest or attend a school board meeting—but they will contribute money or time to help children learn. That matters.

There are some important implications of this work. First, there is the possibility that these efforts can have a practical positive impact on the students which they serve. There are many programs and schools (though not all such efforts) that have documented records of effectiveness. As such, there is at least the promise that some of the unmet needs might be met through more of these efforts.

There are also political and democratic implications for this phenomenon of black churches coproducing education. These projects provide vehicles for individuals to participate in public life. They are outlets for public engagement. That in turn has the potential to push these individuals to become even more engaged in public life. One participant told me that after tutoring students she was amazed at the "shockingly poor academic skills" of the students she worked with. Thus, engaging gives one more information that might spark greater contributions. Furthermore, those who engage may develop an enhanced sense of efficacy, which may also lead to greater participation.[42] Students of civic engagement have also pointed out that participation makes individuals more effective—in that they develop skills and interpersonal networks that enable them to be more effective in working to address issues that they care about.[43]

Another possible democratic impact extends to the students. To the extent that coproducers may shape the content of education, these projects may be shaped to foster a particular political awareness and politically relevant skills. This was seen with the freedom schools and the citizenship schools of the Civil Rights Movement. As Myles Horton suggested, contributions came not only from the teachers and providers of the facilities, but also the students who understood themselves as participating in a political mobilization. Their individual learning was tied to community empowerment. That may very well be a lesson that could translate to contemporary efforts. It is notable that the "freedom school" is a model that continues to resonate with black churches and church leaders.

But coproduction can also have a limiting effect. One might focus on a narrow program—tutoring four or five kids a week for example, versus pushing to transform the broader school system. It could in a sense be an "exit option" for the would-be activist. Rather than push for system reform, the activist or the church works with a charter school, for example. They find it easier and more promising to carve out a smaller space and seek to impact those students, rather than facing the frustration of trying to reform a seemingly impervious public school system. Their effort might be helpful to the students of the charter school, but ultimately there are less resources and fewer advocates and activists available for the effort to improve outcomes for all children.

This brings us back to Child First. As noted, this was an effort that was rooted in community organizing. While they had an impressive set of accomplishments initially, their efforts focused on the dozen schools they were present in—not on system-wide reform. They were able to accrue political influence and power, but that political capital was not directed toward the broader system and had little impact on the majority of students in the system. That changed over time, however. In recent years Child First and BUILD allied with other education activists to form the Baltimore Education Coalition. This group then used the BUILD organizing model and political strategy to push local and state officials on systemic reform. Their efforts culminated with a state commitment to invest $1.1 billion for the construction and renovation of schools in Baltimore City. Thus, we have a project that was initially narrowly focused, but ultimately served as the foundation for a push for a reform that will have system-wide impact.

In the United States and elsewhere the reluctance (or inability) of the state to address the needs of distressed communities suggests that productive engagement ought to be a conscious strategy, even though such efforts cannot replace the state. The various examples reviewed in this chapter illustrate that there is a reservoir of public spiritedness that can be tapped to help meet community needs. Tapping that reservoir though, will require institutions and institutional practices that encourage community contributions. Whether it was the matching requirements of the Rosenwald program that encouraged black contributions through the promise of added support, or charter school laws, institutional practices might draw out community contributions.

The history of black churches and education shows that productive engagement has at times had a major impact. But, can this type of engagement play a key role in addressing the major challenges facing black communities today? Can they impact systemic challenges? Perhaps. First, advocates and activists need to recognize that there are many people who would be willing to engage in such efforts. In fact, there may be more who are willing to contribute to productive engagement or coproductive efforts than might be willing to participate in other ways (marching, protesting, etc.). The challenge is to craft strategies that can tap that reservoir in a way that can be impactful. This will require that the leaders of such efforts consciously seek to maximize the effectiveness of these projects and seek to weave these small or narrow projects (programs, individual schools, etc.) together as part of a broad strategy for change. Importantly, "effectiveness" of such efforts must be understood in three ways: impact on the issue being addressed (education of young people), sustainability over time, and the democratic impacts in terms of enhancing and cultivating democratic participation.

Church led efforts at coproducing education reveal a vibrant realm of public engagement often overlooked by those who decry the lack of civic engagement. Ultimately, these examples reveal an impulse toward transforming social and political landscapes facing black people—what I see as a latent democratic potential—that may well be a source of civic capacity for solving community problems. While not sufficient to completely replace the role of the state, such efforts do have the potential to address some of the unmet needs and may lead to expanded forms of civic participation and political involvement.

Notes

1 The city government was a leader in the reinventing government movement.
2 Donn Worgs, "Food for Starved Minds: The Mobilization of African Americans for Education" in *Education as Social Action: Knowledge, Identity and Power*, ed. Ashok Swain (New York: Palgrave McMillan, 2005).
3 Donn Worgs, "Public Engagement and the Coproduction of Public Education" in *Public Engagement for Public Education*, ed. Marion Orr and John Rogers (Stanford, CA: Stanford University Press, 2011).
4 Elinor Ostrom, "Crossing the Great Divide: Coproduction, Synergy, and Development," *World Development* 24, no. 6 (1996).
5 Macedo, Stephen et al. *Democracy at Risk: How Political Choices Undermine Citizen Participation and What We Can Do About It* (Washington, DC: Brookings Institution Press, 2005).
6 Robert Putnam, *Bowling Alone: The Collapse and revival of American Community* (New York: Touchstone, 2001); Theda Skocpol and Morris Fiorina (ed.), *Civic Engagement in American Democracy* (Washington, DC: Brookings Institution Press, 1999); Matthew Crenson and Benjamin Ginsberg, *Downsizing Democracy: How America Sidelined Its Citizens and Privatized Its Public* (Baltimore: Johns Hopkins University Press, 2004).
7 Andrea Williams, *Self Taught: African American Education in Slavery and Freedom* (Chapel Hill: University of North Carolina Press, 2005); Vincent Franklin, *Black*

Self-Determination: A Cultural History of African American Resistance (Brooklyn, NY: Lawrence Hill Books, 1992); Evelyn Brooks Higginbotham, *Righteous Discontent: The Womens' Movement in the Black Baptist Church, 1880–1920* (Cambridge, MA: Harvard University Press, 1993); Jessica Gordon Nembhard, *Collective Courage: A History of African American Cooperative Economic Thought and Practice* (University Park, PA: The Pennsylvania State University Press, 2014).

8 James Anderson, *The Education of Blacks in the South, 1860–1935* (Chapel Hill: University of North Carolina Press, 1988); Williams, *Self Taught*; Worgs, "Food for Starved" and "Public Engagement."

9 Anderson, *The Education*, 5.

10 Ibid.

11 Ronald Butchart, *Northern Schools, Southern Blacks, and Reconstruction: Freedmen's Education 1862–1875* (Westport, CT: Greenwood Press, 1980).

12 This was largely the result of the efforts of Black legislators who made education a top priority—before they were ultimately cast out of electoral politics at the end of the nineteenth century; W. E. B. DuBois, *Black Reconstruction in America* (New York: Touchstone, 1995).

13 Richard Fuke, "The Baltimore Association for the Moral and Educational Improvement of the Colored People 1864–1870," *Maryland Historical Magazine* 66, no. 4 (1971): 369–404.

14 In Mississippi, for example, Span describes counties where all of the Black schools were torched, including some schools that were burned, rebuilt and burned again; Christopher Span, *From Cotton Field to Schoolhouse: African American Education in Mississippi, 1862–1875* (Chapel Hill: University of North Carolina Press, 2009).

15 Robert Margo, *Race and Schooling in the South, 1880–1950: An Economic History* (Chicago: University of Chicago Press, 1994).

16 Overall, $4.3 million came from Rosenwald, $4.7 million from Blacks, $1.2 million from white donors, and $18 million from districts. The Rosenwald contribution served to leverage state contributions which eventually increased over time. Mary Hoffschwelle, *The Rosenwald Schools of the American South* (Gainesville: University Press of Florida, 2006).

17 Hoffschwelle, *The Rosenwald*; Anderson, *The Education*; Elgin L. Klugh, "Reclaiming Segregation-Era, African American Schoolhouses: Building on Symbols of Past Cooperation," *The Journal of Negro Education* 74, no. 3 (Summer 2005): 246–259; Michelle Baumi, and O. L. Davis, Jr., "From School House to Hay Barn to Museum: The Columbia Rosenwald School in Brazoria County, Texas," *American Educational History Journal* 35, no. 2 (2008): 279–291; Carter J. Savage, "Cultural Capital and African American Agency: The Economic Struggle for Effective Education for African Americans in Franklin, Tennessee, 1890-1967," *The Journal of African American History* 87 (Spring 2002): 206–235.

18 See Anderson, *The Education*.

19 Jill Titus, *Brown's Battleground: Students, Segregationists, and the Struggle for Justice in Prince Edward County, Virginia* (Chapel Hill: University of North Carolina Press, 2011).

20 Polly Welts Kaufman, "Building a constituency for school desegregation: African American women in Boston, 1962–1972," *Teachers College Record* 92, no. 4

(Summer 1991): 619–631; Leonard Moore, "The School Desegregation Crisis of Cleveland, Ohio, 1963–1964: The Catalyst for Black Political Power in a Northern City," *Journal of Urban History* 28, no. 2 (January 2002): 153.

21 Myles Horton, who was heavily influenced by the Social Gospel, founded the Highlander Folk School in 1932. Modeled after Dutch folk schools, Highlander provided workshops and training sessions for labor and civil rights activists. It played a key role in the Civil Rights Movement.

22 Myles Horton, and Palo Freire, *We Make the Road by Walking* (Philadelphia, PA: Temple University Press, 1990).

23 Ibid.

24 John Rachal, "We'll Never Turn Back: Adult Education and the Struggle for Citizenship in Mississippi 'Freedom Summer'," *Adult Education Quarterly* 50, no. 3 (May 2000) 166–197.

25 Ibid.

26 Charles Cobb, "Prospectus for a Summer Freedom School Program," in *Teach Freedom: Education for Liberation in the African American Tradition*, ed. Charles Payne and Carol Sills Strickland (New York: Teacher's College Press, 2008).

27 Rachal, "We'll Never Turn Back."

28 Interview with Charlie Cobb, March 2015.

29 Septima Poinsett Clark, "Citizenship and Gospel," *Journal of Black Studies* 10, no. 4 (1980): 461–466.

30 Clark, "Citizenship," 463.

31 Ibid., 464.

32 G. Bohrnstedt, et al., *School Composition and the Black–White Achievement Gap* (NCES 2015-018). U.S. Department of Education (Washington, DC: National Center for Education Statistics [NCES], 2015). Retrieved March 21, 2017 from http://nces.ed.gov/pubsearch; Frank Adamson and Linda Darling-Hammond, *Addressing the Inequitable Distribution of Teachers: What It Will Take to Get Qualified, Effective Teachers in All Communities* (Stanford Center for Opportunity Policy in Education ~ Research Brief, 2011). Retrieved March 21, 2017 from https://edpolicy.stanford.edu/sites/default/files/publications/addressing-inequitable-distribution-teachers-what-it-will-take-get-qualified-effective-teachers-all-_1.pdf; U.S. Department of Education Office for Civil Rights (2016), *2013-2014 CIVIL RIGHTS DATA COLLECTION*. Retrieved March 21, 2017 from https://www2.ed.gov/about/offices/list/ocr/docs/2013-14-first-look.pdf.

33 Maryland State Department of Education (MSDE), *2016 Maryland Report Card* (2016). Data Retrieved on March 21, 2017 from http://reportcard.msde.maryland.gov/index.aspx?K=13AAAA.

34 Though many summer camps are primarily recreational, many are designed to be academic with the stated purpose of supporting the education of children in their communities.

35 Marion Orr, "BUILD: Governing Nonprofits and Relational Power," *Policy Studies Review* 18, no. 4 (2001): 71–90.

36 Orr, "BUILD: Governing."

37 Bohrnstedt, et al., *School Composition.*

38 Ibid.

39 MSDE, *2016 Maryland Report Card.*
40 Jessica Meyers, "Charter Schools with Ties to Religious Groups Raise fears about Funds' Use," *The Dallas Morning News*, November 22, 2010.
41 There were reports that the pastor paid himself over $200,000 a year to run the school. Ultimately the indictments (and subsequent guilty pleas) were related to padding enrollment numbers in order to garner more funds form the government. While the pastor died before his prosecution, his wife, brother and daughter were each sentenced to prison time for embezzlement and fraud. Meyers, "Charter Schools"; Harvey Rice, "3 Sentenced in Charter School Scam—Relatives Get Prison Terms for Bilking State and U.S. of $6 million," *Houston Chronicle.* September 3, 2005, p. B9.
42 Harry C. Boyte and Nancy Kari, *Building America: The Democratic Promise of Public Work* (Philadelphia, PA: Temple University Press, 1996).
43 Boyte and Kari, *Building America*; Worgs, "Public Engagement."

8. *The Reconnectional Hope: Interfaith Transformation of Recidivism to Regeneration of Community*

Ronald E. Peters

> Now faith is the assurance of things hoped for, the conviction of things not seen.
>
> —Hebrews 11:1

Introduction: Recidivism, A Feeder to Mass Incarceration

For nearly a generation the United States has been the world leader in incarcerating people, with nearly half of those locked up drawn from only 6% of its population: black males.[1] African-descended communities across the globe are suffering effects of political, economic and social inequities whose consequences include alarming levels of disease, unemployment, incarceration, and systemic violence which leads to rough destabilization of their family life and communities. Currently, more than 10.4% of the country's black males between the ages of 25–29 are in prison, compared to 2.4% of Hispanic and 1.2% of white males in the same age group.[2] The devastation of this reality on the poor generally and upon black people particular is incalculable. Nearly 6 of every 10 minor children of incarcerated parents in the United States today (58%) are less than 10 years old.[3]

Recidivism is the rate at which former inmates are rearrested and return to incarceration. In the United States, this rate is 67% during the first three years following release.[4] This phenomenon is a significant, but seldom mentioned contributor to growth of the nation's mass incarceration industry. This situation disproportionally undermines healthy family relationships and communal wellbeing among black people reinforcing patterns of entrenched inequality.

This volume's use of the metaphor of landscaping provides a helpful way to understand how this persistent and debilitating reality must be engaged. Landscaping, in its best sense, ordinarily focuses on utilitarian as well as aesthetic aspects of making a yard or other piece of land more environmentally uplifting, life-sustaining, and attractive by altering the existing terrain in some way to enhance the quality of life for all affected by its territory. This chapter examines one interfaith approach to "landscaping" the environmental and experiential spaces occupied by black people caught into the mass incarceration industry such that the recidivism cycle in the United States is interrupted and its disproportionately negative impact upon black community life is reduced.

Parental Proverbs: A Clue to Discovering Successful Strategies of HOPE

As a youngster, my formative years were framed against a backdrop of homegrown proverbs my parents frequently quoted to emphasize tenets they expected my siblings and me to remember. One of Mom's favorite sayings *I can't hear what you're saying for watching what you're doing*, was often repeated when my behavior or school grades did not meet family expectations. Dad, who often taught by asking thought-provoking questions, always reminded my siblings and me concerning a problem that *If someone can get you to ask the wrong question, the answer you get won't matter* (because it will be irrelevant to the problem at hand).

Both these parental proverbs inform the challenge to be faced in engaging the thorn-ridden landscape of the United States' incarceration industry and environment of recidivism. When considering the plight of "the least of these" (Matthew 25:31–40) in black and other communities of color, the historic importance of articulated civic values like "equal opportunity for all" is challenged by Mom's proverb *I can't hear what you're saying for watching what you're doing*. Dad's proverb, *If someone can get you to ask the wrong question, the answer you get will not matter*, is also helpful regarding consideration of mass incarceration because too frequently, we seem to ask the *wrong* questions: *What's wrong with those people*? or *Isn't it awful*? However well researched and cleverly presented, the responses to such questions will not matter because they are the wrong questions.

Concerning the reduction of recidivism among black people and other communities of color in the United States, the *right* questions should include *How can we undo this tragic and costly dilemma? How can we move beyond warped and narrow jargon of maintaining "law and order" and "getting 'criminals' off the streets" that feeds recidivistic attitudes, expectations, and behaviors toward strategies to reduce recidivism and help reconnect community in uplifting ways?* This chapter explores a little researched strategy that appears to offer hope of "a more excellent way" (1 Corinthians 12:31) of landscaping this tortured social and experiential space through interfaith and public sector collaboration. This is what the organization, entitled *Foundation of HOPE* (acronym for *Helping Open People's Eyes*), seeks to embody through its functioning. This pre-release education and post-release aftercare support program affiliated with the Chaplain's office in the Allegheny County Jail in Pittsburgh, Pennsylvania has achieved impressive results for more than seven years.

The Foundation of HOPE: Addressing Recidivism

The success of this faith-inspired strategy, housed in the Allegheny County Jail (ACJ) in the city of Pittsburgh, Pennsylvania appears to hold impressive potential for redirecting the lives of persons overwhelmingly vulnerable to becoming but another recidivistic casualty in the United States' powerful incarceration industry. Articulating its mission, the *Foundation of HOPE* says it seeks to *empower incarcerated and released individuals to restore their relationship with their God, rebuild their lives and reconcile to their community.*[5]

Although Pittsburgh was listed as one of "the best cities for relocation" in 2012 and one of the "happiest cities" in which to work in 2013, challenges of young adults living in the city's predominately African American communities such as Arlington Heights, Beltzhoover, Garfield, Hazelwood, Homewood, Hill District, or Lincoln-Larimer reflect different realities. In fact, in 2011 the Pittsburgh Region had the 11th highest unemployment rate among African Americans in the top 40 regions in the nation.[6] Pittsburgh's black unemployment was 19% at the time or 2.6 times the white percentage. The needs of young adults, especially between ages 18–29 have been at epidemic levels for years. Unemployment for this demographic, especially men, varies from 30 to 60% depending upon region. In Pittsburgh, the overall unemployment among African Americans in 2013 was near 45%.[7]

In the Upper Hill, for example, the median age in 2014 among males and females was 31.6 and 35.5 years respectively. The median income was $22,556.[8] These statistics help explain the ongoing and acute issues involving substandard housing stock, health, education, and incarceration challenges, that diminish sustainable healthy families or other social relationships in such environments.

Each year, the Allegheny County Jail admits about 25,000 people. The current, but growing average population of the jail is about 2,600 individuals, which suggests that about 22,400 persons are released from the jail annually. Nationally the average recidivism rate in the United States is 37% within one year of release and 67% in three years. In Allegheny County, the one-year year recidivism rate is 33%; the three-year rate is 52%.[9] While lower than national rates, high recidivism rates in Allegheny County—particularly in poor and African American neighborhoods—remain a serious problem. Since roughly half ACJ inmates are African American, this "caste" (to use Alexander's phrase),[10] once released, faces incredible odds to overcoming or avoiding realities that contributed to their becoming recyclable candidates for incarceration.

How the Program Works

The Foundation of HOPE provides intensive faith-based discipleship reflection, practical resources, and one-on-one mentoring to the men and women incarcerated in the county jail that assists them in the process of rethinking choices and options for the future. Through choice awareness and spiritual enhancement training, the program gives those recently released from jail an opportunity to rebuild their lives through exposure to life enhancing values based on faith in God and away from forces that, otherwise, ordinarily would lead them back to incarceration.

Roots of the HOPE are grounded in an ecumenical dialogue of various Protestant and Catholic traditions known as Christian Associates of Southwestern Pennsylvania (CASP) that in 1985 contracted with the County Jail to facilitate chaplaincy services for all faith groups at the jail. Funded by CASP, the Chaplain's Office serves inmates of all faith traditions. As such, the HOPE program's interfaith approach to reducing recidivism serves not only a wide variety of Protestant traditions, but also includes Buddhists, Catholics, Jehovah's Witnesses, Jewish, Islamic, and Native American traditions. In 2002, the Chaplain's Office established project HOPE as a faith-based pre- and post-release program for inmates. The maximum stay at the county jail is typically about 2 years as residents await adjudication in court, although the actual length of time may be longer. Following court, inmates may be released (found not guilty or placed on probation), sentenced to more time in jail, or transferred to prison (State or Federal).

Because the Chaplain's Office took seriously the fact that persons incarcerated in the County Jail are "temporary" residents with the overwhelming majority ultimately released for return to society, an effort to help reduce the high rate of recidivism was initiated and the HOPE approach was born. The HOPE approach seeks to intervene in this increasingly counter-productive cycle of repeated jail returns by addressing some of the social and spiritual self-perception issues that appear to characterize the majority of jail residents, first-timers and returnees.

A strategy was envisioned to address this issue involving a three-component *continuum of care*, that begins first with certain *pre-release activities* followed by *aftercare services* post-release that intentionally connects former residents with a church, mosque, synagogue, or temple as appropriate. Finally, a faith-grounded, pre-screened, trained (for the mentoring task), and *dedicated mentor* is assigned to the released individual and support is given for improving job readiness, employment search, and such.

HOPE's Functional Approach

The uniqueness of the HOPE approach lies in its intrinsically life-affirming values reflected in four core operational values: *transitional chaplaincy, transformative education, tenured mentoring, and tactical prevention.* During pre-release, *transitional chaplaincy* (unselfish interest in the wellbeing of another) and *transformative education* ("problem-posing/solution-discovery" rather than "transfer of information" pedagogy) function to prepare ACJ residents for their return to society. Post-release is where former ACJ residents experience what can be referred to as *tenured mentoring* (not tenuous, but ongoing and committed encouragement, advice, nurture, and support). *Tactical prevention* (strategic collaboration among communal stakeholders to stop incarceration before it starts) is the fourth and perhaps most effective operational value.

These four life-affirming values assist HOPE participants toward successful acquisition of effective communal interdependence that strengthens the individual and society as a whole.

The first part of the *pre-release* engagement of the inmate is referred to here as *transitional chaplaincy.* This type of chaplaincy differs from "traditional" chaplaincy that sometimes can resemble the "medical model" (medical expert/patient) or "social worker" (social resource expert/client) approach to interaction with inmates. The socioeconomic demographics from which the overwhelming majority of jailed persons are drawn make them highly suspicious of "social workers" whose concern for their welfare is ordinarily perceived as disingenuous. As such, traditional chaplaincy approaches can limit the effectiveness of interactions, reducing them to just another exchange between a pseudo-authority figure, at best, and the "caged" individual.

Transitional chaplaincy, by contrast, recognizes the spiritual, social, and legal dilemma of the inmate in a way that, over time, can foster more genuine interactions, laying the groundwork for potentially healthful self-evaluation and life-goals reassessment within the incarcerated resident.[11]

Second, the *pre-release* interaction is framed by what can be called *transformative education* experiences. This type of pedagogical approach seeks to avoid mistakes all too common in educational approaches that complicate the learning environment even before students enter the classroom.[12] Understandably, persons with poor educational achievement are overly represented among the incarcerated and determined effort is required to help those genuinely desiring to critically reevaluate their situation and move forward toward more constructive futures.

Transformative education is an approach that addresses this situation. It is a type of instruction reflecting Paulo Freire's dialogical teaching methods that avoid "banking in teaching" (transfer of information from teacher to student in a way that does not recognize or validate the experiences/information inherent in the student). Freire emphasizes dialogical teaching methods that affirm the student's intellect (personhood) by the teacher, thus rendering pedagogical interaction between "teacher" (who is also a student, learning from the experiences of the *student*-teacher) and "student" (who also is a teacher, learning from the experiences of the *teacher*-student).[13] This approach helps restore the sense of personhood within the incarcerated resident and encourages self-reassessment in learning that nurtures positive aspirations as new life skills are learned.

Third, once released from jail, *tenured* (not *temporary) Aftercare* is structured for society's new returnee. Because of the tenuous nature of life in poor and socially challenged environments especially where race and/or cultural subcultural realities further complicate existence, there is a clear lack of permanency in life. People necessarily move from place to place for lack of resources to insure permanency due to unemployment, unsustainable, unhealthy or dangerous relationships or deteriorating environments, and the list of reasons goes on. In this context, the tenuousness of existence and social susceptibility to displacement, criminal activity, and danger is further undermined by ongoing change among those who would be "helpers" (neighbors, teachers, principals in schools, charitable, social work, police and/or probation personnel, and religious individuals).

Because the parade of changing "helpers" can be constant, it becomes increasingly difficult to create and sustain healthy, trusting, and viable relationships. The capacity to "trust" others after innumerable failed relationships poses a real challenge to moving forward in life with any degree of confidence, however well intended. Against this backdrop, connecting with someone especially trained to creatively engage persons seeking to successfully emerge from this experiential reality is vitally important. The HOPE program has taken on this challenge by doing just that with the provision of especially trained "tenured" mentors drawn from faith traditions. Mentors are recruited and trained with particular attention to the variety of religious traditions from which mentees come, whether Roman Catholic, Pentecostal, Islamic, Baptist, and such. Moreover, a significant feature of aftercare services includes a series of weekly meetings for returning citizens and their supporters—mentors, family members, friends, and such—called *PIRC (Positive Initiative to Reinforce Change).* Through group dialogue, opportunity is given for cultivation of enhanced self-confidence in building trust as re-entrants and supporters together explore ideas in a safe and affirming atmosphere that holds mutual respect and genuine accountability in relationships as intrinsic social and spiritual values.

Finally, *tactical prevention* has been emphasized through its interfaith collaborative networks as the organization broadened its efforts to reduce recidivism by taking measures to prevent incarceration before it begins. In 2017, the Foundation of HOPE expanded its outreach into the area of prevention, focusing on youth and young adults, ages 12-to-26 during these especially vulnerable years.

The *HOPE Diversion Program* was initiated to give young people who commit a nonviolent, low-to-medium offense the opportunity to remain in the community with the support of family, school, and other stakeholders in their success while addressing their needs rather than allowing them to be prosecuted, convicted, or incarcerated. This communal approach to restorative justice emphasizes repairing the harm to the individuals involved "as community"/ as "village" as a preventive and diversional step to incarceration and a possible recidivistic cycle of functioning thereafter. By partnering with local law enforcement, juvenile probation, the city's Housing Authority and County District Attorney's Office along with identified family members, and other community stakeholders, the *HOPE Diversion Program* serves as a possible alternative to prosecution for eligible youths. Since its inception, 94% of the referred youth who received some type of service did not recommit any offenses.[14]

Moving Forward in HOPE

As implemented over the past seven years, the HOPE strategy not only interrupts the recidivistic cycle for those individuals emerging from and continually threatened by return to jail or prison, but also helps to heal and strengthen host communities bedeviled and exploited by social realities that feed the incarceration industry cycle. Additionally, through its *Diversion Program*, it seeks to stop entrance to incarceration and the recidivism cycle before it begins. Although anecdotally noted, initial results have been impressive. These results have been buttressed by encouraging individual stories coming to the Chaplain's attention, including the growing length of time between some individual's re-arrest, and the non-return of several former recidivism veterans. By 2006, the warden had taken notice of the strategy and designated an entire jail housing unit (or "pod") as the project HOPE Pod for men. In March 2009, a HOPE Pod was added for women. Both have a 90-person plus capacity.

During the *pre-release phase* of the program, any inmate, regardless of religious affiliation, ethnic group, or age can be enrolled in the program. Ordinarily, a person should be closer to the end of his/her jail time prior to considering enrollment and relocation to the HOPE pod. Inmates accepted into the HOPE program move on the Pod section,[15] exclusively dedicated to this group of residents. Participants must learn the values, responsibilities, and privileges of community living in the jail. Once admitted and relocated to the HOPE Pod, there is a high standard of accountability to the wellbeing of the Pod community expected and mutual support for all is a primary value.

All program activities take place in this Pod as it sets the context for a new sense of community not only within the jail, but for beyond incarceration upon return to society. Participants meet over a ten-week period for over 120 hours of class and group work. Each class requires homework and participation. Participants live together, addressing interpersonal relationship skills, addiction and recovery issues, anger management, accountability and character development, self-analysis, spiritual development and recognition of one's relationship to God, life skills, parenting skills, job-related values, and more. At the end of each cycle of classes, participants who have passed the final exam receive a certificate of completion and a letter for court certifying their completion. A formal graduation ceremony is held in the jail for those completing the program and program volunteers and the new mentor are invited inside the jail and on the Pod to attend the ceremony. This is part of strategy to reintegrate jail residents with family members "on the outside" who also have suffered due to an incarcerated loved-one (loss of job/income, embarrassment, child-rearing stress, housing, and such).

Participants who graduate from the program and wish to remain on the housing unit are eligible to take supplemental graduate courses. Those demonstrating leadership qualities are selected as "Servant Leaders" who assist with setting up for and facilitating small groups, encouraging their sense of successful responsibility for post-release life.

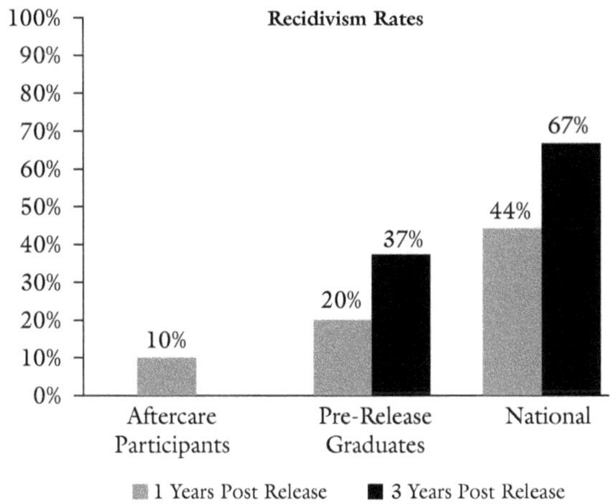

Figure 8.1: Foundation of HOPE Recidivism Reduction 2006–2012 One & Three Year Success Rates vs National Avg.

Following release from jail, the *Aftercare and post incarceration mentorship* phase of the HOPE strategy supports participants. Prior to release from ACJ, HOPE participants are matched with a mentor who will follow them through interaction for at least a year beyond their most recent incarceration experience. Mentors offer former jail residents' friendship, support, and other practical assistance in helping them make a healthy transition to society especially as this may involve establishing new social networks. This may include joining "mentees" at recovery meetings, encouraging them in housing and job searches, meeting their families, or inviting them to fellowship with the mentor's faith-community (church, mosque, synagogue, or temple) or going with them to explore other communities of faith if not reconnecting to a former one.

Results[16]

Between 2006 and 2012, more than 1,350 men and 750 women participated in the HOPE Pre-Release program. Among program graduates, the resulting one-year recidivism rate was less than half the national rate: HOPE grads = 20%; nationwide = 44%. HOPE three-year recidivism rates were similarly impressive, reducing recidivism by nearly half: HOPE grads = 37%; nationwide = 67%. Within one year of release, 90% of HOPE Aftercare participants *do not recidivate* compared to the 44% national recidivism rate (see Figure 8.1 above).

Additionally, these successes produce significant cost savings for society. According to an independent report concerning the Foundation of HOPE program by the ACJ Collaborative[17] published in 2008, the average cost per bed per day at the ACJ was $68.87 or $25,137.55 annually in 2008, far more than $18,400 annual per pupil cost (second highest in Pennsylvania) spent by the City of Pittsburgh in 2011–2012 to educate one child.[18] This same report also noted that for every one dollar invested in support services and programs for former inmates over the period 2006 through 2008, the HOPE program saved the County over $26 million by reducing the percentage of individuals returning to the ACJ. Since 2010, more than 200 male and female HOPE Aftercare graduates have achieved a one-year recidivism rate of 9.5% instead of the 44% national rate.

Conclusion

Without question, the Foundation of HOPE's interfaith approach to reducing recidivism demonstrates that reconnecting the formerly incarcerated to healthy networks of faith and family strengthens the individuals helped and offers hope toward the reconnection of communities in ways that socially, economically, and spiritually enhances the quality of life in society as a whole. As one social justice network put it:

> Faith communities should be models of safe and sacred spaces where formerly incarcerated persons can gather to lead and address the situations they confront, the causes and effects of choices they made, and connect with believers in Christ who model, mentor, and help them mold their lives toward new healing. This effort has the potential to reconnect and strengthen families, and assist in the reduction of violence while offering help and hope to "the least of these" in the community and society.[19]

Notes

1 Ronald E. Peters, *Urban Ministry: An Introduction* (Nashville: Abingdon, 2007), 165.
2 Statistics from a July 2003 report of the Department of Justice, 950 Pennsylvania Avenue, N.W., Washington, DC taken from the website: http://www.usdoj.gov. July 2013.
3 Jeremy Travis, Elizabeth M. Cincotta, and Amy L. Solomon, *Families Left Behind: The Hidden Costs of Incarceration and Reentry* (Washington, DC: Urban Institute/Justice Policy Center, 2003). Website: http://www.urban.org/UploadedPDF/310882_families_left_behind.pdf, 1.
4 Foundation of HOPE, Bureau of Justice Statistics Study of 300,000 release inmates quoted in Foundation of HOPE (2012) [Brochure] (Pittsburgh, PA: Foundation of HOPE, 2012), 2.

5 Foundation of HOPE, *Program Flyer in the Chaplain's Office, Allegheny County Jail* (Pittsburgh, PA: Foundation of HOPE, 2013.
6 Harold Miller, *Futures Business Consultant, LLC and Adjunct Professor of Public Policy and Management at Carnegie Mellon University's Heinz School of Public Policy and Management* (2013). See http://www.pittsburghfuture.blogspot.com/2013/05/african-americans-are-being-left-behind.html / accessed August 2014.
7 Miller, *Futures Business.*
8 City of Pittsburgh, PA Neighborhood Data: See http://www.city-data.com/nbmaps/neigh-Pittsburgh-Pennsylvania.html#N62 / accessed August 2014.
9 Foundation of HOPE, *Program Flyer.*
10 See chapter 1, Alexander, "The Rebirth of Caste," 20.
11 Howard Zehr *Changing Lenses: A new Focus for Crime and Justice* (Scottdale: Herald Press, 2005). See chapter. 10, "A Restorative Lens," 177–184. Also see essay on "Shape of Ministry in Prison," 79–81, in *Black Men in Prison: The Response of the African American Church*, ed. Gayraud Wilmore (Atlanta, GA: ITC Press, 1990).
12 The history and present context of this reality are found in classic educational resources as Jonathan Kozol's, *Amazing Grace: The Lives of Children and the Conscience of a Nation* (New York: Crown, 1995); and *Shame of the Nation: Restoration of Apartheid Schooling in America* (New York: Random House, 2006).
13 This is an approach to pedagogy first articulated by Paulo Freire especially for oppressed groups wherein both teacher and student are benefitted with greater insight into solution-oriented skills that are life-enhancing through mutual sharing of information from life experience. See Paulo Freire, *Pedagogy of the Oppressed* (New York: Continuum, 1996).
14 Quoted in May 13, 2019 email sent by Jody Raeford, Foundation of HOPE Executive Director.
15 The Allegheny County Jail facility is constructed to house residents in various sections called "pods," with each containing a self-enclosed environment of occupants who share certain open spaces in common: leisure and group activities.
16 Except as otherwise noted, the chart and all statistics quoted in this section are from the Foundation of HOPE brochure, *Providing Excellence in Faith-Based Pre- and Post-release Care and Chaplaincy for Incarcerated and Released Individuals* (Pittsburgh, PA: Foundation of HOPE, Allegheny County Jail, 2012), 2–3.
17 The Allegheny County Jail Collaborative (ACJC) is a cooperative partnership of county government agencies, initiated in 2000 by the Allegheny County Department of Human Services (DHS), and includes court officials along with County social and health service providers in collaboration with faith-based community organizations, ex-offenders and their families, and the community at large. The ACJC was formed in response to county leadership observations that not enough was being done for former inmates to support their successful reentry into the community. The ACJC's primary goals are to increase public safety and reduce recidivism. See http://www.alleghenycounty.us/dhs/jail.aspx.
18 http://triblive.com/news/education/3971459-74/district-board-consultants#axzz3Ep6cwEnh / September 21, 2014.
19 *Bearing Witness: A Nation in Chains: A Report of the Samuel DeWitt Procter Conference* (Chicago: SDPC, 2013), 32.

9. *Leadership Succession Practices in African Independent Churches in Zimbabwe: The Case of Zion Apostolic Faith Mission Church*

Clemence Makamure and Vengesai Chimininge

The nature of leadership in Africa in both religious and political arenas is demanding a complete overhaul. There is a need to improve leadership succession practices and adopt leadership capacity that can strengthen agility and growth of the future generation. In fact, one of the greatest challenges facing Africa today is the problem of succession. There are more uncertainties about the future of most organizations beyond the current leader. Leaders come and go leaving no successor or a succession plan in place. Leadership succession problems have formed an integral part of the life of African Independent Churches. History has revealed that a succession problem would always arise after the death of the principal leaders. The subject of leadership has formulated the black religious landscaping in Africa and in the United States. Daneel reiterated that the death of the founder of an Independent church, more than any other occasion, brings conflicting issues to the surface.[1] The Zion Christian Church of Samuel Mutendi had thirteen schisms between 1929 and 1961, though none succeeded in drawing away large numbers. After the death of Samuel Mutendi in 1976 there was a serious schism. Daneel identified three major schismatic groups which emerged soon after the death of "man of God." These groups are as follows: the ZCC under the leadership of Reuben Mutendi whose headquarter is at Mandadzaka in Bikita district and secondly the ZCC under the Episcopal of Gierson Matenda with its headquarters at Garare under Chief Nyamhondo in Mwenezi district. The last one is the group of Nehemiah Mutendi's faction which is the main board, comprising the bulk of senior ministers using Mbungo and Defe Dopota as major centers.[2]

After the death of David Masuka of Zion Apostolic Church in 1950, several *Ndaza* bishops broke away and formed their own churches.[3] According to Hastings, these include Makamba who carried the majority of the church congregates and led his own church known as the Zion Apostolic Church. Bishop Sharara in Buhera also broke away and started his own church and so did Kudzerema who led the faction in Dewure area in Gutu.[4] The other group was led by David Masuka Junior but this was the smallest group of the breakaways. The succession problems in the Zion Apostolic Church led to escalated wrangles which lasted for 8 years and the church disintegrated until it was revived in 1959 by Bishop Zebedee Mutingwende and Amos Mufundirwa under the name Zion Church of God. The church has however, managed to maintain its headquarters in Bikita where it started in 1922. There have been also leadership succession problems in the African Apostolic Church of Johanne Marange between Noah Taguta and Clemence Momberume. The African Apostolic Church of Johanne Marange experienced its first break away in 1963 after the death of its founding figure Johanne Marange. Squabbles arose when Arnold Taguta appointed Abero Momberume the eldest son of Marange as the successor. This did not auger well with Simon Mushati the then deputy founder and he broke away and formed his own church.[5] In 1992 Abero passed away and Noah Taguta the son of Arnold Taguta usurped church leadership and declared himself the chief priest. This displeased Clement Momberume the biological son of Abero who also was eying the post. This sparked a prolonged leadership wrangle in the church which is still raging at the time of this writing. The case has been brought to the attention of the chiefs' courts and even the high court of Zimbabwe but all these efforts have been to no avail.

There have also been schisms and leadership wrangles in other African Independent Churches like the Apostolic church of Johanne Masowe, the African Congregation Church, the Ethiopian Church, the Church of Mai Chaza and many others. All these wrangles have at times resulted in bloody fights and struggles which explains the fact that there is indeed a leadership crisis in African Independent Churches in Zimbabwe. More to this almost all African Independent Churches had to suffer schisms and leadership wrangles which further explain that there is a crisis in leadership. So, from this brief history of selected African Independent Churches in Zimbabwe, it can be seen that the death of a principal leader results in prolonged leadership succession problems. This chapter is thus meant to discuss leadership succession practices in African Independent Churches in Zimbabwe paying particular attention to the Zion Apostolic Faith Mission Church. In the Zion Apostolic Faith Mission Church there are current raging power wrangles between Jameson and Ezra Shoko. These succession problems started after the death of Dorius Pedzisai Shoko the then current Bishop.

Methodological Concerns

Sociological and the phenomenological methods were utilized for this study. The sociological method was handy because it is concerned with describing and explaining social behavior, social structures and interactions in relation to the environment.[6] It is therefore suitable in this research, which endeavors to comprehend the discussion on leadership succession practices in African Independent Churches in Zimbabwe. The phenomenological approach was particularly significant because it is concerned with seeing a phenomenon, behavior or religion as the adherents see them, rather than imposing any sort of external value judgment. In fact, the phenomenological approach provided a means for investigating the way people come to know reality.[7] Through the process of *epoche*, the researcher was able to gather data after the suspension of any value judgments and preconceived notions about the beliefs, practices and leadership systems of the Zion Apostolic Faith Mission.[8]

Historical Background of the Zion Apostolic Faith Mission in Zimbabwe

The Zion Apostolic Faith Mission Church was founded by Andreas Pedzisai Shoko in 1931. Born in Museva rural in Chief Gororo area, Shoko was educated by the Dutch Reformed Church to become a kraal school teacher-assistant at Zunga School.[9] Owing to the poor conditions of work, Shoko left teaching to become a herd-boy at N.C. Peter Forrestall's farm where he was offered "better" wages.[10] As working conditions worsened in Zimbabwe, Shoko joined the exodus to the South in 1923 as a frustrated man.[11]

While in South Africa, Shoko and another migrant laborer Samuel Mutendi were baptized by "Edward of Basutholand" a secessionist leader for the Zion Apostolic Faith Mission (ZAFM) who had broken away from Bishop Mahlangu's Zion Apostolic Church in 1920.[12]

Edward incorporated them into his church and on return to Chivi in 1931 Shoko started preaching and converting many to his church. He concentrated his preaching activities in the Southern part of Chivi district near his home in Museva. Shoko was constantly using the Nyuni range of mountains to conduct his sermons and healing practices and in a very short time he gathered a large following.[13] His charismatic skill, eloquence and his original way of relating the gospel symbolically attracted many that had failed to find meaning in the bureaucracy and teachings of the Dutch Reformed Church. He held open meetings and baptized children. All these moves by Shoko were a threat to the Dutch Reformed Church which began to register very poor attendance at church and school.[14]

Angered by the fair success of Andreas Shoko, the colonial administration was quick to react and took the opportunity to rally the support of the chiefs using "moralist" propaganda. In 1933 a meeting was convened in the presence of chiefs, headmen and "their people" where it is alleged that they all unanimously condemned Andreas' church on the grounds of his age-then hardly 25 years old. At the meeting the elders requested that Shoko's activities be banned. The state reacted accordingly and Andreas was not only warned but was actually "punished for his offense."[15] It is vital to note that some of the traditional circles were growing uncomfortable with Shoko's activities especially his idea of taking women and girls to nightly prayer meetings. In 1948 ZAFM church experienced the first schism led by Jeremiah who broke away to form his own ZAFM in Chief Shindi's area at the southern end of the district.[16] There were two other consecutive breakaways by Rueben and Ruka Changa in 1949 and 1950 respectively. However, it appeared many of these secessionists had personal agendas against Shoko and as it turned out most disappeared into oblivion while others re-joined him. Shoko nonetheless kept the flag of his revolution flying undeterred.

Andreas Pedzisai Shoko died in 1985 and his son Dorius Pedzisai Shoko succeeded him as Bishop in the same year. He was installed in the position following the church's succession tradition based on the September 27, 1949 covenant between Samuel Mutendi, David Masuka and Andreas Shoko, representing the three Zion churches in Zimbabwe, which dictates that "upon the death of a bishop, the late bishop's eldest son from his first wife takes over the throne and is supposed to be ordained by the remaining two bishops or their successors at the deceased bishop's memorial service."[17] However, the decree of the 1949 covenant was disputed by some of the members of the Zion Apostolic Faith Mission and this caused the 1985 schism between Dorius and Zakaria Shoko. Zakaria started his church and led the Zion of the robe (Ndaza) in Dare area under Chief Shindi.[18] Zakaria claimed that he was the rightful heir to church leadership because he was close to his father as compared to Dorius. Dorius on the same issue claimed rights to the throne by virtue of being the eldest son of the Bishop with his first wife as was dictated by the 1949 covenant. The leadership succession dispute between the two led to the schism which made Dorius to lead the main group of the Zion

Apostolic Faith Mission church. He led the church until his death in October 13, 2012 in a car accident.

Dorius had three wives, 27 children and more than 50 grandchildren. Because of his untimely death, Dorius had not trained any successor neither had he put in place any succession plan or practice. After his death, two of his sons were locked in an acrimonious legal battle to take over leadership of the church. According to the interview information that the researchers of this chapter gathered, the two sons of Dorius who are Jameson and Ezra went into a violent fight which is even raging today.[19] Following Shoko's death, Ezra was appointed the new bishop on the basis that their father had spoken by word of mouth and written in his will that Ezra should take over the church leadership.

Ezra was ordained by Zachariah Shoko a brother and rival of Dorius Shoko. Jameson being the eldest surviving son of Dorius had the support of the 1949 Zionist covenant, custom and tradition to the throne. Jameson also had the support of the leader of the Apostolic Christian Council of Zimbabwe (ACCZ) president Reverend Johannes Ndanga. Vital to note is the contention that before the death of Dorius, Jameson had a misunderstanding with his father. According to deacon Muringo, Jameson was accused of revolting against his father and seemed to be running another church within the same ZAFM. This move made Dorius excommunicate him together with those who were supporting him. This is the reason why his father had appointed Ezra by word of mouth to succeed him.[20]

Jameson argued that the appointment of Ezra by the Council of High Priests was violating the Zionist tradition. Jameson denied that there was ever such an appointment made by word of mouth and there was no written confirmation to that effect. The two brothers went further to interfere with each other's church's activities by sending their sympathizers to violently attack each other's followers while they conducted services. It is important to note as well that the two brothers, Jameson and Ezra Pedzisai Shoko, have different mothers, with Ezra coming from the lower house. This being the case, under the degree of the 1949 covenant Ezra was not supposed to be the successor of Dorius.

The wife of the late Andreas Shoko said that Jameson is the legitimate successor of Dorius since according to her he was appointed by Andreas before his death. This implies that if Jameson was of old age by the time Andreas Shoko died, he could have succeeded him rather than Dorius. This implies that in his leadership period, Dorius never used his father's church regalia. The wife to Andreas Shoko took the regalia from where she had hidden it on the anointing of Jameson as the successor of Dorius.

From the historical background we can see that Ezra was not supported by the 1949 Zionist Covenant as well as Apostolic Christian Council of Zimbabwe. The younger claimant to the throne, Ezra Pedzisai alleges that Ndanga the leader of Apostolic Christian Council of Zimbabwe (ACCZ) is using his political connections in ZANU PF and in particular Mujuru to subvert his father's will.[21] The Apostolic Christian Council of Zimbabwe is an African Independent Church ecumenical movement which regulates the operation of African Independent Churches in Zimbabwe. Ezra reiterated that, "Ndanga is using the name of Vice President Mujuru to cow everyone to submit to his whims. It is a shame he deliberately uses the ACCZ's name to achieve his objective. It is against what my father wanted."[22]

Ndanga poured cold water on the claims accusing the younger heir of being childish and working against Christian values. Ndanga said "By resorting to the courts to solve religious cases Ezra is going against the grain of what governs Christianity."[23] Ndanga went on to say, "Succession in the church is clearly defined by their constitution that the eldest son takes over but they want to overturn that for reasons best known to themselves." He even denied that he is using his political connections in the issue of leadership succession in this church. Ndanga said his relationship with ZANU PF is simply that they are both indigenous in scope and character. For him as an organization they support a government that recognizes priesthood just as King David would govern with the priests.

Ezra, on the other hand, accused Ndanga and the ACCZ of poking their nose where they are not wanted. He said, "It's not their (ACCZ) business to determine who leads the church. In any case who is Ndanga to challenge my father's will? I am not claiming to be the heir, I am one." So, the untimely death of Dorius Pedzisai Shoko in a car accident sparked a heavy schism as his two sons Jameson and Ezra Pedzisai Shoko fight over church leadership. The wrangles resulted in church leaders appealing to political protection and this caused a lot of annihilation in the church.

The Concept of Leadership in African Independent Churches (AICs)

Leadership is the key to the understanding of African Independent Churches (AICs). Leadership in AICs is adapted to Shona people's traditional patterns of authority. The notion of inherited leadership or formation of a new tribal unit in the event of congregation squabbles and conflicts is the order of the day. Natural leadership traits such as good conduct, friendly heart, disciplined behavior and charisma often outweigh spiritual and educational qualifications. Rather, in AICs the principal leader is the sum and substance of the whole movement. He is the man in whose hands the future of the church lies. He is deified and is believed to have some mystical powers. The principal leader is regarded as the savior. He is taken as a chief (*ishe*). He is regarded as having direct contact with the supernatural through dreams, visions and speaking in tongues. All in all, leadership in African Independent Churches resembles that of a chief among the Shona people. The leader is at the head of the trichotomous legal system in AICs. He is the senior judge and is assisted by high-ranking clergy and overseers (*Vatariri*). The principal leader is also known as the bishop, archbishop or great bishop. He is the sole leader of the church and everything has to cascade from him to the rest of the adherents. The church is solely in the hands of the principal leader and in most cases the church is taken as his family property. This is the major reason why the issue of inheritance leadership plays a role in the succession of the principal leaders after death. The church is viewed as an extended family property and most office bearers in AICs are relatives of the principal leader. The principal leader is thought to have supernatural powers and this helps him to have a total control over the church. At the same time the attribution of supernatural powers to the principal leader creates a ground for succession problems after his death because those who feared to challenge him would have time to do so. AICs have the principle that the principal leader has to be respected and obeyed completely in every aspect of life. He is the law giver who could not be overruled. He is the one other office bearers fear and he holds ultimate control over the appointment of office bearers. According to deacon Muringo, it is the ability of the principal leader to heal the sick, exorcise evil spirits, and raise the dead and performing miracles which caused people to flock to him.[24] The principal leader then from this narration is "the church." If the principal leader is not there, there is no church.

There are also other leadership offices in AICs and these include: Warden (muongamiri), Minister (*mufundisi*), Evangelist (*muvhangeri*), Deacon (*mudhikoni*), Preacher (*mushumiri*), steward (*gosa*) and overseer (*mutariri*). The bearers of these leadership offices are chosen by the principal leader and in most cases the bearers would be close relatives of the principal leader.

Most African Independent Churches in Zimbabwe consider the following as basic traits for good leadership.[25]

(a) *Moyo munyoro* (a kind heart). This implies that any leader in AICs should be a sympathetic person who is not easily moved to anger.
(b) *Tsika dzakanaka* (good manners). This point to someone leading an exemplary moral life.
(c) *Kubata vanhu zkavakana (to* control people). A good leader should be someone who has the ability to influence others, lead or assert authority.

(d) *Kupa murairo (to* give the law*). A good leader is someone who can lay down the church's laws and induce people to live by it.*
(e) *Munhu ave nenguva yakareba ari musvondo* (Length period of church membership). This implies that a good leader is a person who has been in the church for a long period of time. This means that a good leader is someone who is well versed with the church's practices and one who has had enough time to demonstrate group loyalty.

An analysis of the above traits of a good leader shows that spiritual depth, spiritual maturity, knowledge of the word, persistent prayers and effective preaching are not that vital in determining a good leader. The African Independent Churches put emphasis on the idea that a leader should be a reliable person who can influence and lead others. They consider a person who is not quarrelsome and one who can instill discipline in the church. This implies that charisma plays an integral role in leadership in AICs. The above traits of a good leader are meant to undermine the educational standards or book learning in favor of natural authority leadership talents.

So, leadership in AICs in Zimbabwe is autocratic. It is the principal leader who controls every event in the church. He delegates powers to sub leaders; he holds ultimate control over the appointment of office bearers. The principal leader's supposed mystical powers provide a dimension of authority and directness of control. He has to be respected and obeyed completely. He is the one who any office bearer fears. His authority, words and actions should not be questioned. In all cases after the death of the principal leader, the succession problem would ensue as the contesting candidates will be claiming that each is the rightful heir. In the case of ZAFM, one is claiming that he was chosen by the deceased bishop while the other insists that tradition should be decisive in selecting the true successor. From these remarks, it appears that leadership succession practices can be interpreted, applied and seen differently. More so, leadership succession practices are proving to have a great impact on church's disintegration following the death of a principal leader.

Leadership Succession Practices in the Zion Apostolic Faith Mission

There are a number of leadership succession practices that the Zion Apostolic Faith Mission Church accepts as authentic. Below we have a discussion of some of these practices and we also mention the problems that each practice has to the church at large.

The major succession practice in this church is Tradition. Here leaders are chosen following the cultural customs of kingship. In this succession practice inheritance plays a major role. Traditionally, the eldest son of the king succeeds him after death. In the church scenario, the bishop is seen as a king and his inheritance should be shared according to the African traditional culture. The 1949 Covenant which decreed that upon the death of a bishop, the late bishop's eldest son from his first wife takes over the throne and is supposed to be ordained by the remaining two bishops or their successors at the deceased bishop's memorial service was formulated following the traditional Karanga way of choosing the king's successor. In the church scenario, the covenant has it problems in that it does not consider the issue that the first son from the first wife should be a Christian in the first place. This implies that even if the first son is not a Christian he can succeed the dying bishop using the concept of African cultural practices. More to this, fighting, witchcraft and even assassination can play vitally as the successors to be are thriving to take leadership. This was the case in the ZAFM where Jameson is supported by tradition and the Apostolic Christian Council of Zimbabwe. Ezra on the other hand, had the support of the Council of High Priests even though he is from the lower house and is not even the first born to that lower house. As the situation stands today, Jameson Shoko decries the violence and his faction has applied for a peace order against their rival Ezra Shoko. In an interview Jameson said,

> We are definitely not happy with what happened because a church should not be a place for fighting, but for praying. We are going to apply for a peace order against the Ezra Shoko group because they came and disturbed us as we were praying[26]

This implies that following tradition, leadership can be usurped or acquired by trickery or force and in most cases this has resulted in succession disputes that involve genealogical controversies that is questioning the legitimacy of the persons claiming to be the successors to the principal leader. So, while tradition is the most used method - in leadership succession in ZAFM, it has its own problems and in most cases it has led to disputes, violence and annihilation within the church. All these often lead to power wrangles and schism. Tradition which in ZAFM is seen in the face of the 1949 covenant has often caused division and succession problems in the Zionists in Zimbabwe. After the death of Samuel Mutendi, Bishop David Masuka ordained Ruben in opposition to Nehemiah Mutendi following the 1949 declaration. Vital to note is the contention that Samuel himself had appointed Nehemiah to be his successor by word of mouth but he was younger than Rueben.[27] David Masuka working under the dictates of the 1949 covenant anointed Rueben and this sparked the greatest schism in the Zion Christian Church ever. Upon his death Dorius also appointed a younger brother Ezra by word of mouth and this was against the dictates of the 1949 covenant. This implies that the very people who were supposed to guard and apply the 1949 covenant are the ones who broke it and as a result succession problem looms as the brothers would be fighting over legitimacy to the throne.

The other practice used by the ZAFM in choosing the successor is the use of the constitution. This practice has come as a result of social change among the African communities. The influence of religious organizations like the Theological Education by Extension has led some leaders to appoint leaders following the constitution as Dorius did before he died through the word of mouth. The Zion Apostolic Faith Mission church constitution states that one should be:

- the eldest son of the bishop from his first wife if he is to succeed him
- a member of the church
- living a morally upright life

So, it was through the constitution that Dorius had chosen Ezra as his successor. Even though Ezra was not the first born to Dorius, he had other qualifications which made Dorius to appoint him as his successor. Ezra as seen by his supporters has been working with his father in conducting church issues as compared to Jameson who rebelled against his own father before he died. However, the constitution of ZAFM and the appointment of Ezra as the successor is against the 1949 covenant which was made by the Zionist founders in Zimbabwe. More to this, the practices itself undermine the African cultural values which forms the foundations of African initiated churches.[28] So, the use of the constitution to appoint the successor has its own problems in the ZAFM church. The traditionalists in the church do not support this practice and this is the major reason why Ezra is not supported by the elders of the church.

Political intervention seems to play a role in the succession practices of the ZAFM church in particular and the AICs in general. It is interesting to note that in Zimbabwe currently, the political affiliation and the role of the ecumenical body which in this case is the Apostolic Christian Council of Zimbabwe (ACCZ), override all other succession practices which are traditional and constitutional. The political situation in Zimbabwe does not allow anyone who is not pro-ruling party to lead in any situation. The AICs have become the breeding ground of political leaders' supporters. Most politicians attend the gatherings of AICs so that they will have ample time to solicit for votes in these churches because the churches attract a lot of people. As a means to gain support, politicians help some AICs to become leaders after the death of the principal leader so as to make sure that the leader will know who puts him in power together with his supporters on the voting days. In most cases politicians support the leader who will be pulling a large number of the church or one who is on the disadvantaged side and they will elevate him to power and thereafter ask him to support them. This succession practice has problems in that it does not look at the religious affiliation of the candidate to succeed the bishop as was the case with Jameson. More so, the practice has problems in that the church will be turned slowly into a political parlor other than a place of worship.

Charisma is the other way of assuming leadership in the Zionists churches in Zimbabwe after the death of the principal leader. A charismatic leader is someone who gathers followers through dint of personality and charm, rather than any form of external power or authority.[29] In most cases a charismatic leader pays much attention to the people they are talking to at any one moment, making them feel like they are, for that time, the most important people in the world.

Charismatic leaders pay a great deal of attention in scanning and reading their environment, and are good at picking up the moods and concerns of both individuals and larger audiences.[30] They hone their actions and words to suit the situation. Charismatic leaders use a wide range of methods to manage their image and may engender trust through visible self-sacrifice and taking personal risks in the name of their beliefs. They show great confidence in their followers. They are very persuasive and make very effective use of body language as well as verbal language.

Religious leaders, too, use charisma by focusing strongly on making the group very clear and distinct, separating it from other groups. In doing so, they create an unchallengeable position for themselves. Charismatic leaders seek to instill both commitment to ideological goals and also devotion to themselves. Despite their charm and apparent concern, the charismatic leader may well be somewhat more concerned with themselves than anyone else. A typical experience with them is that whilst you are talking with them, it is like being bathed in a warm and pleasant glow, in which they are very convincing. Yet afterwards, the sunbeam of their attention is moved elsewhere. This is the practice that Ezra is using. As a lecturer, he is eloquent and verbose and is managing to conquer the minds of the large group of the church. Since he is backed by the Council of High Priests, he has managed to occupy the church's premises and is using his charisma to lure more adherents to his side.

The Church's vote as a leadership succession practice in ZAFM is not as vitally important since it is overridden by other practices like tradition, constitution and charisma. However, the adherents have to some extent the liberty to choose their own successor but the process has to be in line with either the church's tradition or constitution.

Appointment by word of mouth by the deceased principal leader seems to be one of the ways through which successors are chosen in ZAFM. The principal leader can say by word of mouth who his successor would be or can write a will to that effect. This is the kind of situation in the Ezra Shoko issue. For him, the words of mouth by the father should stand as true and legitimate. This method was also used when Samuel Mutendi died. Samuel chose Nehemiah by word of mouth but he was not his first son from the first wife. This means Samuel Mutendi who is one of leaders who formulated the 1949 covenant did not follow it himself. However, it can be argued that as in the case of Dorius Shoko these leaders would choose their heirs who are not the first sons because the first sons will not be Christians or will not be following their fathers' footsteps. Using the Esau and Jacob story, if the first child from the first wife is not a Christian he will not be considered as a first child because for them he does not exist if he is not following the father's religious steps.

Recommendations

Ubuntu should be the most prevalent method in the succession issues of the ZAFM. From a leadership perspective, Ubuntu requires that leaders model the way for others. As a role model, the leader legitimizes his or her leadership by a commitment to such African values as honesty, sincerity, truthfulness, compassion, empathy, dignity, and respect for others.[31] Values reflect the most basic characteristic of adaptations that guide individuals in deciding into which situations they should enter and what they should do in them.[32] By committing to ethical behavior, the leader models ethical values and characteristics for others. One should not expect others to exhibit ethical behavior if one cannot oneself demonstrate it. Ethical values are critical to the success of an enterprise, because they serve to guide an entrepreneur on ethical issues.

The Ubuntu leadership framework requires that leadership not only inspires a shared vision but also has a vision for the future that offers direction for others. Enterprise is communal, with the derived benefits shared rather than accruing to the individual. Outcomes for the group are more important than individual goals. At the same time, decision making under the principle of Ubuntu is circular and inclusive. Polyocular vision, as opposed to monocular vision, allows for multiple viewpoints, and diversity of perspectives. Differences in what is normal and acceptable are allowable.

Applying Ubuntu to leadership succession contributes to changing and transforming the world. Leaders search for opportunities to initiate change through people. Rather than being forced on people, change comes through a process of openness and transparency; people come to accept change. Decisions to change come by consensus rather than inheritance, constitution or declaration and there should be circularity in the decision-making process. The process is iterative, and decisions are revised as many times as necessary before the final one is made. By using Ubuntu, the church will be gradually transforming to meet the challenges of a changing global environment.[33]

An important organizing element of Ubuntu is interconnectedness and interdependency. No man or woman is an island, and as such it is important for people in leadership to recognize this aspect. Building relationships with others is a hallmark of good leadership in general, but an absolute necessity for Ubuntu. In building relationships one builds trust thereby fostering collaboration and reciprocity. By accepting our interconnectedness, a leader operating from the principles of Ubuntu will also have the desire to empower others. Empowerment of others means strengthening others, allowing them to act on their own initiative and believe in themselves.

Another leadership principle derived from the concept of Ubuntu is the notion of collectivism and solidarity. The African social culture is generally collectivist, in which the needs of the community or society trump the needs of the individual. We can also think of it by way of the gestalt principle of organization whereby the whole is greater than the sum of its parts. A collectivist mentality encourages teamwork and a noncompetitive environment. Such an environment promotes solidarity and a spirit of working together toward common goals and the good of the church as a whole.[34] Ubuntu will to some extent reduce leadership wrangles, schisms and blood fighting in the church. The church leader who demonstrates Ubuntu will empower others to act and nurture their growth and creativity through mentoring and building relationships. Ubuntu recognizes the contribution of others and further empowering them.

So, the church lessons from Ubuntu are that collective responsibility is key to church leadership succession practices. Squabbles and schism can dissipate the church's energy and diminish its ability to unite people. Collective responsibility also applies to the fair distribution of benefits and efforts. When some people are perceived as unjustifiably benefitting more than others from the church's collective efforts, this will lead to resentment and strained relationship, adversely affecting team spirit and church performance.

The other recommendation to AICs is that they should be able to plan leadership succession in advance. AICs must plan for succession in good time, and have a clear and effective system for identifying their successors. The successors must undergo well thought through programs that will prepare them to take charge of the church when their times come. In line with this, the principal leader must ensure that appointments to leadership positions are conducted with complete transparency and accountability. The process followed to select new leaders must leave the people in the church satisfied. The churches must have succession plans well in advance to ensure smooth transitions from one leader to the next. All in all, AICs need to train successors who will lead people to the targeted position.

AICs should thrive for teamwork for the benefit of the people when a leader dies and a new leader is to be chosen. Church leadership should not be determined by political leaders but by the religious people themselves. Greed should not be part of leadership succession system. Whoever has been chosen should be supported for the furtherance of the church.

More to all of the above, AICs should adopt a better hermeneutical approach in their understanding of the Bible in so far as leadership succession practice is concerned. This will reduce chances for schism, wrangles and violence in churches. There is a need for uniform policy on succession practices in AICs in general and ZAFM in particular. The issue of traditional succession practices should not be accommodated in the church. Rather, the church should not be taken as a family property for this has potential for destabilizing the family and the church at large. The principal leader should not impose or appoint his successor at the expense of the legitimate one. AICs should not have divergence leadership succession methods. There should be uniformity in the way leaders succeed leaders in African Independent Churches.

Notes

1 M.L. Daneel, *Old and New in Southern Shona Independent Churches*, Vols. 1–2 (The Hague: Mouton, 1974).
2 Ibid.
3 A. Hastings, *The Church in Africa 1450–1950* (Oxford: Clarendon Press, 1994), 22.
4 Ibid.
5 Jules-Rosette Benetta, "Prophecy and Leadership in the Maranke Church," in *African Christianity: Patterns of Religious Continuity*, ed. G. Bond, et al. (New York, 1979), 109–136.
6 James L. Cox *Expressing the Sacred: An Introduction to the Phenomenology of Religion* (Harare: University of Zimbabwe Publications, 1992), 15.
7 Ibid.
8 Chitando Ezra, *Sprit-Type Churches as Holistic Healing Movements: A study of the Johane Masowe Wechishanu Church* (Unpublished B.A. Honors diss., Harare: University of Zimbabwe, 1989).
9 M.L. Daneel, "African Independent Church Pneumatology and the Salvation of All Creation," *International Review of Mission*, 82,326 (1993): 143–166.

10 Gerald Chikozho Mazarire, "The Rise and Fall of the Dutch Reformed Church (DRC) in The Victoria Circle 1888–1950: A Dissenting View of the Church's Alleged Invention of Chikaranga with Particular Reference to the Chibi Circuit," *New Dimensions in History Seminar Paper No. 5* (Department of History, University of Zimbabwe, May 28, 2004).
11 M.L. Daneel, *Quest for Belonging: An Introduction to the Study of African Independent Churches* (Gweru: Mambo Press, 1987).
12 T.O. Ranger, *The African Voice in Southern Rhodesia* (London: Heinemann, 1970).
13 Mazarire, "The Rise and Fall," 20.
14 Ibid.
15 Ibid.
16 M.L. Daneel, *Old and New in Southern Shona Independent Churches: Leadership and Fission Dynamics*, Vol. 3 (Gweru: Mambo Press, 1988).
17 Daneel, *Old and New*.
18 Tranos Mugari, *Interview* by Clemence Makamure. Leadership. April 13, 2019.
19 Muringo Mugove, *Interview* by Clemence Makamure. Leadership. March 14, 2019.
20 Ibid.
21 Shoko Ezra, *Interview* by Clemence Makamure. Leadership. March 15, 2019.
22 Ibid.
23 Ndanga Johanes, *Interview* by Clemence Makamure. Leadership Succession. March 19, 2019.
24 Muringo Muringo, *Interview* by Clemence Makamure. Leadership Succession. March 14, 2019.
25 M.L. Daneel, *Old and New in Southern Shona Independent Churches*, Vol. 1 (The Hague: Mouton, 1971).
26 Shoko Jameson, *Interview* by Makamure Clemence. March 15, 2019.
27 M.L. Daneel, "The Growth and Significance of Shona Independent Churches," in *Christianity South of the Zambezi*, Vol. ii, ed. M.F.C. Bourdillon (Gweru: Mambo Press, 1977).
28 Daneel, *Quest for Belonging*.
29 Chiku Malunga, *Understanding Organisational Leadership through Ubuntu* (London: Adonis and Abbey, 2009).
30 Malunga, *Understanding Organisational Leadership*.
31 Ibid.
32 Ibid.
33 Ibid.
34 Ibid.

10. The Place of Women in African-Initiated Churches in Zimbabwe: The Case of Zionist and Apostolic Churches

VENGESAI CHIMININGE AND CLEMENCE MAKAMURE

Introduction

There are so many Zionist and Apostolic Churches in Zimbabwe. These churches are categorized as African-Initatied Churches (AICs). Daneel identified three major groups of Zionist Churches which are the Zion Christian Church, Zion Apostolic Church and Zion Apostolic Faith Mission.[1] Under the Apostolic Churches there are several of them, but the major ones are the Johanne Marange Apostolic Church, African Apostolic Church, and Johanne Masowe Apostolic Church. Togarasei noted that "demographically, AICs in Zimbabwe have now taken over a significant percentage of the Christian population in urban areas. This is evidenced by the fact that during the weekends, shades of trees are turned into seas of red, white, blue and all sorts of colors of religious regalia."[2] For Gunda, such a move summarized the impact of AICs in Zimbabwe.[3] Very little research has been done in terms of the role of women in these churches. Therefore, the focus of this chapter is to assess the place of women in AICs in Zimbabwe with special reference to the Zionist and Apostolic churches in Chivi district. The chapter examines how traditional culture has been used to subjugate women in these churches.

Methodology

The study made use of the phenomenological method as a chief paradigm in data collection and analysis. The method is sometimes known as the comparative method to the study of religion. According to Cox the phenomenology of religion as a research paradigm requires the researcher to begin by suspending or bracketing previous ideas, thoughts, opinions, and beliefs of a community you are studying.[4]

By doing so, the researchers observe the phenomena of religion as they appear rather than as they are understood through opinions formed prior to observation. Academic theories about the nature, function, purpose or meaning of religion must also be suspended or bracketed.[5] This study applied *epoche*, empathy, describing and naming the phenomena in collecting, presenting and analyzing data to do with the role of women in AICs in general and Zionist and Apostolic Churches in particular. This method is an enterprise that is preoccupied with bringing to the fore differences and similarities between two or more entities, be it historical epochs, personalities, events or components. In this case the position of women in the Zionist and Apostolic churches in Chivi District of Masvingo province. Before we examine the place of women in Zionist and Apostolic churches, it is better for us to have a general picture of the issue of gender in Zimbabwe.

Gender Inequality in Zimbabwe: An Overview

The fact that Zimbabwe is a signatory to the international convention on Millennium Development Goals particularly its concentration on goal number three persuaded the authors of this chapter to do situational analysis of gender inequality in Zimbabwe. This is done in such a way that we see whether AICs in Zimbabwe are contributing to the government program of trying to reduce gender inequality. A recent survey by the Southern African Gender Protocol Alliance (SAGPA) noted that women in Zimbabwe still lag behind their male counterparts in critical areas such as education, economic empowerment and the advancement of their rights.[6] In a report titled *Southern African Development Community (SADC) Gender Protocol 2012 Barometer: Zimbabwe*, produced by the "Zimdiaspora: voice of the voiceless" underscored that "the regional gender body points out that Zimbabwe has allocated meager resources towards achieving gender parity, hence its low ranking despite government boasting of making considerable strides in developing a normative framework to advance women's status and rights as citizens. Less than 1% of the allocations in the 2012 national budget are for advancing gender equality and women's rights." Social critics say the quantum of representation of women is not necessarily about quantity, but about their contribution to the quality of their lives that is an issue which even women serving in cabinet or parliament have failed to effectively address.[7] This has been necessitated by the traditional setup of

Zimbabwe society which was and still is patriarchal in nature. However, there are efforts being done by the government of Zimbabwe to uplift women in all spheres of life ranging from education, politics and economics. In education there are various Non-Governmental Organizations which are there to support girl child education and these are the Campaign for Female Education (CAMFED), Forum for African Women Educationalists Zimbabwe (FAWEZ) and others.[8]

In politics women are elected as counselors, members of Parliament (MPs) as well as appointed as ministers and district administrators. This is why the vice president of the Republic of Zimbabwe, Joice Mujuru, is a woman. Women's representation in Parliament more than doubled from 17% following the 2008 general elections, to 35% in the elections on July 31, 2013. Zimbabwe now joins the ranks of more than 30 countries worldwide that have used a special electoral quota system to increase women's representation in Parliament to at least 30%, which is considered the minimum for collective action.[9] As a result, women now comprise 124 of the 350 MPs in Zimbabwe's new Parliament, including 86 women in the National Assembly—60 in the reserved seats and 26 elected directly to the 210 constituency seats.[10]

In the economic sector there are so many women playing key roles in Zimbabwe. It is very unfortunate that the percentage of women in the business sector is unknown. However, what is so clear according to the ZimTrade database is that women are mostly active in the processed foods, arts and crafts, services, horticulture, cosmetics and clothing and textiles and even engineering. However, most women with registered companies who are manufacturing are concentrated in Harare and Bulawayo. Those who are outside these two cities are mainly into agricultural business. Currently there are no statistics as to how much women in businesses are contributing towards GDP. However, there has been the realization that women contribute significantly towards GDP and employment since the economic woes of 2007 and 2008. Women played a critical role and ensured the survival of families through cross border trade. These informal businesses need to be formalized so that their performances are captured in the mainstream of statistical data collection, so that authentic figures regarding women businesses contribution to GDP can be ascertained.[11]

In religion, particularly in Pentecostal churches women are ordained as pastors, deaconess and some as bishops. For instance, Mrs. Eunor Guti is the current Bishop of Zimbabwe Assemblies of God (ZAOGA). Be that as it may, it should be noted that although there is a great change on the status of women in politics very little has changed in AICs especially in Zionist and Apostolic Churches.

Status of Women in Africa Initiated Churches

Ethnographic and historical studies of women and religion have thoroughly documented patterns of women's exclusion from positions of significant religious leadership. In many African societies, women have active religious lives, yet ecclesiastical hierarchies rarely include women, and official or great traditional religious concepts generally reflect men's and not women's priorities and life experiences. Scattered throughout the world and centuries, however, there are instances of religious traditions in which women have been the leaders, most participants in congregations, and in which women's concerns have been central.[12]

In the available literature, the most puzzling issue is the immense power and influence which female leaders often wield in these churches, contrary to male dominance in the mainstream churches. In some of these churches, prophetesses have left indelible marks on the African continent, for example, Alice Lakwena of Uganda and Mother Jane Bloomer of Freetown. Several scholarly works have been published on the causative and development of AICs in Africa and Zimbabwe. Ndeda in Kenya explored the connections between gender and the independency Christian ideology in the formation of new social relations as well as affirmation of traditional relations of domination between men and women.[13] Molobi also examined the marginalization of women and patriarchy in AICs in South Africa. He discovered that in South Africa women in AICs have initiated and established their own churches.[14]

In Ivory Coast, Marie Lalou was inspired by a dream to start a cult so women have ceremonial leadership and a clear sense of gender roles is maintained. In the movement of William Harries Wade women become leaders and gender roles are well balanced but polygamy is not renounced. Such independent churches believe that it is the Holy Spirit that raises people to positions of authority irrespective of gender. There is Mary Akatsa of Kawangware and Maria Aoko of Legio Maria who carved a niche for themselves in Kenya's religious history.[15] Bengt Sundkler says that from early times the church was like a women's movement. It functioned as a women's liberation movement long before that term was invented. Indeed, he points out numerous examples of churches in South Africa where women excelled as leaders, but he also gives instances of the efforts of women that have failed to be fully recognized and appreciated just because of gender. An example is that of Grace Tshabala who brought great revival in her church but was just described as "after all she was merely a woman."[16] Her husband and other Zionist leaders admitted, "Yes, they can pray all night but of course man's prayer is stronger, for he is the head and leads in everything." Perhaps in South Africa, the fact that women lead as presidents of churches, while others carry both the financial burdens and evangelistic outreach, is Zionist great contribution to African society. Zion gave women a central and honored position, in healing activities, in worship and social life of the church. New emotional contacts of care and concern were found where women and men could meet on equal terms. These terms were regarded as those of the ultimate authority, the Holy Spirit.[17]

Status of Women in Shona Traditional Religion

It should be noted that the status of women in AICs in Zimbabwe can be well understood if we look at the status of women in Shona Traditional Religion as well as the biblical interpretation of these churches. Traditional Shona society was patriarchal in nature and family setup was extended in nature. Daneel, an expert in the study of the Shona independent churches, published three volumes entitled "The Old and New" where he examined the relationship between Shona traditional culture (The Old) and AICs (The New) and he discovered that there is continuity of the old traditional practices in AICs.[18] According to Chimininge, a lot of beliefs and practices in AICs are adopted from Shona culture.[19] This means that traditional forms of education, leadership, governance and religion of the Shona society shape the organizational nature of AICs.

However, there is need to note that there is ambivalence on the status of women in traditional Shona society. On one hand, women were devaluated and treated as second class citizens. For instance, women were not involved in decision making. They were not allowed to own land and property, participate in family council (*dare*) since they were treated as aliens (*vatorwa*). Their duties were to gather food, bear and keep children. Women were living under the control of the extended family. The boy child enjoyed a special place in African traditional cultures. He represents the potential of the lineage to grow. Therefore most families in AICs preferred sending the boy child to school at the expense of the girl child. This entails that a boy child is empowered in these churches.

In Shona traditional society, women were not allowed to be chiefs (*Ishe*), headman (*mambo*) village head (*sabhuku*) neither were they allowed to inherit their father's estate. AICs also borrowed this practice from the Shona conception of governance and leadership and applied it to their churches. As a result, women are not allowed to be bishops, priests, deacons, preachers or enter into the church with uncovered or unveiled head.[20] Furthermore, they are not allowed to attend church services when they are in their menstrual periods or with a new baby less than a month old. The interviewee Misias Hadzikamwi a Minister in the Zion Christian Church argued that "all these teachings are based on our culture which is in agreement with the Deutronomistic and Leviticus laws."[21]

On the other hand, Sackey noted that in African traditional society women were valued since they were given space for leadership. In West Africa for example, women functioned as mediums, diviners, prophetesses, medicine persons, herbalists and priestesses. They owned deities, cults and shrines.[22] However, among the Shona the girl child was considered an asset only to the extent that she will bring bride-wealth (*pfuma*) to her parents.[23]

Be that as it may, we can see that the Shona tradition culture is very ambiguous on the role of women in society since on one hand it supports while on the other hand it inhibits women's leadership roles. What then is the biblical understanding of the status of women in AICs?

The Bible and Women in AICs

Daneel argued that AIC founding fathers like Samuel Mutendi of the Zion Christian Church, Andreas Shoko of the Zion Apostolic Faith Mission Church, Peter Makamba of the Zion Apostolic Church, Johanne Marange of the Apostolic Church and many others discovered that certain biblical passages agreed with their African culture.[24] As a result, they used those passages to support their church doctrines. Texts like I Timothy 2:11–14 which says a woman must learn in silence and be completely submissive;" and 1 Corinthians 14: 34–35 which says "As in all the congregations of the Saints, women should remain silent in the churches. They are not allowed to speak but must be in submission as the law says. If they want to inquire about something, they should ask their own husbands at home; for it is disgraceful for a woman to speak in the church" are taken very seriously in the Zionist and Apostolic churches in Chivi district.

Basing on the above biblical texts and Shona traditional culture, the Zionist and Apostolic churches had constructed "institutional masculinities" with gendered space. This is because of their emphasis on role delegation where men are represented by the Petrine symbol whose duty is to perform all the "public" duties of the church which are embedded in the church leadership roles. For the AICs, women are represented by the Marian symbol, where women's roles are confined to the "private sphere" where their role is mainly in the kitchen and motherhood is the central role for women in society.

Shona feminist theologian Tapiwa Praise Mapuranga argues that, the prevailing process from the theology in AICs is that, "women are supposed to be subordinate to men." As a result, AICs present a very difficult situation in which women should be taught whatever they may need to ask from their husbands at home.[25] Luke Guni of the Johanne Marange Apostolic Church argued that placing women in leadership position in and outside the church somehow weakens biblical authority.[26]

The Status of Women in Zionist and Apostolic Churches in Zimbabwe

A feminist theologian Loveness Mabhunu argues that despite the inroads that women have had in AICs in Harare, consideration of personal testimonies and observations have indicated that they still have limited roles in leadership positions.[27] Women are recognized as healers, midwives and prophetesses. But all women in AICs, even prophetesses, are excluded from the church hierarchy. The expression of equality in leadership is denied for women in both Zionist and Apostolic Churches. An interviewee, who is a member of the Johanne Marange Apostolic Church (JMAC) said that the JMAC forbade women from preaching in line with the Pauline Instruction … 1 Timothy 2:11–14.[28] In JMAC prophetesses are also excluded from positions of authority and influence such as occupying positions of secretary general or treasurer.

For Mukonyora, AICs can be labeled as a gendered space because all of them emanated from the so-called patriarchal societies and space is extended towards women.[29] In African Apostolic Church (AAC) of Paul Mwazha, there is clear evidence of gender discrimination against women. Matorofa, a full member of the AAC, said that "in church it is a taboo for a woman to stand in front of men and preach." Women are not allowed to talk in church or to appear as the leaders of the congregation. This is because the church bases its teachings on the books of Deuteronomy and Leviticus as well as some selected passages like 1 Timothy 2:11–15 and 1 Corinthians 14.

In the Apostolic Church of Johanne Marange, women's participation is curtailed even more because of the church's appreciation of Levitical laws. These include, as highlighted by Oduyoye, menstruation avoidances which exclude women who have just given birth and those undergoing their monthly flow of blood. The laws of the church were formulated by men who were very strict on women. As such, women are restricted in worship on natural and biological experiences.

The Apostolic Church of Johanne Marange is one other church that has been noted with some discriminatory characteristics in relation to the status of women in the church. The writers of this chapter observed that subordination of women has been vivified by the church at large as normal and women are taught to be subordinate both in the church and at home. Consequently, there is no leadership space for women since they are not considered as participants in the leadership hierarchies as well as preaching. Biblical passage like Genesis 2 is taken very literal and women are taken as "just helpers of men."

In this regard, it can be argued that the Apostolic and Zionist Churches in Zimbabwe give women opportunity to articulate their voices especially in group identities, and thus, the individual inherent power tends to be outshined in these numbers. As such, it appears that position of women in these churches may be regarded as created only when the less important leadership roles and individual leadership capabilities are concerned. Patriarchal tendencies in the church tend to give the male more chances of accessing leadership, more so even as individuals, rather than in groups.

However, even though women are subordinated in Zionist and Apostolic churches, there are instances where they are recognized. The writers of this chapter discovered that in the Zion Christian Church of Samuel Mutendi, women occupy functional roles like, prophetesses, choristers, healers, and "itinerant preachers," among a variety of other functions. According to Chitando women prophets have played a significant role in the rapid spread of AICs in Southern Africa. Apostolic women in their distinctive white garments and Zionist women in colorful outfits have become an integral part of urban life in the region. Prophecy is an important leadership role for which women are recognized especially in the Zionist and Apostolic churches in Zimbabwe. These AICs believe in the manifestation of the Holy Spirit as a result, they believe that it is the Holy Spirit that raises someone in the position of prophecy. In this regard, both Zionist and Apostolic churches believe that prophesy is a role and not an office. This was supported by Misias Hadzikamwi of the Zion Christian Church that prophecy is momentarily because you can only enter that "office" when you are possessed by the Holy Spirit.

So, in Zionist and Apostolic churches in Zimbabwe, women are allowed to assume ritualistic roles but are excluded from the church hierarchy.

Discussion and Analysis

From the explanation above, one is tempted to ask about the future of women in AICs in general and Apostolic and Zionist Churches in particular. Is it possible for these churches to change their perception of women? It is women who constitute most members within Zionist and Apostolic churches, and they have been central in the emergence of transnational networks that have emerged. Several reasons have been proffered in an effort to explain the dominance of women in AICs. One of the key attractions is the space that has been granted to women in these new religious movements. They can express themselves fully, and occupy key offices as prophetesses and healers especially in the Zionist type. For instance, it is generally noted that the 1950s and early 1960s was a decade of women prophetesses like Alice Lenshina of Lumpa Church of Zambia and Mai Chaza of the Guta raJehovah Church in Zimbabwe. They began the long road of tearing apart the curtain of patriarchy within the church. AICs cultivated a fertile ground for the participation of women. Lilian Dube cited a good example of Mai Chaza of the Guta raJehovah Church (GRJ) (that is the City of God Church) who emerged as a prominent woman who transcends the socio-cultural hierarchy, defying the imposed status of a perpetual minor. She throws into relief the question of the position and status of women in the church. So from that time to the present women leadership status in AICs runs parallel to that of men. AICs have no doubt made a paradigm shift. This substantiates the claim made by Massey in Mapuranga that gender space "is always in the process of being made. It is never finished; never closed." This being the case, the writers of this chapter noted that the gendered dimension of AICs is always affected by change. Gradually, women are beginning to get space within these settings. Chimininge discovered that in the Zion Christian Church of Samuel Mutendi women, particularly the wives of the bishop and other senior office-bearers, can preach on conferences and church service, such a move was not allowed during the leadership of Samuel Mutendi. Here we see the current bishop in a paradigm shift from the tradition Zion. However, the situation is different when it comes to the Zionist Churches of the sacred cord (Zion *Yetambo*). In this brand of Zion women are not allowed to stand in front of men. They are allowed to preach only in the women conference or council known as *ruwadzano*. But this is done when the high priests (*muongamiri*) and other teachers of the word (*Vafundisi*) are present. Daneel discovered that in these churches there are deep connections between the landscape and women.[30] In the Johanne Masowe Apostolic Church (JMAC), it is argued that women are closely tied to the land and its sacred places. In as much as the earth has healing powers, so do women in these churches play a paramount role in healing ceremonies.

According to Mwaura "AICs are said to particularly provide women with a chance to recover their traditional status and positions that had been undermined by the teachings of the mission churches ... AICs are also regarded as sites of women's liberation. They have provided women with a forum where they find liberation from ever present fears of witchcraft and other forces that undermine their well-being." This is also true of the Johanne Masowe Apostolic Church, as documented by Mukonyora. Mukonyora says that "Besides attending the prayer meetings in large numbers, they were active participants in ritual activities, especially at healing ceremonies where woman-oriented matters of fertility and the protection of life, with their corresponding feminine religious symbols, took centre stage."

Researchers of this chapter observed that within the Apostolic and Zionist churches the issue of empowerment, space and land provisioning to women still needs to be given high consideration. Apostolic and Zionist churches can still be regarded as gendered spaces necessarily because equality of the sexes coexist with complete male monopolization of leadership roles, religious laws and authority in community affairs. For this reason, this chapter recommends that for Zionist and Apostolic churches to survive the wave of social change there is need to address the issue of the liberation of women. In this case both men and women need to develop a consciousness of gender related issues. AICs need to consider, understand and evaluate both long term and historical effects and current realities. In a way, both the Bible and traditional teachings need to be understood and evaluated, as far as the status of women is concerned. Men also need to be liberated from the attitudes and structures that bind them. This implies that male and female liberation are two sides of the same coin; both are necessary for liberation and wholeness in the true church of Christ.

AICs in Zimbabwe should form ecumenical movements like those in South Africa which can teach their members to change their mind set. They should work with other Interdenominational movements of women in evangelical and Pentecostal churches so that they can learn from them. Finally, there is need for increased education for both men and women through training in theological and leadership programs. The theological education will assist the leaders and lay people in AIC to read and reinterpret the Bible for it to be contextually relevant. As a result, members of the AICs in general and the Zionist and Apostolic sects will be able to reinterpret their cultural practices in order for it to be in line with changes taking place in the world.

Conclusion

The unequal status of women in the Zionist and Apostolic churches in Zimbabwe is unchanged. Women were excluded from leadership positions in the church because male leaders were not open to change and created no space for them. However, women in other AICs have made considerable efforts to prove that the sharing of power by men with women is vital to normal life. The situation is not only confined to AICs but even in various Christian denominations, women have been striving to open up the churches' hierarchies to the participation of women and to increase women's representation in church and decision-making bodies. Those who do not find an immediate scope of advancement within the church are potential seceders (like Mai Chaza of the Guta Rajehovah Church—City of God Church) unless new positions are created for them with new responsibilities.

What we are saying is that women's roles in AICs vary tremendously. Some AICs were founded on fundamentalist principles which promote a traditional or even regressive social position of women while others are welfare oriented as practiced in the Zion Christian Church of Samuel Mutendi. Consequently, it should be noted that with the modernization and globalization processes and the general shift or change in society using technology in recent years, the status of women in several AICs is left unchanged. With special reference to Zionist and Apostolic churches in Zimbabwe our observations and experiences are that despite some changes on the healing ministry women are still occupying lower posts as compared to men.

Notes

1 M.L. Daneel, Old and New in Southern Shona Independent Churches: Leadership and Fission Dynamics, Vol. 3 (Gweru: Mambo Press, 1988): 273.
2 Lovemore Togarasei, "Modern Pentecostalism as an Urban Phenomenon: The Case of the Family of God Church in Zimbabwe," *Exchange* 34 (2005): 349–375.
3 Regies Masiiwa Gunda, "From Text to Practice: The Role of the Bible in Daily Living of African People Today," *Bible in Africa Studies* 4 (2011).
4 James L. Cox, *Expressing the Sacred: An Introduction to Phenomenology of Religion* (Harare: University of Zimbabwe, 1996), 26.
5 Ibid., 27.
6 http://www.zimdiaspora.com/index.php?option=com_content&view=article&id=11371:zimbabwe-remains-ravaged-by-gender-inequality. Retrieved on June 13, 2014.
7 Ibid.
8 Ibid.
9 http://www.unwomen.org/en/news/stories/2013/9/zimbabwe-women-mps-sworn-in#sthash.Cslw8HEI.dpuf. Retrieved on January 12, 2014.
10 Ibid.
11 Ibid.
12 Sered Susan Starr, *Priestess, Mother, Sacred Sister: Religions Dominated by Women* (New York: OUP, 1994).
13 M.A. Ndeda, "Nomiya Luo Church: A Gender Analysis of the Dynamics of an African Independent Church among the Luo of Siaya District in the Twentieth Century and Beyond," in *Gender, Literature and Religion in Africa*. Codesria Gender Series 4 (2005): 49–78,.
14 Victor Molobi, "The Marginalization of Women in the African Initiated Churches in South Africa, 1882 to 2006, Pretoria," *Research Institute for Theology and Religion*, UNISA, 2008.

15 B. Sundkler, *Bantu prophets in South Africa* (London: Oxford University Press, 1961).
16 Ibid.
17 Ibid.
18 M.L. Daneel, *Old and New in the Southern Shona Independent Churches*, Vol. 1 (The Hague: Mouton, 1971).
19 Vengesai Chimininge, *An Analysis of Myths and Rituals Associated with the Origins and Development of Zion Christian Church of Samuel Mutendi in Zimbabwe* (Pretoria: University of South Africa, 2012).
20 Tenson Muringo, *Interview*, by Vengesai Chimininge, Women and in Shona Traditional Religion. March 10, 2014.
21 Misias Hadzikamwi, *Interview*, by Vengesai Chimininge, Women and in Shona Traditional Religion. March 10, 2014.
22 B.M. Sackey, *New Directions in Gender and Religion: The Changing Status of Women in African Independent Churches* (Oxford: Lexington Books, 2005), 200.
23 Misias Hadzikamwi, *Interview*, by Vengesai Chimininge, Women and in Shona Traditional Religion. March 10, 2014.
24 M.L. Daneel, *Quest for Belonging: An Introduction to the Study of African Independent Churches* (Gweru: Mambo Press, 1987).
25 Tapiwa Praise Mapuranga, *AICs as a Gendered Space in Harare, Zimbabwe: Revisiting the Role and Place of Women* (Pretoria: UNISA Press, 2009), 303–317.
26 Luke Guni, *Interview*, by Vengesai Chimininge, Women in Apostolic Churches. March 16, 2014.
27 Loveness Mabhunu, "Revolting against the Biblical and Traditional Stereotypes of Women? Women Prophets in African Initiated Churches," in *Faith in the City: The Role and Place of Religion in Harare*, ed. L. Togarasei and E. Chitando (Uppsala: Swedish Science Press, 2010).
28 Luke Guni, *Interview*, by Clemence Makamure, Women in Apostolic Churches. April 13, 2014.
29 Isabel Mukonyora, *Wandering a Gendered Wilderness: Suffering and Healing in an African Initiated Church* (New York: Peter Lang, 2007).
30 M.L. Daneel 1979:29

11. *Pick Up Your Cash and Follow Me: Pentecostalism, Prosperity and Socioeconomic Empowerment in Southwest Cameroon*

DANIEL PRATT MORRIS-CHAPMAN

There has been much research concerning whether or not Christianity has a positive socioeconomic impact. In this chapter, I want to examine these questions from within the Cameroonian context—exploring whether some of the expressions of Pentecostalism found within this nation have empowered people economically. Moreover, I also want to probe whether the emphasis these churches place on self-enterprise has had a social impact—particularly regarding women.

Inner-Worldly Asceticism

In *The Protestant Ethic and the Spirit of Capitalism* (1904)[1] Max Weber argued that the rise of Protestantism played an essential role in the development of capitalist societies. In particular he maintained that the emphasis Calvinism places on confirming ones divine election implanted an "inner-worldly asceticism" which gave way to an important spiritual dimension.[2] Building upon Weber's thesis Peter Berger maintains that any religion which contains a variant of this "inner-worldly asceticism" can be "economically functional" within the current global capitalist system.[3] By way of example, Berger indicates that Pentecostals who connect piety with personal prosperity, rather than viewing holiness as separation from the world, can be tremendously "economically functional."[4]

Studies in South Korea resonate profoundly with Berger's analysis. In that context the expansion of this tradition has coincided with earth-shattering economic development.[5] Examples like this lead some writers to the conclusion that there is a connection between Pentecostalism and economic progress.[6] However, the advance of Zimbabwe's Pentecostal churches has been followed by economic stagnation.[7] This provokes the question as to whether the South Korean example is normative and indicates that in different contexts there are a variety of political and Pentecostal actors in play.

Like Zimbabwe, Cameroon faces a number of serious political, social and economic challenges. Since the mid-nineteen eighties, Cameroon has been in the grip of a serious economic recession.[8] Within the context of this financial turmoil Cameroon has witnessed a sudden increase in Pentecostal churches. The theme of this volume is black religious landscaping and the chapters therein query whether and how religious organizations seek to make their communities more habitable, more just. What impact, if any have the new Pentecostal churches had on the Cameroonian religious landscape? Before exploring the potential socioeconomic ramifications of these religious developments, it is necessary to introduce the terms Pentecostalism and Prosperity Gospel more fully.

Pentecostal-isms

Defining "Pentecostalism" is no easy task. The term can represent a series of renewal movements going right back to the beginning of Christianity.[9] However, in its modern form Pentecostalism can be aggregated into three stages: (1) classical Pentecostalism, (2) the charismatic movement and (3) neo-Pentecostalism. Classical Pentecostalism, shaped by the Wesleyan Holiness tradition,[10] began with the Azusa Street Revival (1906) which emphasized *glossolalia*,[11] asceticism and moral purity (examples include denominations such as the Assemblies of God).[12] The charismatic movement pertains to the period following the 1960s when Pentecostal phenomena were embraced by (non-Pentecostal) groups within the Baptists, Methodists, Anglicans, Roman Catholics and others.[13] The term neo-Pentecostalism differentiates classical Pentecostalism from newer independent churches which have tended to emphasize a doctrine of prosperity.[14] In its most basic form this "Health and Wealth" gospel promoted by neo-Pentecostals holds that God wants to physically bless Christians so that they not only develop spiritually but flourish financially. Advocates thus proclaim that the divine covenant entitles Christians to claim these blessings as a new birth right.[15]

This account of the different kinds of Pentecostalism can be misleading for a number of reasons. First, the distinction between classical and neo-Pentecostalism is becoming increasingly blurred. While this distinction might have held in the past there are several cases in which conventional Pentecostal churches have begun to propagate a prosperity message of health and wealth.[16] Conversely there are newer independent churches which advocate a classical form of Pentecostalism.[17] Secondly the stages identified above imply that the Holy Spirit's renewal of the Church is causally linked to Asuza Street.[18] While its extensive media output has had an enormous impact[19] the emergence of global Pentecostalism cannot be reduced to being merely yet another export of American capitalism. As Asamoah-Gyadu points out, in his work *African Charismatics* (2005), when modern Pentecostal history is viewed from an "intercultural" perspective it is documented that around the time of Azusa, and before, there were "Pentecostal outbursts" in India, the Caribbean and West Africa which have no causal link with contemporaneous developments in the United States.[20] Thirdly, it is important to note the plurality of prosperity messages available. Even if it is acknowledged that American groups such as the Faith Gospel[21] have had an enormous global impact,[22] African heirs to this message have received their inheritance within particular socio-cultural circumstances.[23] Figures such as the Nigerian Pastor Benson Idahosa (who studied these ideas in Dallas),[24] interpreted this teaching in a context where evil spiritual forces have material manifestations (poverty and sickness) is rarely disputed.[25] From this perspective, the idea that God provides believers with power to overcome malevolent spirits in order to attain holistic (material and soteriological) wellbeing resonates profoundly.[26]

Pentecostal-Charismatic Christianity

At this juncture it is apparent that there is considerable nuance surrounding the word Pentecostalism. Nevertheless, the Ghanaian theologian Asamoah-Gyadu denotes seven characteristics common to what he terms "Pentecostal-Charismatic Christianity":

- (i) Charismatic Leadership
- (ii) Urban-centered congregations
- (iii) Exuberant Worship styles
- (iv) Use of Multi-Media technology
- (v) Extensive use of media for advertising programs
- (vi) An internationalism—reflected in the names given to churches
- (vii) Proclaiming a message of success and social mobility.[27]

These tendencies, inspired by Pentecostal developments in Ghana, are all present in the Cameroonian context. Thus, I will utilize the terms

"Cameroonian Pentecostal-Charismatic" (CPC) as a general term referring to recent[28] Pentecostal developments in Cameroon.[29] However, so as facilitate a discussion of the socioeconomic implications of CPC churches, I will also employ Amos Yong and Nimi Wariboko's analysis of the different prosperity paradigms and their possible links to economic renewal in *Pentecostalism and Prosperity* (2012).[30]

Cameroonian Pentecostalism and Prosperity

Kumba, in South West Cameroon, is situated in a part of the country that has suffered considerably from a lack of government investment. According to Mbaku:

> Critical areas such as health care, higher education, roads railways and other forms of communication, rural electrification, and water in the [western] Anglophone region of the country [have been] totally neglected. Most of the industrial development ... was primarily in the French-speaking [eastern] part of the country.[31]

Amos Yong indicates that the theme of prosperity is especially important to Christians living in contexts like this. In his "Typology of Prosperity Theology" Yong contends that people enduring these realities naturally view salvation from the particularities of their economic, material and physical needs. Thus, people who do not have access to medical professionals are more likely to understand "Good News" to entail tangible wellbeing—even prosperity. Moreover, people in these situations will be drawn to faith if they have witnessed real, concrete, transformation in the lives of others:

> [These] People have experienced God as saviour not only in their bodies but also in the concrete circumstances of their lives. They believe that God is providing them with jobs; enabling them to pay their bills; rescuing them from debilitating debts; promoting them in the workplace, the church, or the public domain; bringing about a higher quality and standard of life—in short that God hears their prayers and transforms their situation.[32]

Ruth Marshall reinforces Yong's analysis, arguing that in many African countries, "economic decline and the struggle for material survival" form the "backdrop of the conversion experience." Marshall contends that, amidst this individual and collective despair, many people are attracted to these churches because they offer practical solutions to both individual and social problems.[33] These findings resonate with the responses I got from residents interviewed in Kumba—the headquarters, and birthplace for the majority of CPC groups in Cameroon.[34]

While conditions in Kumba are very difficult, residents I interviewed informed me that the ministries offered by CPC churches offered them a sense of "hope"—regardless of whether these hopes were realized. Those interviewed were especially appreciative of the healing ministry offered by their churches—stressing that this gave them "hope" when hospital bills were out of reach. All said that their churches encouraged them to stop drinking and had motivated them to work hard in order to achieve success. Even where the promise of prosperity remained unfulfilled, those I interviewed attributed the small gains that they had made to their regular tithing. While it is difficult to define the subtle emphases within CPC churches Nimi Wariboko's discussion of the "Pentecostal Paradigms of National Economic Prosperity in Africa"[35] is helpful for categorizing the kinds of prosperity message I have encountered in Kumba. Wariboko's discussion of a "spiritualist paradigm," which attributes hardship to spiritual causes, and a "covenant paradigm," in which prosperity depends upon a contractual relationship between human giving and the divine response, are particularly helpful in this context.[36]

For example, I was taken to *Revival Ministry International Church* by my friend. Here the preacher called upon the congregation to give. He stated that the more you give the more you will be financially endowed. The preacher brought a large yellow book to the front. He related that in this book he had a record of all the special offerings people had made. Quoting Hezekiah's recovery from illness (2 Kings 20) the preacher said *God keeps records of your tithe ... Hezekiah was going to die ... But then he prayed, and God changed his mind. You see at that moment God consulted his records and when He did ... God could see that Hezekiah had been faithful in tithing*. Following this the preacher called upon the congregation to *give 10 000 and God will give you 100 000.*[37] At this moment my friend went to the front and contributed about a tenth of his weekly earnings. This was recorded in the yellow book. Later, when I asked him how the experience made him feel, he told me that he believed giving in this way would have an impact on his life. He explained that he was struggling to afford the high cost of prescription drugs in the hospital and he was convinced that God would either provide him with more income or would heal him.

This understanding resonates with Wariboko's "covenant" Pentecostal paradigm which holds that God blesses individuals according to the covenant of giving. Essentially this paradigm views financial giving as a demonstration of one's faith.[38] Hence if poverty is being caused by lack of faith, someone who gives will activate a magical release—a divine source of wealth through the activation of a metaphysical law which connects prosperity to giving.

A slightly different perspective was offered by a Nigerian resident in Kumba who spoke to me about his congregation *Dominion Chapel.* He explained that he had been struggling to renew his residence card. This is a serious and common problem in Cameroon where security services are considerably obtrusive and a failure to carry identification can often lead to incarceration or unreasonable financial penalties (bribes).[39] While the delay in obtaining these papers can be readily attributed to the administrative chaos caused by endemic corruption in the country, I found it interesting that he was convinced that malevolent spiritual forces had prevented him from obtaining his permit. He linked these difficulties to a *marabout*—someone in league with the devil who can use supernatural powers—who he claims had impaired his ability to progress. To reinforce his bewitchment, he relayed that he had spent days outside the immigration office and had been frequently harassed by police—who at roadblocks frequently extort money from passengers on public transport who do not have identification. He was convinced that these experiences were due to demonic forces. He claims he only received his visa when these wicked forces were frustrated by his pastor's prayers for his deliverance.

This perspective echoes what Wariboko describes as a "Spiritualist" Pentecostal paradigm. While this paradigm has similarities with the "Covenant" paradigm it offers a deeper philosophical analysis by attributing individual hardship to an ontology of spiritual agents which need to be expunged from the Continent. However, critics of this position argue that it distracts individuals from identifying the political causes of their situation.[40]

The difficulties faced by people like this stem from the fact that Cameroon is one of the most corrupt nations on earth.[41] Government workers frequently demand 30% "kickbacks" before giving companies contracts for national infrastructure projects.[42] This has stunted economic development considerably.[43] Moreover, corruption has impeded administration. For example, Henry Kam Kah, who refers to his homeland as a "gluttonocracy," argues that the political elite do not appoint civil servants on the basis of merit but rather on what they can get out of them; whether that is money or political canvasing. This inevitably (regularly) leads to people obtaining positions which they have no ability to fulfill—some are even illiterate.[44] These practices render administration ineffective.[45]

The effect of this upon the national economy is disastrous. Since the mid-nineteen eighties, Cameroon has been in the grip of a serious economic recession.[46] Though external factors cannot be ignored,[47] most commentators agree that these economic problems are the result of poor governance and systemic corruption.[48] For example Jua and Mbaku argue that the economic crisis was foreseen[49] hence, while it could not necessarily have been prevented, measures could have been taken to mitigate its effects—it need not have had such a lasting impact.

This state of affairs raises the following question—what role do CPC churches play within this political landscape? While the Presbyterian and Roman Catholic churches in Cameroon have ceaselessly pressed for democratic reforms (some of their critical members have even been jailed) the CPC churches have largely refused to get involved in political issues or debates.[50] This silence is curious when one considers the claim, made by many commentators, that the economic crisis has been exacerbated, and even prolonged, by the government's reluctance to introduce democratic reforms.[51] In effect, while CPC churches preach prosperity, it might be argued that they have failed to address the main obstacle to its realization.[52]

Pentecostalism and Grassroots Social Transformation

Thus far it seems that CPC churches, while offering positive answers to the despair and destitution faced by Cameroonians, have failed to lobby for the democratic reforms needed to resolve the economic crisis in Cameroon. As a result, one might conclude from this that the impact of this religious tradition upon Cameroonian society has been negligible. Nevertheless, research from other African nations indicates that the emphasis Pentecostal-Charismatic Christianity places on personal transformation does have a positive social impact—particularly upon the lives of women. Writing on the Nigerian context, Ruth Marshall implies that these churches offer believers an alternative way of being:

> Most born-again Christians do not bribe officials, nor sanction or even tolerate such behaviour, not simply because doctrine proscribes it but because they are now part of a community and the possessors of a belief system which empowers them not to, makes them the condition for continued membership.[53]

The emphasis these groups place on being "born again" brings people to have a profound personal transformation which, inevitably, has social implications. This conversion experience typically involves a reversal of destructive and reckless behavior. In addition to being morally pure, converts are encouraged to be time-conscious, disciplined and hardworking; to conduct all their working life in an honest and upright manner.[54] In addition to this, Marshall argues that these Nigerian churches have made a practical contribution to the empowerment of women. She writes:

> Being born again provides women, especially younger women, with strategies for escaping the all too pervasive phenomenon of being forced to exchange

> sexual favours for things which they feel and society promises should be theirs by merit ... within the born-again community fornication is a sin for either gender. This is one of the most strongly emphasised aspects of living a "life in Christ", and ... the mere fact that it has such prominence in the discourse constitutes a powerful resource in the hands of women.[55]

Marshall argues that in Nigeria these Christians offer an alternative subculture in which women can flourish.[56] Marshall considers that the new communities provided by these churches enable:

> an opportunity to construct a space in which [women] can move with relative freedom and dignity, to gain a measure of control over their sexual and family lives, and from there use their positions to gain more influence in the sphere of labour outside the home.[57]

In addition to the above Marshall argues that these churches tend to stress the nuclear family over and above the extended family. This, she argues, releases women from unreasonable financial and other societal pressures.[58]

Writing on the Southern African context David Maxwell makes similar observations. exploring the connection between the Assemblies of God Africa (AOGA) and Zimbabwean society[59] Maxwell argues that once a person is "born again" they are conditioned by a "re-socialization" process which:

> ... captures born-agains and takes control of their lives ... the believer is taught how to budget. Money is saved by other means too. There is a rejection of secular entertainment ... The new focus of the believer's social life becomes the church: an unending round of bible studies, prayer meetings ... Re-socialisation is reflected in the physical transformation of the believer. Smartness and cleanliness are encouraged.[60]

In sum, people are encouraged to attend church activities regularly.[61] This not only takes them away from activities (gambling, alcoholism) which Berger terms economically "dysfunctional"[62] but imparts moral values which facilitate economic mobility.[63]

In addition to this, Maxwell contends that members are actively encouraged to improve their financial situation. While not everyone becomes rich the emphasis that is placed upon wealth creation empowers men, and more importantly, women financially. The AOGA has actively encouraged women to generate income. Maxwell writes:

> The vending of cheap food stuffs and clothes initially within the religious community but later outside it, to finance the expansion of that community ... is not a new doctrine. [However] The practice was perfected by one of ZAOGA's co-founders ... who taught that women should "prosper the church," and indirectly themselves, by "using their hands." .... [This] enthusiastic promotion of talents ... has systematised women's production.[64]

These observations indicate that within the Zimbabwean context these churches have been a vehicle for the empowerment of women and men by reorientating them away from practices with negative economic consequences and instilling a strong socioeconomic code of conduct within them.[65]

The above resonates with the Cameroonian context. For example, while CPC churches have failed to engage meaningfully in political activism, Robert Akoko argues that they do make a very important contribution to society and often have schools, hospitals and banks which provide real jobs for members.[66] Moreover, as in the other contexts discussed, the emphasis CPC churches place upon being "born again" liberates men, and women, from economically "dysfunctional" activities and structures. According to Akoko:

> For women, particularly those less educated or poorer individuals, becoming "born-again" is an assurance that their position in the family and their relationship with their husband guarantees mutual respect, marital fidelity and sharing of family responsibilities. Husbands are less likely to abuse their wives or cheat on them, giving them instead respect assisting in child rearing and spending plenty of time with the family, thereby avoiding unnecessary expenditure out of the home on drinking, entertainment, or other women. Marital problems are often taken to the Pastor for adjudication. The Pentecostal stress on the nuclear family relieves the young couple of the pressure from the In-laws, especially the wife. The choice of marriage partner rests on the prospective couple rather than on the family, thereby liberating the young people from unwanted arrangements might otherwise have been made by the family. The proscription of fornication is of advantage, particularly to the young girls, because it enables them resist unwanted sexual pressures, which are regularly brought to bear on them in case they need jobs, good grades or secure relationship. Young women therefore find this community a space where they can move with relative freedom and dignity, as well as fine psychological support.[67]

The above indicates that, in the case of men, being "born-again" discourages them from what Berger describes as negative economic acts such as alcoholism, fornication and gambling.[68] For women it seems that being "born again" may actually provide a "space," an alternative "community," in which they can enjoy a degree of emancipation. As in the Nigerian context, this potentially entails liberation from sexual exploitation. Moreover, the stress CPC churches place on the nuclear family can relieve women from the economic demands that can be made by the extended family.

Akoko's research suggests that CPC churches have made a practical contribution to the empowerment of women. To take an example, the "Woman Ministry"[69] of the Full Gospel Church is specifically charged with uniting women to fight the economic crisis. It does this by challenging women to be strong witnesses at home and encourages them to engage in business that can generate income for their families by training them in needle work, crafts and other useful things that could help them earn much needed income. Akoko points out that empowering women in this way has had an important secondary consequence in that it has enabled mothers to send their children to school and even provide basic health care provision for their families. Moreover, by providing small loans the church has also enabled them to gain the capital necessary to begin small businesses.[70]

A similar perspective was offered by a woman, who attends the Full Gospel Church in Kumba. She complained about health care provision, the lack of doctors and medical equipment in local hospitals. However, she told me that she was particularly appreciative of the practical opportunities afforded to her by her church. When I asked what this entailed, she explained that within the church community she had been engaged in a number of fund-raising activities, such as making dresses and shirts for special church anniversaries. She related that her involvement in these events had helped her learn skills which have been tremendously useful outside the church. She stated that now she has more ability to pay the expenses caused by sickness. Thus, while she complained that health care provision in Kumba was "terrible," her skills in sewing have enabled her to weather family illnesses by providing an additional family income.

The way in which CPC churches assist women is indicative of how the promise of prosperity offered by these churches is often accompanied by real employment opportunities. Though these opportunities are often conditional upon one becoming a member, the training these churches provide offers a tangible response to the alleviation of poverty in Cameroon.[71]

Conclusion

In summary it seems that CPC churches can have a positive socioeconomic impact. As in the other contexts discussed, these Christians are challenged to desist from "negative" economic activities which can deplete financial resources (heavy drinking, etc.). Moreover, CPC churches are actively engaged in wealth creation and both men and women are encouraged to view income generation as a godly enterprise—and are even given the resources to accomplish this. This resonates with a variant of Weberian "inner-worldly" asceticism. However, while these churches might contain—what Berger terms—"economically functional" tendencies, in certain cases a spiritualization of poverty can distract CPC Christians from identifying the political roots of their poverty. Whether or not this spiritualization explains the political silence of CPC churches, in the longer term it is apparent that if there is a continued failure to engage in political activism this could impair the degree to which these groups can bring lasting socioeconomic change to the nation. Nevertheless, it is equally possible that, as their position within society increases CPC churches may also make their voices heard on important political issues.[72]

Notes

1 Max Weber, *The Protestant Ethic and the Spirit of Capitalism*, trans. Talcott Parsons (London: Routledge, [1930] 2001). Weber's thesis is debated. For further discussion see: R H Tawney, *Religion and the Rise of Capitalism* (London: Pelican Books, 1938); Kurt Samuelsson, *Religion and Economic Action: A Critique of Max Weber* (London: Heinemann, 1961).

2 Weber, *The Protestant Ethic*, 73.

3 Peter Berger, "Faith and Development," *Society* (2009): 71, 74.

4 Ibid., 71.

5 In only 30 years South Korea grew from humble rural origins to be a "hyper-urban industrialized" country. Sung-Gun Kim, "Korean Protestant Christianity in the Midst of Globalization: Neoliberalism and the Pentecostalization of Korean Churches," *Korea Journal* (2007): 169.

6 Sung-Gun Kim writes: "[Pentecostal] religion and economic advancement often appear in tandem [This] accurately describes the South Korean situation … neo-Pentecostals, embrace the gospel of success, value and endorse this connection and, in fact, are noticeably more prosperous than people of other faiths or of no faith." Kim, "Korean Protestant Christianity," 164. Martin makes similar observations: David Martin, "Undermining the Old Paradigms," *PentecoStudies* (2006): 37; David Martin, *Tongues of Fire. The Explosion of Protestantism in Latin America* (Oxford: Blackwell, 1990).

7 David Maxwell, "'Delivered from the Spirit of Poverty?': Pentecostalism, Prosperity and Modernity in Zimbabwe," *Journal of Religion in Africa* (1998): 351.

8 Robert Akoko, *"Ask and You Shall Be Given": Pentecostalism and the Economic Crisis in Cameroon* (Leiden: African Studies Centre, 2007).

9 For further discussion see: William K. Kay, *Pentecostalism* (Oxford: University Press, 2011), 1ff.

10 For further discussion see: John Wesley's *A Plain Account of Christian Perfection* (London: Epworth Press, 1952); Donald Dayton, *Theological Roots of Pentecostalism* (Metuchen, NJ: Scarecrow Press, 1987); Vinson Synan, *The Century of the Holy Spirit: 100 Years of Pentecostal Charismatic Renewal 1901–2001* (Nashville, TN: Thomas Nelson, 2001).

11 Speaking in Tongues.

12 Dela Quampah, *Good Pastors, Bad Pastors: Pentecostal Ministerial Ethics in Ghana* (Eugene, OR: Wipf and Stock Publisher, 2014), 2. The early Pentecostals emphasized that (i) after conversion there was a (ii) purification of the heart, and that following this there was a (iii) baptism in the Holy Spirit and eventually (iv) entire sanctification. It is not difficult to see a resonance between these ideas and what has come to be viewed as the essence of the Methodist faith, as captured by Fitzgerald's account of "Wesley's Alls." According to Fitzgerald: "The faith of the early Methodists stands

out in bold relief . . . All men need to be saved . . . All men may be saved . . . All men may know themselves saved . . . All may be saved to the uttermost." W. B. Fitzgerald, *The Roots of Methodism* (London: Epworth Press, 1930), 173.

13 Kay, *Pentecostalism*, 39.

14 Katherine Attanasi, introduction to *Pentecostalism and Prosperity: The Social-Economics of the Global Charismatic Movement*, ed. Katherine Attanasi et al. (New York: Palgrave Macmillan, 2012), 2–5.

15 On this understanding, disease and destitution have been vanquished by Christ's death and resurrection. Believers must therefore claim Christ's authority over their circumstances by remunerating scriptural promises. Attanasi, introduction, 2–5.

16 Robert Akoko, "From Asceticism to a Gospel of Prosperity: The Case of Full Gospel Mission Cameroon," *Journal for the Study of Religion* (2004): 47–66; Akoko, *"Ask and you shall be given,"* 66–100, Quampah, *Good Pastors, Bad Pastors*, 5–7.

17 Tomas Sundnes Dronen, *Pentecostalism, Globalisation and Islam in Northern Cameroon* (Leiden: Brill, 2013).

18 J. Kwabena Asamoah-Gyadu, *African Charismatics: Current Developments within Indigenous Pentecostalism in Ghana* (Leiden: Brill, 2005), 10–11.

19 Kay, *Pentecostalism*, 18.

20 Asamoah-Gyadu, *African Charismatics*, 10–11, 19ff.

21 Essentially the Faith Gospel teaches that through the death and resurrection of Christ Christians can overcome sin, sickness and poverty through positive confession (Romans 10:9). It was notably expounded by the following American writers: E. W. Kenyon, A. A. Allen, Oral Roberts, K. Hagin, K. Copeland, J. Avanzini.

22 Paul Gifford, *African Christianity: Its Public Role* (London: Hurt & Company, 1998), 39, 77.

23 According to Anim, "Despite the significant influence of American neo-pentecostalism in shaping prosperity teaching in the charismatic churches in Ghana, it is important to note that the primal aspirations of prosperity also continue to play a significant role in the shaping of prosperity theology in Ghana. The thriving prosperity teaching in the charismatic ministries is largely because the charismatics have tapped into fertile ground already nurtured by the traditional concept of prosperity, which is to be understood in terms of wealth, longevity, and fertility or procreativity. In African cosmology, the belief in and pursuit of prosperity is paramount. Africans do not 'honor' or accept suffering or poverty. It is a battle they have always sought to fight. The belief in the gods is primarily to ensure prosperity and well-being. The influence of American-type prosperity teaching only served as a catalyst and reinforced what was already prevailing in the matrix of the primal worldview. Thus, local primal considerations offer important perspective in interpreting contemporary African Christianity." Emmanuel K. Anim, "The Prosperity Gospel in Ghana and the Primal Imagination," *Pentvars Business Journal* (2010): 66.

24 Ogbu Kalu, *African Pentecostalism: An Introduction* (Oxford: University Press, 2008), 91.

25 Asamoah-Gyadu, *African Charismatics*, 222.

26 Paul Gifford, *Christianity Development and Modernity in Africa* (London: Hurst & Company, 2014), 13–28.

27 J. Kwabena Asamoah-Gyadu, *'Taking Territories and Raising Champions': \ Contemporary Pentecostalism and the Changing Face of Christianity in Africa 1980–2010* (Accra: Trinity Theological Seminary, 2010), 12.

28 Paul Gifford points out that, as a result of political oppression in Cameroon, the emergence of pentecostalism in this context had been stifled until relatively recently. Gifford, *African Christianity*, 246ff.
29 Asamoah-Gyadu, *African Charismatics*, 12.
30 For further discussion see: Amos Yong, "A Typology of Prosperity Theology: A Religious Economy of Global Renewal or a Renewal Economics?," in *Pentecostalism and Prosperity: The Social-Economics of the Global Charismatic Movement*, ed. Katherine Attanasi et al. (New York: Palgrave Macmillan, 2012), 15–33; Nimi Wariboko, "Pentecostal Paradigms of National and Economic Prosperity in Africa," in *Pentecostalism and Prosperity: The Social-Economics of the Global Charismatic Movement*, ed. Katherine Attanasi et al. (New York: Palgrave Macmillan, 2012), 34–60.
31 John Mbaku, "Economic Dependence in Cameroon: SAPs and the Bretton Woods Agreement," in *The Leadership Challenge in Africa: Cameroon under Paul Biya*, ed. John Mbaku et al. (Trenton: Africa World Press, 2004), 404–405.
32 Here Yong discusses various perspectives on this teaching, examining whether the scriptures promise believers material and spiritual riches. In addition to the contextual perspective he also explores what he terms a "Missional" argument, which states that financial prosperity is imparted for evangelistic purposes. Finally, he offers a synthesis of these different approaches. For further discussion see: Yong, "A Typology of Prosperity Theology," 18–19, 23–24.
33 Ruth Marshall, "Power in the Name of Jesus," *Review of African Political Economy* (1991): 25–27.
34 This is mostly due to its proximity to Nigeria. For further discussions see: Akoko, *"Ask and you shall be given,"* 56.
35 He writes: "These five paradigms are Weberian ideal constructs and as such no one denomination, theologian, or preacher will perfectly conform to any of them. As ideal constructs they draw sharply the distinctive features between the historical patterns for the sake of contrast. These paradigms are very rough preliminary systematizations of theological thinking about Africa's economic development. I am merely coding them to stimulate reflection, indicating logical possibilities for relating theological ideas (mainly in the forms of extended sermons and devotional materials) to the continent's economic crisis, and offering some sort of guidance for the research project of this volume." Wariboko, "Pentecostal Paradigms," 36.
36 He also discusses a "leadership paradigm" in which immoral leadership is blamed for economic problems, a "nationalist paradigm" which views present economic hardship as a result of Africa's colonial legacy, and a "development paradigm" which emphasizes the role of the church in alleviating poverty; Wariboko, "Pentecostal Paradigms," 34–60.
37 10,000 Central African francs is roughly $20.
38 Wariboko, "Pentecostal Paradigms," 54.
39 Gifford, *African Christianity*, 249. I met a lady from Chad who, because she didn't have a residence permit, stayed in and around her house for two years—only going out when necessary.
40 Wariboko, "Pentecostal Paradigms," 45–46.
41 In 1998 and 1999 Transparency International found Cameroon to be the most corrupt country in the world. For further discussion see: "Cameroon," last modified June 1, 2015, http://www.transparency.org/country.

42 Akoko, *"Ask and you shall be given,"* 203.
43 An interview with a local businessman, who wanted to tar a stretch of road between his business and the main road (in order to avoid a three-hour detour), indicates how corruption is an obstacle to economic development. He claims that when he offered to build the road (out of his own pocket) he was asked to give $100,000 in bribes before he could even be given permission to begin the work.
44 Henry Kam Kah, "The Culture of Appointments, Arrogance, and Chop Broke Pottism in Cameroons' Contemporary Governance," *Cameroon Journal on Democracy and Human Rights* (2010): 28–31.
45 As a result of this one can spend an entire day, even two, waiting outside a government office when trying to perform a simple administrative process such as registering a change of vehicle ownership.
46 Akoko, *"Ask and you shall be given"*.
47 Juliette Rousselot, "The Impact of French Influence on the State of Democracy and Human Rights in Cameroon," *Cameroon Journal on Democracy and Human Rights* (2010): 59–71.
48 Though multiparty elections have been held regularly since 1992, repeated irregularities in the nations democratic process have failed to bring the transformative socioeconomic leadership that is sorely needed. For further discussion see: Nantang Jua, "Cameroon: Jump-Starting an Economic Crisis," *Africa Insight* (1991): 162–170; Christophe Dongmo, "The Building of a Dictatorship," *Cameroon Journal on Democracy and Human Rights* (2008): 49.
49 Jua, "Cameroon: Jump-Starting an Economic Crisis," 162–170; Mbaku, "Economic Dependence," 404–405.
50 Robert Akoko and Timothy Mbuagbo, "Christian Churches and the Democratization Conundrum in Cameroon," *Africa Today* (2006): 29–31.
51 Jua, "Cameroon: Jump-Starting an Economic Crisis," 162–170; Dongmo, "The Building of a Dictatorship," 41–50.
52 Nevertheless, Akoko points out that while in Latin America and Zimbabwe neo-pentecostal churches have often sided with oppressive regimes the Cameroonian Pentecostal churches have neither condoned nor condemned the political establishment. Conversely, in Ghana, pentecostal leaders like Mensa Otabil have been highly critical of the Ghanaian government. For further discussions see: Akoko, "Christian Churches and the Democratization Conundrum in Cameroon," 29–30; Mensa Otabil, *Beyond the Rivers of Ethiopia* (Accra: Alter Media, 2004).
53 Marshall, "Power in the Name of Jesus," 30.
54 Martin describes this process as 'Betterment' and emphasizes that this term refers to both moral and economic betterment. He writes: "Beneath the notion of betterment is a broad search for wealth . . . for worth rather than worthlessness, for a clean future rather than the dirt or the past. It is clear from previous investigations that the economic category of 'goods' is part of the moral category of the good. The economic is subsumed within such moral rubrics as prudence and sobriety. The seamless web of living rejects a separation of the economic aspect and treats goods as intimately linked to the gods." Martin, "Undermining the Old Paradigms," 37.
55 Marshall, "Power in the Name of Jesus," 30.
56 This follows a long tradition of Christianity in Africa in which the church has offered a special, alternative, space for women. For further discussion see: Deborah Gaitskell,

"Hot Meetings and Hard Kralls: African Biblewomen in Transvaal Methodism, 1924–1960," *Journal of Religion in Africa* (2000): 279; Farai David Muzorewa, "Though Prayer to Action: The Rukwadzano Women in Rhodesia," in *Themes in the Christian History of Central Africa*, ed. T. Ranger et al. (London: Heinemann, 1975), 256–268.

57 Marshall, "Power in the Name of Jesus," 32.

58 Marshall, "Power in the Name of Jesus," 31. Interestingly, writing in the Ghanaian context, Jane Soothill, argues that solidarity in that context does not facilitate the empowerment of women to the same degree. For further discussion: Jane Soothill, *Gender, Social Change and Spiritual Power: Charismatoc Christianity in Ghana* (Leiden: Brill, 2007), 142ff.

59 Maxwell, "Delivered from the Spirit of Poverty?" 351.

60 Ibid., 353–354.

61 It should also be noted here that, according to Maxwell, the emphasis these churches place upon reading the bible has improved literacy rates.

62 Berger, "Faith and Development," 71.

63 Maxwell writes: 'For some, the doctrines have engendered social mobility. For others, they provide a code of conduct which guards them from falling into poverty and destitution. For all they provide a pattern for coming to terms with, and benefitting from, modernities' dominant values and institutions.' Maxwell, "Delivered from the Spirit of Poverty?" 351.

64 Maxwell, "Delivered from the Spirit of Poverty?" 355.

65 Berger affirms this point and intimates that in addition to financial betterment Pentecostalism may actually be viewed as a form of empowerment in the sense that in many contexts it has led to the emancipation of women: "Conversion to Pentecostalism carries with it a cultural revolution—a turning-away from deeply ingrained traits ... such as concerning the [inferior] status of women .... [Pentecostalism] can be described accurately as a movement that emancipates women." Berger, "Faith and Development," 71–72.

66 Robert Akoko, "New Pentecostalism in the Wake of the Economic Crisis in Cameroon," *Nordic Journal of African Studies* (2002): 363–364.

67 Akoko, *"Ask and you shall be given,"* 58.

68 Berger, "Faith and Development," 71.

69 I cannot tell whether this should be titled "Woman's Ministry." Their notices in Kumba read "Woman Ministry."

70 Akoko, *"Ask and you shall be given,"* 137–139.

71 Ibid., 138.

72 I wish to dedicate this chapter to Very Revd. Prof. J. Kwabena Asamoah-Gyadu.

Conclusion

We began this volume with a discussion about black empowerment in the twenty-first century. In many ways this has been an era of empowerment for Africans and people of African descent the world over. Decades after independence in Africa and the Caribbean, civil rights in the United States, and the end of apartheid in South Africa, black people now have a seat at the table. The chapters in this book, however, have illustrated that the twenty-first century is characterized by the *paradox of empowerment*. While there has been a movement towards black people occupying some of the highest positions of power in government, there are also persistent racial disparities the world over. The vestiges of apartheid, colonialism, slavery, Jim Crow segregation, etc. all continue to plague places where black people find themselves both on the Continent and in the diaspora. Furthermore, there are new inventions of racial oppression that undermine black empowerment that we observed in religious and political institutions throughout the world.

On the Continent, while Africans may have ascended into occupying the above-mentioned "seat at the table," such space is not without surveillance utilized as a form of colonial power. Coloniality as a technology of power is performed by surveilling the democratic electoral processes as well as the economic processes of African nations. Economic monitoring by Western powers operates by rewarding nations that operate within the Western norms of governing and sanctioning those that operate outside of these norms. The call for decolonization and Africanization is an attempt to *denormalize* the normal and challenge the epistemological privilege that pervades the space at the table.

Further adding to the paradox of empowerment in inter-racialized contexts, there is a rise of white nationalism, a harkening back to "old fashioned racism,"[1] anti-immigration policies and a general anti-blackness, as well as continued economic exploitation and police surveillance. Black people in urban and rural spaces around the world are still denied basic services, access to healthy food, quality education and decent housing as a result of "dominant geographies" that have impacted black life.

Despite this, black people continue to exercise agency. They continue to engage in cartographical struggles to create "counter-landscapes—spaces that are inhabitable for their communities to exist, spaces that support social movements for change, and spaces that support just relationships and holistic living. Taken together, the chapters in this volume have shown us the ways in which black people on the African continent and in the United States have identified obstacles and barriers to black freedoms and have constructed counter-landscapes in response to these obstacles. Contributors to this volume provided specific examples of attempts to create counter-landscapes that move communities forward in the project of emancipation.

Tracey E. Hucks' chapter "In Search of a 'Land Language' " established the relevance land has to black empowerment. In this chapter, we were introduced to the significance of land and the struggle for emancipatory space for black people. These struggles are indeed about physical space. Black people have been struggling, over the centuries for a space in which they can bodily exist without fear of violence or violation. But what Hucks' chapter illustrated is that there is a deep relationship between psychic/spiritual space and physical space as black people connect the construction of religious imagination and communal space to these emancipatory physical spaces. Thus, in these chapters we see how creativity and control of physical space enable black communities to engage in struggles that generate new religious, artistic and political networks and structures that support black life.

Chapters within this book, pointed to the ways in which the paradoxes of empowerment are complex, diverse and ubiquitous. Some of the chapters focused primarily on specific examples of black religious institutions' landscaping that result in empowering communities. Other chapters pointed out barriers to empowerment such as indigenous and colonial sexism, vestiges of apartheid, colonialism and slavery, and white supremacist and nationalist theological interpretations. Still others emphasized the complexities of black empowerment and identified factors that can be both barriers to empowerment and tools of empowerment at the same time.

Several of the chapters primarily emphasized the ways in which black religious institutions landscape to empower their communities. For example, in his chapter on education and black churches, Donn Worgs identified the ways in which select black churches in the United States participate in "coproducing" education as a public good—sometimes in tandem with government—other times in place of government (when government fails to act). The examples he provided reveal an impulse toward transforming social and political landscapes facing black people that may be a vibrant source of civic capacity for solving community problems. Driven by their theological orientations, their centrality in black communities and their desire "to be relevant," there is a set of black churches ripe for this activity. Likewise, Ronald Peters identified a faith-based program—Foundation of HOPE—that reduces the recidivism rates of community members caught up in the criminal justice system in Pittsburg, PA. Foundation of HOPE is a model for religious landscaping that takes into account the devastating impact that mass incarceration and recidivism have on black communities. Foundation of HOPE has begun to successfully interrupt the pattern of recidivism and thus promotes community empowerment. In her chapter, Karen Crozier outlined a community strategy of "Peace Circles" (communal discussions or strategizing sessions) that can engage communities in black religious landscaping where in which they can construct new remedies to address the problem of mass incarceration and related issues within the community—ultimately drawing attention to the parallels between the strategies performed during the era of Jim Crow and the contemporary mass incarceration of black bodies.

Still other chapters in the volume highlighted the barriers to black emancipation and empowerment. These authors identified the specific aspects of the dominant white Christian religious geographies that have impacted the religious landscapes of black communities. For example, several of our contributors identified Eurocentric ideologies in ministry and counseling as well as Eurocentric theological constructions as barriers to black emancipation. Some of the authors also illustrated the ways in which gender constructions in *both* white dominant geographies and autochthonous indigenous traditions have served as barriers to establishing and maintaining holistic forms of communal liberation.

For example, in Chapter 3, Itumeleng D. Mothoagae argued that the foundation of white supremacy and nationalism in South Africa are fundamentally linked to the pseudo-understanding of Calvinist Theology from the beginning of white settler arrival. He maintained that though the South African Constitution is regarded as a liberal constitution, there are sections in the Constitution[2] that are aimed at maintaining and sustaining the 1994 accord signed between the African National Congress, National Party, and Freedom Front on the self-determination of the Afrikaners. This, according to Mothoagae, does not redress the ideology of white supremacy and nationalism expressed in settlements such as Orania. Mothoagae further argued that religion has contributed to such ideologies and has continued to shape the identity of the democratic South Africa post-1994.

In another example from the volume, Melinda Contreras-Byrd wrote that religious and healthcare professionals who use Eurocentric methods in counseling, teaching and psychology have not thoroughly understood and, therefore, do not effectively address the toll that oppression has taken on black people and therefore often serve as a detriment to black bodies and black minds. Likewise, Senokoane and Mataboge, in Chapter 4, focused on African youth and argued that colonization and colonialism have produced a Duboisian-like "identity crisis" in these youth. According to the authors, this identity crisis leads to the alienation of young Africans from their African selves which is clearly a barrier to empowerment.

One of the insights that several of the chapters highlighted is the *complexity* of the paradox of empowerment. This can be seen clearly in Daniel Pratt Morris-Chapman's exploration of the impact of the proliferation of the new Pentecostal churches' "prosperity gospel" on community empowerment in Cameroon. Morris-Chapman found that the Cameroonian version of the prosperity gospel leads to a modicum of empowerment by encouraging thrift, hard work and economically productive activity. It also encourages some level of equality for women. At the same time however, the prosperity churches in Cameroon fail to examine or challenge systemic roots of poverty, deprivation and social inequality. Nor do they engage in political activism or challenge government corruption. These are all ultimately barriers to any real community empowerment.

On the other hand, we have Tshehla's examination of the impact of modern Christian missions in Africa and on the Basotho people of South Africa in particular. He illustrated how modern African missions have shaped the religious landscape in Africa in profound ways particularly as it regards the introduction of literacy. Tshehla looked specifically at the Basotho traditions and found that the literacy project was heavily influenced by Christian traditions which were at odds with Basotho traditions. However, Tshehla examined the work of Masotho author, Filemon Rapetloane, and illustrated that the Basotho used literacy and the reconfiguration of Christian religious symbols and ritual to construct counter-landscapes that were more empowering than what was intended by the Christian missionaries.

An examination of African Independent/Initiated Churches (AICs) in the volume provided an additional manifestation of the complexity of the paradox of black empowerment. These churches were developed as a form of resistance against Western colonial-formed Christian churches. They center the African experience, embrace a version of Christianity that speaks to African spirituality and thus seek to create counter religious landscapes for the empowerment of African people. Chimininge and Makamure coauthored two chapters in this volume focused on AIC's and demonstrated that while African people can break away and form independent churches, these churches are not necessarily free from the influences of colonial thinking and still have attributes that serve as barriers to empowerment. For example, in Chapter 9 the authors wrote about leadership succession practices among AICs in Zimbabwe. They pointed out that these churches' failure to prioritize and properly plan for leadership succession serves as a barrier for AICs to empower Zimbabwean communities to counter the impact of colonial Christianity. In Chapter 10 they focused on the role of women in AICs. They illustrated that despite some of the advances that have been made by the Zimbabwean government when it comes to advancing gender equality, in AICs women are still marginalized and still restricted from some leadership roles. Furthermore, the marginalization is often done in the interest of preserving traditional culture. These two examples deepen our perspective about the paradox of empowerment. AICs are still under colonial influence, even if they are emancipated from colonial rule and are actively working to counter the impact of colonialism. In other words, there are indigenous practices and beliefs (in the case of gender equity) that serve as barriers to full empowerment and emancipation.

Clearly the chapters in this book comment on the paradox of empowerment. Some of them described the religious landscaping used to make communities more habitable for the holistic wellbeing of black people and others pointed out barriers to said landscaping. Further, some of the chapters emphasized the complexities of landscaping for empowerment. Now we will turn to a brief examination of South Africa and the United States to further illustrate the paradox of black empowerment.

South Africa, the United States and the Paradox of Empowerment

A brief examination of the United States and South Africa provides additional instructive examples of the paradox of black empowerment. While in both South Africa and the United States, apartheid was dismantled by law in the latter half of twentieth century, vestiges of apartheid, colonialism, and Jim Crow segregation still impact Black people in these places. For example, in the United States, by law Black people have access to the ballot. Yet, many still battle voter suppression efforts when they try to exercise those rights. In recent years efforts have included an array of tactics that disproportionately impact black communities—instituting onerous voter identification laws, purging voting rolls and closing polling sites and various other tactics. These tactics were on full display during the 2020 US Presidential Elections which provided a special set of circumstances, as people were trying to vote safely during the COVID-19 pandemic. The 2020 Elections included an attack on mail in and absentee voting which disproportionately impacted black voters. Yet, despite the suppression tactics and the COVID-19 challenges, black people voted in record numbers. As these black voters were key to the defeat of Donald Trump, their efforts were met with yet another attack on their voting rights after the election. Though their efforts were ultimately unsuccessful, President Trump and his supporters attempted to cast doubt on the legitimacy of the votes cast in key majority black areas in Wisconsin, Georgia and Pennsylvania by demanding recounts, filing lawsuits and seeking to have millions of votes discounted. Voter suppression has real consequences for who is elected to office and the value of their franchise itself.

In both the United States and South Africa, racial disparities in wealth, health, levels of education, mortality, access to affordable housing and a host of other indicators are still readily observable. For example, in 2013 in the United States, the median net worth of the average white household was US $141,900 compared to the median net worth of the average black household—US $11,000. In 2012, the U.S. Census bureau reported that 11% of non-Hispanic whites compared to 28.1% of African Americans were living at, or below the poverty level. Likewise, examining 2014/2015 South African statistics reveals the dire situation that black people face. Black South African-headed households face severe economic disparities when compared to white and Asian-headed households. For example, 11.6% of black South African-headed households were in the upper quintile, compared to 80% Indian-Asian-headed households and 84% of white-headed households.[3] These statistics reveal serious racial disparities in South Africa. They problematize the status quo and highlight the struggles of being black in a country that even while politically governed by blacks, forcing South Africans to ask uncomfortable questions about the extent of the liberation and empowerment they obtained with the end of apartheid.

An important part of the empowerment narrative in the United States is the advancement of the claim that the United States has developed into a post-racial society. That in fact while racism had existed in the past and had been a key defining element of the country, the dismantling of Jim Crow segregation, the election of African Americans to local and statewide office, and the development of a discernable black middle class meant that the United

States is beyond "race" and is in fact, "post-racial." Barack Obama's election as the first black president of the United States has been used as the linchpin in this argument. Surely, a country that has elected a black president cannot be racist. Race is no longer a defining element of one's life's chances. Surely the United States is post-racial. As a result, the racial disparities described above and black suffering in general is seen as a product of black people's own making. According to Keeanga-Yamahtta Taylor, "Black poverty, imprisonment, and premature death are widely seen as the products of Black insolence and lapsed personal responsibility."[4]

In the post-Apartheid/post-Mandela era a similar phenomenon developed in South Africa. A discourse developed that describes South Africa as a "Rainbow Nation." This concept of a Rainbow Nation was underpinned by the Truth and Reconciliation Commission. As an ideological concept it was developed as a tool for promoting multiculturalism and like "post-racialism," to advance the discursive strategy that race, gender and class no longer matter—only the "human race" is of any consequence. Such a premise not only constructs and maintains privileges of the white minority, it also created for them a sense of comfort. Furthermore, like the post-racial construct, the rainbow nation rejects any attempts to deal with the structural inequality that continues to be a pervasive factor in the lives of so many. Such an attempt not only sustains white privilege at the expense of the majority, it also performs as tool to invalidate and silence the lived experiences of oppression. In her book *Memoirs of a Born Free: Reflections on the New South Africa by a Member of the Apartheid Generation* (2018) Malaika wa Azania, ponders the notion of *rainbowism* from the perspective of a young black woman and provides us with an insight from the perspective of the so-called born free generation.[5] Her reflection on her own experience with institutionalized racism offers a view of South Africa that refutes the implied racial liberation of the so-called Rainbow Nation. Her description of her upbringing in a black township afflicted by poverty, disease, and death suggests that the idea of post-racialism is a problematic notion to say the least. Though the country may be described as a rainbow nation/post-racial state, it is still held in the clutches of a de facto apartheid.[6]

In both the United States and in South Africa the post-racial/rainbow/color-blind theories are myths. This discourse ignores the structural reasons for racial disparities and black suffering. Additionally, instead of being post-racial we see a persistence and resurgence of racial animus and white nationalism in both South Africa and the United States that these myths only serve to harbor and exacerbate. Post-racialism then becomes a space that reproduces racial inequality and white nationalist ideologies.

In South Africa, such ideologies are masked as the right to self-determination, operating under the banner of organizations such as AfriForum—a white nationalist organization that promotes the protection of Afrikaner culture as part of its broad agenda. AfriForum has opposed renaming streets (a process that has been used to rid the nation of the monikers that validate/celebrate apartheid and colonialism).[7]

In the United States these ideologies have inspired several overt and high-profile acts of racial violence in recent years such as the murder of nine black church-goers at Emmanuel AME Church by white supremacist Dylan Roof and the murder of Heather Heyer at a gathering of white supremacists in Charlottesville, VA. These bold examples of the persistence and resurgence of white nationalist and white supremacist ideology in South Africa and the United States further refute the argument of a post-racial society. They also point out further the paradox of black empowerment.

At the center of the struggle to address these disparities and post-civil rights and post-apartheid anti-blackness is what Mignolo refers to as "the colonial wound." This "colonial wound cuts across social classes, and it is both racial and patriarchal."[8] An awareness of the colonial wound becomes explicit in twenty-first century movements on South African university campuses such as the #feesmustfall movement (to protest the impending tuition increases at South African institutions of higher education); the #Rhodesmustfall movement (to remove the statue of Cecil Rhodes from public spaces, which served as a celebration of colonialism, imperialism and oppression) and a movement to #decolonise the curriculum (a push to restructure universities to shift from the students consider a Eurocentric and racist curriculum. Decolonizing the curriculum also has as a goal to embrace traditional epistemological orientations as opposed to only Western based epistemology). Led by university students in South Africa, these movements all aimed to revitalize the consciousness of the masses to reevaluate the spaces they occupy. They all have in common the implicit claim that the emancipation against apartheid and exploitation has not yet been achieved. In other words, the movements all imply that black South African liberation and empowerment remain incomplete.

In the United States similar movements such as the uprisings that occurred after the police killings of Mike Brown in Ferguson and Freddy Gray in Baltimore; the national and localized #BlackLivesMatter movements that attempt to address anti-black policing and reform the criminal justice system; Rev. William Barber and the "Moral Mondays" struggles with economic justice, voting rights and health care in North Carolina; efforts to remove Confederate statues and monuments (which venerate people who wanted to protect their rights to own enslaved Africans in the United States) from public spaces and efforts to get reparations for American slavery, reminded us that we still have a distance to go along the path towards recognition of the value of the lives of black people. More recently, #BlackLivesMatter protests in response to the extrajudicial killings of black citizens such as Breonna Taylor and George Floyd have gained more ground as the demands for policing reforms grow louder and more municipalities have actually removed or have renewed debates regarding the removal of Confederate statues. Rev. William Barber is leading a Poor People's Campaign to address issues of poverty. Barber and activists such as Stacey Abrams and LaTosha Brown in Georgia are making important inroads to mobilizing black voters and demanding that the voting rights of black and poor people be protected.

These struggles to address the value of black lives and black bodies, though separated geographically, are connected. As Angela Davis noted, it is important to recognize "that there has been a symbiotic relationship between struggles abroad and struggles at home, relationships of inspiration and mutuality."[9] Furthermore, these movements illustrate the symbolism of space, as they all attempt to metaphorically and physically redefine spaces. This is visible in the movements to remove the Rhodes's statues in South Africa and the Confederate statues in the United States. These statues are viewed as monuments to oppression. Removing them not only alters the physical space but also makes the spaces sites of resistance. Thus, spaces of oppression are transformed into spaces of empowerment. Moreover, they have also functioned as religious spaces and make claims about the inherent value of life in general and black life in particular. They are spaces from where strength and courage are drawn to face brutal systems of white supremacy.

Notes

1 Among others, Michael Tessler refers to old fashioned racism (OFR) in his article, "The Return of Old Fashioned Racism to White Americans Partisan Preferences in the Early Obama Era" in the *Journal of Politics* vol. 75, no. 1, January 2013, Racist attitudes and white identity more a factor in partisanship than any time Post-civil rights movement and before Obama.

2 Article 235 of the South African Constitution recognizes a community's self-determination within the framework of the Constitution and the law.

3 Statistics South Africa, Living Conditions of Households in South Africa. An analysis of household expenditure and income data using the LCS 2014/2015, Republic of South Africa: Pretoria, 2017.

4 Keeanga-Yamahtta Taylor, *From #Black Lives Matter to Black Liberation* (Chicago: Haymarket Books, 2016).

5 The name is used to refer to the generation born after the end of apartheid.

6 Malaika wa Azania, *Memoirs of a Born Free: Reflections on The New South Africa by a Member of The Post-Apartheid Generation* (Auckland Park, South Africa: Jacana Media, 2018).

7 AfriForum a white nationalist organization has attracted significant controversy because of its views, especially its denial that Apartheid was a crime against humanity. On October 30, dozens of mainly white South Africans dressed in black and protested what they call the targeted murder of white South African farmers. The killings are described as "an onslaught" and "a form of terror." Thus, suggesting that whites in South Africa were experiencing victimization and isolation. The Afrikaner cultural group AfriForum, has argued that farm attacks are characterized by torture and specific brutality. Such a notion has somewhat fueled the myth that a "white genocide" is waiting to happen in South Africa. The myth has gained traction among white supremacists around the world, especially among conservatives in the United States. It is also a myth that wraps itself in the apartheid-era flag for comfort.

8 Gaztambide-Fernández Rubén, "Decolonial options and artistic/aestheSic entanglements: An interview with Walter Mignolo," *Decolonization: Indigeneity, Education & Society* 3, no. 1 (2014): 196–212.

9 Angela Y. Davis, *Freedom is a Constant Struggle: Ferguson, Palestine, and the Foundations of a Movement* (Chicago: Haymarket Books, 2016).

Notes on Contributors

Editors

Joy R. Bostic is an associate professor in religious studies and director of the African and African American Studies program at Case Western Reserve University in the United States. She is also a program faculty member for the university's Women and Gender Studies and Ethnic Studies programs. She is the author of *African American Female Mysticism* and chapters and articles on womanist and feminist religion and culture.

Itumeleng D. Mothoagae, PhD, is a lecturer of New Testament and Early Christian Studies in the Department of Biblical and Ancient Studies, at University of South Africa (UNISA) in Pretoria, South Africa. His fields of specialization are New Testament ethics, Bible translation, African Biblical interpretation and cultural studies. His academic interests are Black Theology of Liberation, African ethics and identity studies.

Tamelyn Tucker-Worgs is the Virginia E. Lewis Professor of Political Science, chair of the Department of Political Science and an associate professor of African American studies at Hood College in Frederick, MD, USA. Her current research focuses on morality and black politics. She is the author of *The Black Megachurch: Theology, Gender and the Politics of Public Engagement* and several book chapters and journal articles about black churches and public life.

Contributors

Daniel Pratt Morris-Chapman is a presbyter of the Methodist Church in Britain. He has served as a lecturer in the Anglophone part of Cameroon where he taught at the Presbyterian Theological Seminary (Kumba). He currently serves in a bilingual Methodist congregation in Italy in a church which seeks to bring Migrants and Italians together in worship (Novara, Piemonte).

Vengesai Chimininge is a Senior Lecturer and Programme Leader at Zimbabwe Open University in the Department of Religious Studies and Philosophy. He is currently a Research Fellow in the Department of Politics Philosophy and Religion at Lancaster University, United Kingdom.

Melinda Contreras-Byrd is a New Jersey state licensed psychologist and owner of the Generations Center. She is founder and acting Dean of the AME Ministerial Institute in the Dominican Republic. She presently serves as adjunct professor in the Doctor of Ministry Program of the New Brunswick Theological Seminary. She is an author and poet, an ordained Elder of the African Methodist Episcopal Church, and joins her husband, Rev. Vernon R Byrd Jr. in pastoral ministry at St. Matthew A.M.E. Church in Philadelphia, PA.

Karen D. Crozier is the founder of *Jewel of Justice*, a consultant, training, spiritual direction, and pastoral counseling business which focuses on women's personal and professional development. A former diversity and faculty development administrator, and associate professor of practical theology in Christian higher and seminary education, Karen has published in the areas of race and religion, children's spirituality, and Christian education. In 2021, she released her first book entitled *Fannie Lou Hamer's Revolutionary Practical Theology: Racial and Enironmental Justice Concerns*

Tracey E. Hucks is James D. Vail III Professor and Chair of the Department of Africana Studies at Davidson College. A graduate of Harvard University with a Ph.D. in the study of religion, her recent book, *Yoruba Traditions and African American Religious Nationalism*, complicates classical questions in Africana and religious studies regarding origins, race, and nationalism. She has just completed a coauthored work, *Religious Vocabularies of Africa: Obeah and Orisa in Trinidad*, which engages historical, literary and theological accounts of Africana religious identity in colonial Trinidad.

Clemence Makamure is Lecturer and Programme Leader at Zimbabwe Open University in the Department of Religious Studies and Philosophy. He holds a PhD in Religion and Social Transformation. He has research interests in Religion and Politics, Religion and Development, Human Sexuality, Human Rights, Religion and Environment and Leadership and Ethics.

Mofenyi L. Mataboge is a PhD student at the University of South Africa, in the Department of Philosophy, Practical, & Systematic Theology. He is also a lecturer in the same department.

Itumeleng D. Mothoagae, PhD, is a lecturer of New Testament and Early Christian Studies in the Department of Biblical and Ancient Studies, at UNISA in Pretoria. His fields of specialization are New Testament Ethics, Bible Translation, African Biblical Interpretation and Cultural Studies. His academic interests are Black Theology of Liberation, African Ethics and Identity Studies.

Ronald E. Peters, Ed.D., served as President of Interdenominational Theological Seminary in Atlanta, Georgia and, prior to that, was the Henry L. Hillman Professor of Urban Ministry at Pittsburgh Theological Seminary and founding Director of its Metro-Urban Institute. Currently he serves as a member of the Seminary's Board of Directors. Past President of the Foundation of HOPE, he has lectured throughout sub-Saharan Africa, Asia, the Caribbean and Europe and his publicaitons explore issues in urban ministry and justice advocacy.

Boitumelo Senokoane is an associate professor in the Department of Philosophy, Practical, & Systematic Theology, at the University of South Africa. His research focus primarily in Black Theology of Liberation, and Christian Ethics.

Maarman S. Tshehla, PhD, is a senior lecturer within the School of Religion, Philosophy and Classics at the University of KwaZulu-Natal (UKZN) in Pietermaritzburg, South Africa. He lectures, supervises and publishes in aspects of New Testament Studies, African Biblical Hermeneutics as well as Bible Translation Studies. He has enduring interest in the lives and uses of Africa's mother tongue Bibles, and is currently part of the team engaged in revising the Sepedi Bible on behalf of the Bible Society of South Africa.

Donn Worgs, PhD, is a Professor of political science and Director of African and African American Studies at Towson University. He is author of several articles and book chapters covering such topics as morality and African American politics, neighborhood politics, community development, and education politics. He is also one of the coauthors of the recently published book, *Urban Neighborhoods in a New Era: Revitalization Politics in the Postindustrial City.*

Index

Note: Page numbers followed by "n" refer to notes.

B

C

D

E

F

L

M

N

S

T

U

V

W

Y

www.ingramcontent.com/pod-product-compliance
Ingram Content Group UK Ltd.
Pitfield, Milton Keynes, MK11 3LW, UK
UKHW020210290926
15470UKWH00001B/104

9 781433 172588